Lecture Notes in Computer Science   14337

Founding Editors

Gerhard Goos
Juris Hartmanis

Editorial Board Members

The series Lecture Notes in Computer Science (LNCS), including its subseries Lecture Notes in Artificial Intelligence (LNAI) and Lecture Notes in Bioinformatics (LNBI), has established itself as a medium for the publication of new developments in computer science and information technology research, teaching, and education.

LNCS enjoys close cooperation with the computer science R & D community, the series counts many renowned academics among its volume editors and paper authors, and collaborates with prestigious societies. Its mission is to serve this international community by providing an invaluable service, mainly focused on the publication of conference and workshop proceedings and postproceedings. LNCS commenced publication in 1973.

Bernhard Kainz · Alison Noble · Julia Schnabel ·
Bishesh Khanal · Johanna Paula Müller ·
Thomas Day
Editors

Simplifying Medical Ultrasound

4th International Workshop, ASMUS 2023
Held in Conjunction with MICCAI 2023
Vancouver, BC, Canada, October 8, 2023
Proceedings

Editors
Bernhard Kainz (iD)
Friedrich-Alexander-Universität
Erlangen-Nürnberg
Erlangen, Germany

Imperial College London
London, UK

Julia Schnabel (iD)
Technical University of Munich
Munich, Germany

Johanna Paula Müller (iD)
Friedrich-Alexander-Universität
Erlangen-Nürnberg
Erlangen, Germany

Alison Noble (iD)
University of Oxford
Oxford, UK

Bishesh Khanal (iD)
Nepal Institute for Applied Mathematics
and Informatics Institute for Research
NAAMII
Lalitpur, Nepal

Thomas Day (iD)
King's College London
London, UK

ISSN 0302-9743   ISSN 1611-3349 (electronic)
Lecture Notes in Computer Science
ISBN 978-3-031-44520-0   ISBN 978-3-031-44521-7 (eBook)
https://doi.org/10.1007/978-3-031-44521-7

This Springer imprint is published by the registered company Springer Nature Switzerland AG
The registered company address is: Gewerbestrasse 11, 6330 Cham, Switzerland

Paper in this product is recyclable.

Preface

We are standing at the precipice of a revolutionary era for medical ultrasound. The integration of deep learning and medical robotics is spearheading advancements that promise unprecedented improvements in the precision, pace, and consistency of various ultrasound procedures and interventions. Furthermore, these innovations are broadening the applications of ultrasound across diverse facets of patient care.

The Fourth International Workshop of Advances in Simplifying Medical Ultrasound (ASMUS 2023) carved a niche as a vibrant platform for ultrasound researchers, app developers, and healthcare professionals. This edition showcased presentations and live demonstrations encapsulating ongoing projects, groundbreaking achievements, open-source tools, and collaborative datasets. ASMUS acts not only as a catalyst for fostering novel partnerships but also as a spotlight identifying emergent challenges in ultrasound computing, robotics, clinical applications, and computer-assisted interventions. Notably, ASMUS enjoys the distinction of being the endorsed workshop of the MICCAI Special Interest Group on Medical Ultrasound. This year's event witnessed an influx of 30 stellar submissions. Each manuscript underwent a meticulous double-blind review, drawing feedback from a minimum of two external reviewers complemented by an organizing committee member. The in-depth evaluations were instrumental for the Program Committee, guiding their final selections based on the amalgamation of scientific value, novelty, methodological soundness, and potential clinical ramifications. The result? A selection of 19 exceptional papers that collectively represent the zenith of medical ultrasound. Encapsulated within these contributions are clinical applications spanning obstetrics, cardiology, interventional radiology, and organ transplant surgery. The workshop also showcased pioneering techniques in ultrasound image reconstruction, segmentation, and registration. Further, pressing topics like the utilization of AI with synthetic data, robotics, and noise mitigation were brought to the fore.

We were fortunate to have both emerging talents and stalwarts of the ultrasound community grace ASMUS 2023, leaving their indelible mark as authors and participants. Our heartfelt gratitude goes out to every reviewer, committee member, author, and participant who poured their expertise and passion into making this event an unparalleled success. As we reflect upon the milestones achieved, our eyes are set on the horizon, eagerly anticipating the innovations and collaborations this promising era of medical ultrasound will usher in.

September 2023

Bernhard Kainz
J. Alison Noble
Julia Schnabel
Bishesh Khanal
Johanna Paula Müller
Thomas Day

Organization

Program Chairs

Bernhard Kainz   Friedrich-Alexander-Universität
Erlangen-Nürnberg, Germany, Imperial
College London, UK
Julia Schnabel   Technical University of Munich, Germany
Bishesh Khanal   NAAMII, Nepal

Organizing Committee

Alison Noble   University of Oxford, UK
Stephen Aylward   Kitware, USA
Yipeng Hu   University College London, UK
Purang Abolmaesumi   University of British Columbia, Canada
Dong Ni   Shenzhen University, China
Emad Boctor   Johns Hopkins University, USA
Andy King   King's College London, UK
Ana Namburete   University of Oxford, UK
Thomas van den Heuvel   Radboud University, The Netherlands
Wolfgang Wein   ImFusion, Germany
Parvin Mousavi   Queen's University, Canada
Alberto Gomez   King's College London and Ultromics, UK
Veronika Zimmer   Technical University of Munich, Germany

Delivery Team

Thomas Day   King's College London, UK
Mischa Dombrowski   Friedrich-Alexander-Universität
Erlangen-Nürnberg, Germany
Johanna Müller   Friedrich-Alexander-Universität
Erlangen-Nürnberg, Germany
Matthew Baugh   Imperial College London, UK
Zachary Baum   University College London, UK

Advisory Board

Gabor Fichtinger	Queen's University, Canada
Kawal Rhode	King's College London, UK
Russ Taylor	Johns Hopkins University, USA
Chris de Korte	Radboud University, The Netherlands
Nassir Navab	Technical University of Munich, Germany
Reza Razavi	King's College London, UK
Joseph V. Hajnal	King's College London, UK

Program Committee

Valentin Bacher	University of Oxford, UK
David Stojanovski	King's College London, UK
Mischa Dombrowski	Friedrich-Alexander-Universität Erlangen-Nürnberg, Germany
Johanna Müller	Friedrich-Alexander-Universität Erlangen-Nürnberg, Germany
Alison Noble	University of Oxford, UK
Weitong Zhang	Imperial College London, UK
Ang Nan Gu	University of British Columbia, Canada
Helena Williams	KU Leuven, Belgium
Zhen Yuan King's	College London, UK
Thomas Day	King's College London, UK
Alberto Gomez	Ultromics, UK
Bernhard Kainz	Friedrich-Alexander-Universität Erlangen-Nürnberg, Germany, Imperial College London, UK
Bishesh Khanal	NAAMII, Nepal
Qingjie Meng	Imperial College London, UK
Johannes Paetzold	Technical University of Munich, Germany
Veronika A. Zimmer	Technical University of Munich, Germany
Zeju Li	Imperial College London, UK
Yipei Wang	University of Oxford, UK
Jerome Charton	Massachusetts General Hospital, USA
Alexander Gleed	University of Oxford, UK
Wietske A. P. Bastiaansen	Erasmus MC, The Netherlands
Andy King	King's College London, UK
Constantin Jehn	Friedrich-Alexander-Universität Erlangen-Nürnberg, Germany
Athanasios Vlontzos	Spotify, UK

Zhe Li	Friedrich-Alexander-Universität Erlangen-Nürnberg, Germany
Cheng Ouyang	Imperial College London, UK
Simon Heilig	Friedrich-Alexander-Universität Erlangen-Nürnberg, Germany
Wolfgang Wein	ImFusion GmBH, Germany
Luisa Neubig	Friedrich-Alexander-Universität Erlangen-Nürnberg, Germany
Franciskus Xaverius Erick	Friedrich-Alexander-Universität Erlangen-Nürnberg, Germany
Aaron Fenster	Western University, Canada
Zachary Baum	University College London, UK
Marc Vornehm	Friedrich-Alexander-Universität Erlangen-Nürnberg, Germany
Madeleine Wyburd	University of Oxford, UK
Daniel Roth	Friedrich-Alexander-Universität Erlangen-Nürnberg, Germany

Sponsors

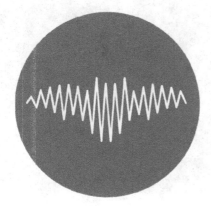

ThinkSono

ThinkSono Ltd. https://thinksono.com/

Ultromics Ltd. https://www.ultromics.com/

ImFusion GmbH. https://www.imfusion.com/

Contents

Advanced Imaging, Segmentation, and Ultrasound Techniques

Predictive Analysis, Learning, and Classification

Diagnostic Enhancements and Novel Ultrasound Innovations

Advanced Imaging, Segmentation, and Ultrasound Techniques

Ultrasound Video Segmentation with Adaptive Temporal Memory

He Zhao[1]([✉]), Qianhui Men[1], Alexander Gleed[1], Aris T. Papageorghiou[2], and J. Alison Noble[1]

[1] Institute of Biomedical Engineering, University of Oxford, Oxford, UK
he.zhao@eng.ox.ac.uk
[2] Nuffield Department of Women's and Reproductive Health, University of Oxford, Oxford, UK

Abstract. Automated segmentation of anatomical structures in fetal ultrasound video is challenging due to the highly diverse appearance of anatomies and image quality. In this paper, we propose an ultrasound video anatomy segmentation approach to iteratively memorise and segment incoming video frames, which is suitable for online segmentation. This is achieved by a spatio-temporal model that utilizes an adaptive memory bank to store the segmentation history of preceding frames to assist the current frame segmentation. The memory is updated adaptively using a skip gate mechanism based on segmentation confidence, preserving only high-confidence predictions for future use. We evaluate our approach and related state-of-the-art methods on a clinical dataset. The experimental results demonstrate that our method achieves superior performance with an F1 score of 84.83%. Visually, the use of adaptive temporal memory also aids in reducing error accumulation during video segmentation.

1 Introduction

In obstetric ultrasound, it is crucial to efficiently identify and segment various anatomical structures in the fetomaternal environment including the placenta and maternal bladder. This is because the mutual position between these two anatomies can indicate obstetric complications and thus inform the safest mode of delivery [11,15]. Such anatomy location and morphology analysis typically involve a large amount of manual effort, which is expensive due to the required expertise and is prone to inter- and intra-observer variation. Automated segmentation of the placenta and bladder can provide valuable information for computer-aided diagnosis. However, it is difficult to define the boundaries of such maternal anatomies because of high variations in shape and low contrast of the ultrasound video.

Several works [5,12,14,18,20,21] have attempted automated segmentation of maternal anatomies. A typical approach is to employ a 2D network for single image segmentation [7], such as U-Net [13] and its variations. For instance, four U-Net-based networks are used in [21] to segment a placenta image from

B. Kainz et al. (Eds.): ASMUS 2023, LNCS 14337, pp. 3–12, 2023.
https://doi.org/10.1007/978-3-031-44521-7_1

multiple views of 3D ultrasound volumes. They further propose a multi-task learning approach [20] of placenta position prediction to complement the placenta segmentation task. A coarse-to-fine segmentation pipeline is introduced in [5], where the initial anatomy segmentation is generated by a U-Net model and refined by conditional random field as a recurrent neural network. In [18], a multi-object segmentation network is proposed to segment anatomies in an ultrasound volume. The current ultrasound segmentation methods focus solely on individual timestamp and do not take into account the temporal relationship, leading to inadequate and inconsistent segmentation. Recently, a video-based segmentation method is proposed [3] to recognize breast lesions, where a 3D convolutional network with the additional temporal dimension over images is modelled to reconstruct the segmentation from a pseudo mask. However, their method requires the entire video to be observed, which makes it not applicable to online video streams.

In this paper, we propose a video-based approach for online segmentation by modelling the temporal dynamic behaviour of ultrasound video. We follow the protocol of one-shot video-object segmentation (OS-VOS) [1]: given only the first-frame annotation, the model conducts a closed-loop prediction that automatically segments subsequent frames. Our approach utilizes a memory network [10,19] to store the temporal information of ultrasound video. Inspired by [2] to update states in RNN, we propose a skip gate mechanism on the memory network, and the memory is further selected by a scoring function [8]. Then, a combined pixel and region loss encourages the model to consider both local and regional information, thus facilitating segmentation of accurate shape and boundary. The contributions of our paper are summarized as follows: 1) We propose a spatio-temporal model for ultrasound video segmentation with a memory bank, which provides new insight for video segmentation by effectively utilizing information from preceding frames. 2) An adaptive temporal memory module is proposed to update the memory bank with a skip gate, which reduces the error accumulation and maintains temporal consistency. 3) A combined pixel and region loss is proposed to learn the shape and boundaries of segmented regions. An investigation of our approach on an unseen anatomy, *i.e.*, fetal head, illustrates the generalisability of our approach to other anatomical structures.

2   Method

Our goal is to segment multiple objects in incoming video frames by referring to the first-frame segmentation. The idea of our model is to use the historical sequential information retrieved from an adaptive temporal memory bank to assist in accurate segmentation of the current frame. The current frame $I_t \in \mathbb{R}^{W \times H \times 3}$ and the preceding frames $I = \{I_i | i = 1, ..., t - 1\}$ are considered as query and memory, respectively. As shown in Fig. 1, the complete framework consists of three parts: a spatial feature extraction module $\mathcal{F}$ with two encoders E_Q and E_M used for extracting the spatial representations of query and memory frames; an adaptive temporal memory module which updates from temporal

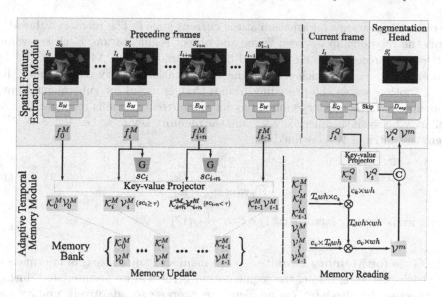

Fig. 1. Flowchart of our architecture. It has three components: the feature extraction module for spatial feature learning by encoder E_M and E_Q; the adaptive temporal memory module controlled by a skip gate mechanism for memory update and memory reading; and a segmentation head with skip-connection decoder D_{seg}. $\otimes$ denotes matrix inner-product and © represents the concatenation operation.

dependencies of memory frames I and their predicted masks S'; and a segmentation head, fusing retrieved memory embedding $\mathcal{V}^m$ and query embedding $\mathcal{V}_t^Q$ to predict the current frame segmentation.

2.1 Spatial Feature Extraction Module

The memory encoder E_M takes both the preceding frame I_i and its predicted segmentation mask S_i' as input, and outputs spatial features $f^M = \{E_M(I_i, S_i')|i = 0, \ldots, t-1\}$, where S_i' helps to identify the spatial features of related targets from the background. Different from E_M, the query encoder E_Q only takes the current frame I_t as input and produces a feature map $f_t^Q = E_Q(I_t)$. Other than an extraction layer in E_M to deal with the segmentation input, E_M and E_Q share the same model structure of a ResNet-50 [6] as the feature extraction backbone.

2.2 Adaptive Temporal Memory Module

Memory Construction and Reading. After the spatial feature extraction module $\mathcal{F}$, each of the spatial features f^M from memory and f_t^Q from the query is embedded into a *key* matrix $\mathcal{K} \in \mathbb{R}^{w \times h \times c_k}$ and a *value* matrix $\mathcal{V} \in \mathbb{R}^{w \times h \times c_v}$ by two convolutional layers, where c_k and c_v are the corresponding embedded channel dimensions, respectively. $\mathcal{K}$ is learned to retrieve the relevant feature embedding from the spatial information stored in $\mathcal{V}$. The query value $\mathcal{V}_t^Q$ focuses on the object appearance information at the current time t. The memory value $\mathcal{V}_i^M$ learns the relationship between frame and object segmentation. Each key-value pair from a preceding frame is stored in the memory bank $\mathcal{M} = \{(\mathcal{K}_i^M, \mathcal{V}_i^M)\}$ with size $|\mathcal{M}| = T_n$, which records the segmentation history and encodes the object motion across the preceding frames that is useful for subsequent frame segmentation. The memory embedding for the current frame is retrieved by the similarity between the query key $\mathcal{K}^Q$ and the memory key $\mathcal{K}^M$, i.e., $\mathcal{V}^m = W\mathcal{V}^M$, where the entry of W is defined as:

$$\omega_j = \frac{\exp(z\mathcal{K}_t^Q \cdot \mathcal{K}_j^M)}{\sum_l \exp(z\mathcal{K}_t^Q \cdot \mathcal{K}_l^M)}. \tag{1}$$

Here z is the scaling factor that is set to $\frac{1}{\sqrt{c_k}}$ [17].

Skip Gate for Memory Update. As the memory bank consists of information from each preceding frame, the segmentation error will be accumulated during this process. To alleviate this problem, we propose to adaptively update the memory bank with a skip gate mechanism. The key insight is to introduce a score function to control the temporal information flow that preserves the memories only with frames given a high segmentation confidence. The skip gate G for the memory update is implemented by a trainable convolutional network to predict a confidence score sc from the memory feature f_i^M at time i with $sc_i = G(f_i^M) = G(E_M(I_i, S_i'))$. Here, G consists of three convolutional layers, two fully-connected layers, and a sigmoid function such that the predicted score is within the range of $[0, 1]$. The role of G is as a regression function to predict the confidence level of the correspondence between the frame and its predicted segmentation. Only the frames with a confidence score larger than a predefined threshold τ are used to update the memory bank. During inference, the proposed skip gate also reduces the burden of the memory bank to enable fast segmentation.

2.3   Segmentation

Segmentation Head. During segmentation, the predicted mask is generated by decoder D_{seg} from both the query value $\mathcal{V}_t^Q$ at the current frame t and the retrieved memory value $\mathcal{V}^m$ of the past frames $i < t$. The decoder is built based on three ResBlock with skip connections. The initial ResBlock merges $\mathcal{V}^m$ and $\mathcal{V}_t^Q$ to extract comprehensive spatial information for the current segmentation, and the decoder output is interpolated to the size of I_t as the predicted segmentation mask.

Training. The overall objective function $\mathcal{L}$ is a combination of two loss components: a segmentation loss $\mathcal{L}_{seg}$ and a confidence loss $\mathcal{L}_{sc}$, i.e., $\mathcal{L} = \mathcal{L}_{seg} + \mathcal{L}_{sc}$. The detailed construction of each loss component is explained next.

Segmentation Loss. We consider both the local and global errors in the generated segmentation mask with a pixel loss and a region loss, respectively. The pixel loss is constructed from the cross entropy between the corresponding segmented pixels, which aims to identify each pixel independently. The region loss is IoU-based to minimize the mismatched area between two segmentation masks. Additionally, the inclusion of region loss also helps to alleviate the foreground and background imbalance present in ultrasound images. Combining the two losses, the segmentation loss $\mathcal{L}_{seg}$ is given by

$$\mathcal{L}_{seg} = \underbrace{-\sum_n (s_n log(s'_n) + (1 - s_n) log(1 - s'_n))}_{\text{pixel loss}} + \underbrace{\frac{\sum_n s_n s'_n}{\sum_n (s_n + s'_n - s_n s'_n)}}_{\text{region loss}}, \quad (2)$$

where s_n and s'_n stands for the nth pixel in the segmentation ground truth S and prediction S', respectively.

Confidence Loss. The skip gate G predicts the segmentation confidence based on the image and segmentation features. To train network G, the ground truth of confidence score of each frame segmentation is defined as the IoU between the segmentation prediction and its corresponding ground truth. The segmentation confidence loss $\mathcal{L}_{sc}$ for optimizing the skip gate is defined as:

$$\mathcal{L}_{sc} = (sc - IoU(S, S'))^2 \quad (3)$$

where $sc = G(E_M(I, S'))$ is the output from skip gate network.

3 Experiments and Results

The dataset used in this paper consisted of 15 ultrasound video scans from the CALOPUS project [16] that used a U-shaped video sweep protocol to scan from the maternal right to left over the top of the pelvis. The videos were randomly split into 11 for training and 4 for test. Each video is approximately 20 s containing around 200 frames after downsampling, with a video frame size of 1008×784. For each video frame, a manual segmentation annotation of the placenta and maternal bladder was available as ground truth. To increase the robustness of automated segmentation, we randomly selected three frames in temporal order with resized shape of 448×448 as one training sample. The model was trained with an Adam optimizer for 200 epochs with a decayed learning rate of $2e^{-5}$. During inference, a whole video sequence is iteratively segmented given the manual annotation of the starting frame as reference.

3.1 Evaluations

We compared our method with three image-based models which only use the current frame to predict the segmentation mask: U-Net [13], ResNet34 [6] and

Table 1. Quantitative performance of image- and video-based segmentation methods evaluated by the F1-score, accuracy, Jaccard Index, Hausdorff distance, and contour accuracy.

Protocol	Method	F1-score ↑	Accuracy ↑	Jaccard ↑	Hausdorff ↓	Contour ↑
Image-based	U-Net [13]	62.51	97.67	52.93	83.60	26.57
	ResNet34 [6]	64.25	96.48	50.69	97.24	21.04
	TransU-Net [4]	68.00	97.52	59.15	77.84	34.24
Video-based	STM [10]	82.50	99.20	73.15	46.16	39.29
	Ours	**84.83**	**99.39**	**76.25**	**33.73**	**40.03**

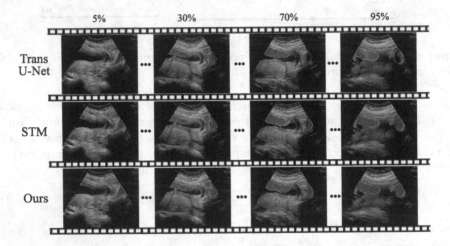

Fig. 2. Qualitative results of video segmentation. Red: placenta; Green: bladder. The white boundary line is the segmentation ground truth of each object. Different frame positions are shown as the percentage of the video length. (Color figure online)

TransU-Net [4]; and a video-based segmentation model under OS-VOS protocol [1] – Spatio-temporal Memory Network (STM) [10]. Table 1 compares these methods with our approach using five segmentation metrics: F1-score, accuracy, Jaccard Index, Hausdorff distance, and contour accuracy. Among those metrics, Hausdorff distance and contour accuracy inform about the object boundary and shape which are important in our clinical application.

First, we observe that the two video-based methods achieve higher overall scores than image-based methods, which suggests that the information from prior video frames is helpful during the video segmentation process. Compared with video-based STM, our approach with adaptive temporal memory achieves superior performance with an improvement of F1-score by 2.8%. Our approach also achieves the lowest Hausdorff distance (33.73 pixels) and the highest contour accuracy score (40.03%). The accurate shapes and border regions of placenta and bladder are important indicators for fetal diagnosis. For instance, the distance between the lower boundary of placenta and the bottom of bladder can be used

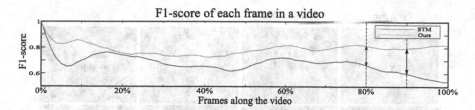

Fig. 3. The quantitative comparison (F1-score) between STM and our approach with adaptive memory module on each frame along the video.

Table 2. Ablation studies for different experimental settings.

Method		F1-score ↑	Accuracy ↑	Jaccard ↑	Hausdorff ↓	Contour ↑
Latest frame only		73.18	99.18	64.52	43.94	32.20
First & latest frames		78.21	99.30	69.70	37.93	34.35
Preceding frames	w/o ATM	82.50	99.20	73.15	46.16	39.29
	w/o region loss	81.45	99.37	72.85	35.53	37.42
	Ours	**84.83**	**99.39**	**76.25**	**33.73**	**40.03**

to differentiate normal and abnormally-located placentae [9]. Figure 2 shows typical visual segmentation results for TransU-Net, STM, and our approach. The TransU-Net segmentation results are less consistent and less accurate compared to the video-based methods, as it only considers the current frame appearance and ignores segmentation history. Within the video-based methods, the segmentation error for STM quickly accumulates as prediction progresses - *c.f.* the result at 70% and 95% of the whole video. Figure 3 illustrates the F1-score of each frame along a video. It can be observed that the model without adaptive memory (*i.e.*, STM) experiences a significant decrease in performance for the later frames in the video. By keeping only the memory with high segmentation confidence in the temporal domain, our approach does not suffer the same performance degradation.

3.2 Ablation Study

Temporal Memory Bank. We first analyze the influence of using temporal information. Four scenarios are compared in this experiment: 1) only the latest frame (the frame before current frame) used as memory; 2) the first annotated frame and the latest frame as memory; 3) all preceding frames as memory without adaptive temporal memory (denoted as *w/o ATM*), and 4) preceding frames with adaptive temporal memory (*Ours*). The quantitative and qualitative results are shown in Table 2 and Fig. 4, respectively. The model with only the latest frame as memory produces the lowest F1-score (73.18%) and fails to segment the bladder. The performance increases to 78.21% by adding the first frame into the memory, since the first annotation is a key reference to inform the model with the position of the segmentation. With more preceding frames

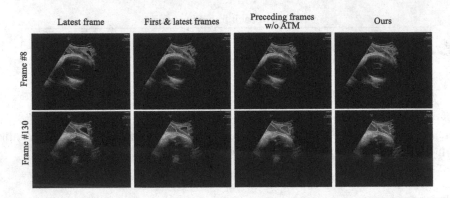

Fig. 4. Qualitative comparisons under different memory settings.

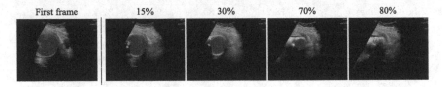

Fig. 5. Visual results on unseen anatomy (fetal head) segmentation.

included (as in *w/o ATM*), the temporal dependencies and the motion of objects in video are modelled in the memory. This allows the model to recall and leverage information from previous frames to generate a plausible prediction on the current frame. Adding the adaptive temporal memory mechanism (as in *Ours*) further boosts segmentation performance, which utilizes the skip gate to encourage incorrectly segmented frames to be discarded. This enables the model to self-check and rectify its own errors, resulting in a more accurate segmentation.

Pixel and Region Loss. We tested the model with different loss terms. The results are reported in the last two rows of Table 2. The model with both pixel and region loss (shown as *Ours*) achieves stronger metric scores in terms of regional evaluation, *i.e.,* Jaccard Index and contour accuracy. This demonstrates that the region loss encourages the model to pay more attention to the whole area and thus anatomical structure, resulting in more precise object boundaries.

Sensitivity of First-Frame Annotation. It is of interest to qualify the model robustness towards the variations of the first-frame annotation. For a test video, first-frame masks of placenta and bladder from three individuals are served as reference in addition to the ground truth segmentation. The standard deviation of their F1-scores is 0.7 and the average Pearson correlation coefficient is 0.89. This statistical analysis indicates that our model is robust to the first-frame annotation and can produce reasonable results with inter-variations of reference frame annotations.

Unseen Anatomy Segmentation. To investigate generalisability, we tested our segmentation model on unseen anatomy, *i.e.*, the fetal head. An example result is shown in Fig. 5. Segmenting the fetal head in ultrasound video is challenging due to the significant inter-frame shape changes. Our model still generates valid head segmentation masks over time when given the annotation of the first frame.

3.3 Conclusions

In this paper, we have proposed an automated ultrasound video segmentation method which exploits temporal continuity over video frames. A memory bank is constructed by a memory encoder to extract and store the association between a frame and its segmentation over time. A skip gate is proposed to control the memory module update resulting in an adaptive temporal memory bank for retrieval. Our approach provides new insight using the preceding frames in a memory bank for online video stream segmentation, and it achieves state-of-the-art performance on the placenta and maternal bladder. Experiments on video of an unseen fetal head show the potential of our model to be applied to other ultrasound anatomical segmentation tasks.

Acknowledgments. We acknowledge the ERC (ERC-ADG-2015 694581, project PULSE), the Global Challenges Research Fund (EP/R013853/1, project CALOPUS), EPSRC Programme Grant (EP/T028572/1, project VisualAI), and the InnoHK-funded Hong Kong Centre for Cerebro-cardiovascular Health Engineering (COCHE) Project 2.1 (Cardiovascular risks in early life and fetal echocardiography).

References

1. Caelles, S., Maninis, K.K., Pont-Tuset, J., Leal-Taixé, L., Cremers, D., Van Gool, L.: One-shot video object segmentation. In: Proceedings of the IEEE Conference on Computer Vision and Pattern Recognition, pp. 221–230 (2017)
2. Campos, V., Jou, B., Giró-i Nieto, X., Torres, J., Chang, S.F.: Skip RNN: learning to skip state updates in recurrent neural networks. In: International Conference on Learning Representations (2018)
3. Chang, R., Wang, D., Guo, H., Ding, J., Wang, L.: Weakly-supervised ultrasound video segmentation with minimal annotations. In: de Bruijne, M., et al. (eds.) MICCAI 2021. LNCS, vol. 12908, pp. 648–658. Springer, Cham (2021). https://doi.org/10.1007/978-3-030-87237-3_62
4. Chen, J., et al.: Transunet: transformers make strong encoders for medical image segmentation. arXiv preprint arXiv:2102.04306 (2021)
5. Gleed, A.D., et al.: Automatic image guidance for assessment of placenta location in ultrasound video sweeps. Ultrasound Med. Biol. **49**(1), 106–121 (2023)
6. He, K., Zhang, X., Ren, S., Sun, J.: Deep residual learning for image recognition. In: Proceedings of the IEEE Conference on Computer Vision and Pattern Recognition, pp. 770–778 (2016)
7. Huang, Q., Huang, Y., Luo, Y., Yuan, F., Li, X.: Segmentation of breast ultrasound image with semantic classification of superpixels. Med. Image Anal. **61**, 101657 (2020)

8. Huang, Z., Huang, L., Gong, Y., Huang, C., Wang, X.: Mask scoring R-CNN. In: Proceedings of the IEEE/CVF Conference on Computer Vision and Pattern Recognition, pp. 6409–6418 (2019)
9. Jauniaux, E., Collins, S., Burton, G.J.: Placenta accreta spectrum: pathophysiology and evidence-based anatomy for prenatal ultrasound imaging. Am. J. Obstet. Gynecol. **218**(1), 75–87 (2018)
10. Oh, S.W., Lee, J.Y., Xu, N., Kim, S.J.: Video object segmentation using space-time memory networks. In: Proceedings of the IEEE/CVF International Conference on Computer Vision, pp. 9226–9235 (2019)
11. Oppenheimer, L., et al.: Diagnosis and management of placenta previa. J. Obstet. Gynaecol. Can. **29**(3), 261–266 (2007)
12. Qi, H., Collins, S., Noble, A.: Weakly supervised learning of placental ultrasound images with residual networks. In: Valdés Hernández, M., González-Castro, V. (eds.) MIUA 2017. CCIS, vol. 723, pp. 98–108. Springer, Cham (2017). https://doi.org/10.1007/978-3-319-60964-5_9
13. Ronneberger, O., Fischer, P., Brox, T.: U-net: convolutional networks for biomedical image segmentation. In: Navab, N., Hornegger, J., Wells, W.M., Frangi, A.F. (eds.) MICCAI 2015. LNCS, vol. 9351, pp. 234–241. Springer, Cham (2015). https://doi.org/10.1007/978-3-319-24574-4_28
14. Schilpzand, M., et al.: Automatic placenta localization from ultrasound imaging in a resource-limited setting using a predefined ultrasound acquisition protocol and deep learning. Ultrasound Med. Biol. **48**(4), 663–674 (2022)
15. Self, A., Gleed, A., Bhatnagar, S., Noble, A., Papageorghiou, A.: Vp18. 01: machine learning applied to the standardised six-step approach for placental localisation in basic obstetric ultrasound. Ultrasound Obstetr. Gynecol. **58**, 172–172 (2021)
16. Self, A., et al.: Developing clinical artificial intelligence for obstetric ultrasound to improve access in underserved regions: protocol for a computer-assisted low-cost point-of-care ultrasound (calopus) study. JMIR Res. Protocols **11**(9), e37374 (2022)
17. Vaswani, A., et al.: Attention is all you need. In: Advances in Neural Information Processing Systems, vol. 30 (2017)
18. Yang, X., et al.: Towards automated semantic segmentation in prenatal volumetric ultrasound. IEEE Trans. Med. Imaging **38**(1), 180–193 (2018)
19. Zhou, T., Li, L., Bredell, G., Li, J., Unkelbach, J., Konukoglu, E.: Volumetric memory network for interactive medical image segmentation. Med. Image Anal. **83**, 102599 (2023)
20. Zimmer, V.A., et al.: A multi-task approach using positional information for ultrasound placenta segmentation. In: Hu, Y., et al. (eds.) ASMUS/PIPPI -2020. LNCS, vol. 12437, pp. 264–273. Springer, Cham (2020). https://doi.org/10.1007/978-3-030-60334-2_26
21. Zimmer, V.A., et al.: Towards whole placenta segmentation at late gestation using multi-view ultrasound images. In: Shen, D., et al. (eds.) MICCAI 2019. LNCS, vol. 11768, pp. 628–636. Springer, Cham (2019). https://doi.org/10.1007/978-3-030-32254-0_70

An Automatic Guidance and Quality Assessment System for Doppler Imaging of Umbilical Artery

Chun Kit Wong[1(✉)], Manxi Lin[1], Alberto Raheli[1], Zahra Bashir[2,3], Morten Bo Søndergaard Svendsen[2,4], Martin Grønnebæk Tolsgaard[2,4], Aasa Feragen[1], and Anders Nymark Christensen[1]

[1] Technical University of Denmark, Kongens Lyngby, Denmark
{ckwo,anym}@dtu.dk
[2] University of Copenhagen, Copenhagen, Denmark
[3] Slagelse Hospital, Slagelse, Denmark
[4] CAMES Rigshospitalet, Copenhagen, Denmark

Abstract. Examination of the umbilical artery with Doppler ultra-sonography is performed to investigate blood supply to the fetus through the umbilical cord, which is vital for the monitoring of fetal health. Such examination involves several steps that must be performed correctly: identifying suitable sites on the umbilical artery for the measurement, acquiring the blood flow curve in the form of a Doppler spectrum, and ensuring compliance to a set of quality standards. These steps are performed manually and rely heavily on the operator's skill. In this work, we propose an automated pipeline as an assistive system. By using a modified Faster R-CNN network, we trained a model that can suggest locations suitable for Doppler measurement. Meanwhile, we have also developed a method for assessment of the Doppler spectrum's quality. The proposed system is validated on 657 images from a national ultra-sound screening database, with results demonstrating its potential as a guidance system.

Keywords: Fetal Ultrasound · Umbilical Artery · Doppler Imaging

1 Introduction

Ultrasound is widely used for routine monitoring of fetal health. In the third-trimester, ultrasound screenings are utilized to monitor potential growth restrictions of the fetus and the blood supply through the umbilical cord (UC). These screenings examine several anatomical standard planes formally defined in guidelines [2] developed by the International Society of Ultrasound in Obstetrics and

---

C.K. Wong and M. Lin—These authors contributed equally to this work.

Supplementary Information The online version contains supplementary material available at https://doi.org/10.1007/978-3-031-44521-7_2.

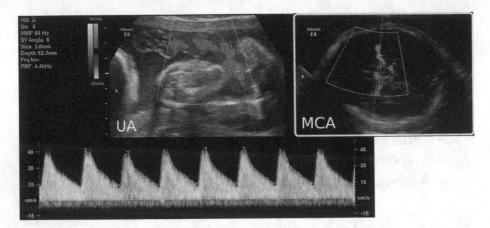

Fig. 1. Examples of Doppler ultrasonography in obstetrics. **Left:** Umbilical Artery (UA) including the spectral Doppler waveform. **Right:** Middle Cerebral Artery (MCA). Note how on the MCA, the vessel is running parallel to the long axis of the vessel's segmentation, making angle estimation from segmentation straightforward. In UA, however, the vessels are usually intertwined, which means the angle cannot be trivially inferred from the segmentation.

Gynecology (ISUOG), which aims to ensure accurate measurement. In practice, conducting such examinations while adhering to the guidelines is technically demanding and often relies on operator experience. However, due to the shortage of sonographers, third-trimester screenings are often performed by clinicians not specialized in ultrasound acquisition [3,11]. To assist clinicians in acquiring high quality images, this paper presents an automatic system for operator guidance in assessment of the umbilical artery (UA), which is crucial for monitoring of the fetal blood supply, but challenging to image optimally due to the high variance in orientation of the UC.

Examination of blood flow with ultrasound is performed over two steps: identifying and placing a measurement gate on a suitable site with color Doppler imaging, followed by measuring the blood flow curve in the form of spectral Doppler waveform with pulsed Doppler (see Fig. 1). These waveforms, which allow assessment of UA as well as the middle cerebral artery (MCA), play an important role in the third-trimester ultrasound screening [7]. A number of machine learning-based techniques have been used to support analysis of Doppler waveforms [5,9]. Hoodbhoy et al. [5] identified fetuses at increased risk of adverse perinatal outcomes with multiple kernel learning. Naftali et al. [9] built a support vector machine, a K-nearest model, and a logistic regression model for identifying unseen UC abnormalities from the waveforms. While these studies show a clear potential for AI-based diagnosis, they were conducted using waveforms acquired by experienced clinicians. As noted by Necas [10], even with the availability of guidelines, mistakes are still commonly observed in practice.

Table 1. ISUOG guidelines on using Doppler ultrasound in obstetrics

Criterion	Description
Anatomical site	the Doppler signal must be measured in a free loop of the UC
Angle of insonation	the angle to the blood flow should be less than 30°, indicating a near-vertical presentation of the blood vessel
Image clarity	the resulting Doppler signal should be clear, without artifacts and with an accurate trace
Sweep speed	resulting Doppler signal should have 3–10 waveforms visible
Dynamic range	in the resulting Doppler signal, the waveforms should occupy more than 75% of the y-axis

Meanwhile, acquisition of an optimal Doppler waveform requires consistent, manual adjustment of various parameters, which increases the mental load on the operator [14]. This motivates research in automation of the ultrasound acquisition procedure. In this direction, MCANet [14] was developed to propose positions for measurement gate placement. In contrast to MCANet, we consider Doppler measurement at the UA, and are, to the best of our knowledge, the first to address this problem. In addition, we also introduce a study protocol for assessing the quality of the acquired Doppler waveforms. In summary, our contributions are **1)** an automatic detection of appropriate sites for UA Doppler measurement, taking both location and insonation angle into account, and **2)** an automated evaluation of the Doppler waveforms to ensure sufficient quality.

2 Method

We propose an image analysis pipeline that is based directly on the ISUOG guidelines (see Table 1). The first two criteria relate to the presentation of UA in the chosen ultrasound plane, whereas the remaining three criteria relate to the quality of the resulting waveforms. As such, the ISUOG criteria align well with a 2-step process. First, we assist the ultrasound operator by giving feedback on the presentation of the UA and suggesting a suitable gate location for measuring the Doppler spectrum. Next, we consider the resulting spectrum, either accepting or rejecting the combination of ultrasound plane and gate. In this way, we ensure that the examination maintains a high quality, while also giving the operator feedback on potential problems in the image acquisition.

2.1 Deep Learning-Based Processing of Color Doppler Images

As a first step in our pipeline, we need to identify a vessel, and a gate location within the vessel. This vessel needs to be an artery (as opposed to a vein) satisfying the first two ISUOG criteria. While it might seem trivial to segment vessels that are colored red and blue and measure their angle, Fig. 1 illustrates how this problem is significantly harder for the UA, where the vessel twists and turns around itself, than it is for the MCA. We tackle this as a modified object detection problem where, instead of just detecting potential gate locations within vessels as being acceptable or not, we add a regression head to the detection algorithm in order to encode its angle (see Fig. 2).

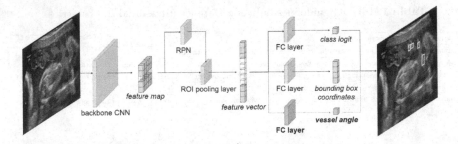

Fig. 2. Network architecture: Faster R-CNN with an extra sibling FC layer branch added for vessel angle prediction.

We base our UA gate location algorithm on the Faster R-CNN object detection algorithm [12]. Faster R-CNN first generates a feature map using a backbone CNN network, which is fed to a Region Proposal Network (RPN) to propose candidate regions of interest (ROIs). Then, an ROI pooling layer is employed to extract, pool, and flatten features corresponding to the proposed ROIs, which are finally passed to two sibling branches of fully connected (FC) layers for classification and bounding box regression of the proposed ROIs. The loss function proposed in the original paper is given by:

$$L_{FasterRCNN}(\{p_i\}, \{t_i\}) = \frac{1}{N_{cls}} \sum_i L_{cls}(p_i, p_i^*) + \lambda \frac{1}{N_{reg}} \sum_i p_i^* L_{reg}(t_i, t_i^*) \quad (1)$$

where p_i is the predicted probability that the i-th proposed ROI at the predicted coordinates t_i is a valid object, with p_i^* and t_i^* as the corresponding ground-truths. The log loss L_{cls} is normalized by the batch size N_{cls}, and the smooth L1 loss L_{reg} by the number of proposed ROIs N_{reg}, with λ balancing the terms.

In our setting, we want to detect potential gate locations that satisfy both the anatomical site and angle requirements of the ISUOG criteria. To achieve this, the standard classification branch predicts whether the anatomical site criterion is fulfilled. Then, we enrich the Faster R-CNN model with an extra sibling FC layer branch to predict the underlying vessel's angle at each proposed ROI.

To train this modified model, we included another term in Eq. 1 to regress the predicted angle against ground truth annotations (see Fig. 4a):

$$L(\{p_i\}, \{t_i\}, \{a_i\}) = L_{FasterRCNN}(\{p_i\}, \{t_i\}) + \mu \frac{1}{N_{reg}} \sum_i p_i^* L_{reg}(a_i, a_i^*) \quad (2)$$

where a_i and a_i^* are the predicted and ground truth angle of the i-th proposed ROI, and μ is another balancing factor. λ and μ are set to 1 and 10, respectively.

Locating Source of Ultrasound Beam. The vessel angle estimated using our modified Faster-RCNN network indicates the vessel's direction (see Fig. 4b). However, the angle of insonation needed to assess the second ISUOG criterion refers to the angle of the vessel with respect to the direction of the ultrasound beam.

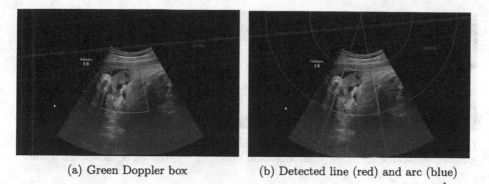

(a) Green Doppler box   (b) Detected line (red) and arc (blue)

Fig. 3. Locating source of the ultrasound beam by using the green Doppler box. (Color figure online)

Hence, to assess whether the angle is acceptable and give suitable feedback to the operator, we need to determine the direction of the ultrasound beam and use it to calibrate the angle prediction from the network.

We begin with determining the direction of the ultrasound beam by utilizing the green Doppler box, which becomes active during color Doppler acquisition (see Fig. 3a). A binary mask of the green Doppler box is first obtained by color thresholding on the RGB pixels, followed by enhancing the mask using a watershed transform [6]. Next, a Hough line detection algorithm [1] is used to identify the two radial line segments on each side of the box. The ultrasound source is located at the intersection between the two line segments. As an extra step to prevent erroneous detection, we verify that we are able to detect the two arc lines with Hough circle detection when the center location is constrained to be at the intersection point from the previous two Hough lines (see Fig. 3b).

Determining the Angle of Insonation. Next, from the identified location of the ultrasound source, it is straightforward to compute a vector map pointing at the direction of the ultrasound source from each pixel (see Fig. 4c). By expressing the vessel angle predicted by the network as another vector, the angle of insonation can be easily calculated using the law of cosine.

Based on the above, we obtain a detection algorithm that proposes, to the operator, gate locations fulfilling both anatomical and angle requirements. This algorithm is developed using images acquired with different models of GE scanners. Adjustments for cross-vendor applications is expected to be minor, since it is a convention in Doppler ultrasound to use variations of red and blue while encoding flow directions [2].

2.2 Processing of Pulsed Doppler Spectrum Images

From the suggested gate locations (see Sect. 2.1), an operator could choose the best one for spectrum acquisition with pulsed Doppler. Next, we present our processing to assess the quality of the resulting spectrum.

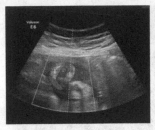
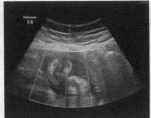
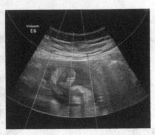

(a) Expert annotated boxes and tangential lines   (b) Model predicted boxes and tangential lines   (c) Vectors pointing in direction of ultrasound source

Fig. 4. Different stages in processing Color Doppler image.

Segmentation of the Doppler Spectrum. Prior to analyzing the Doppler spectrum, all irrelevant visual confounders, such as tracing lines indicating measurements made by the scanner (see Fig. 1), are first removed from the image to prevent bias in our method. Since the confounders are all colored, they can be delineated from the grey spectrum by identifying pixels with large variance across the color (i.e. RGB) channel, and removed by inpainting with biharmonic functions.

Next, the spectrum is segmented using a random walk segmentation algorithm [4], as watershed is found to be insufficient. From the mask of the segmented spectrum, the envelope of the spectrum can be identified from the boundary. Then, the x-axis line of the spectrum is detected using the Hough line detection algorithm, and used to remove anything below and fill any holes above.

Identification of Individual Waveforms. From the spectrum segmentation, peaks and valleys are detected along the upper envelope. To avoid over-detection, the envelope is Gaussian-smoothed prior to running the detection algorithm. Besides that, the detected peaks (and valleys) are forced to have a minimum distance of 70 pixels between each other. Individual waveforms are then identified with the rule that a complete waveform starts and ends at valleys with a peak in between. From that, the sweep speed is said to be optimal if there are 3–10 individual waveforms in total.

Determining Waveform Properties. Having identified individual waveforms, we need to quantify their quality in order to assess whether the waveform as a whole satisfies the last three ISUOG criteria. To obtain this, the spectrum image pixels are first rescaled to floating point values between 0 and 1. Using the spectrum segmentation, we mask out the relevant part of the spectrum to compute the mean intensity of pixels in each individual waveform. Two threshold values are defined to classify the waveform as having good, moderate, or poor clarity (see Fig. 5). In our experiment, these thresholds are set empirically, together with a clinician, to 0.56 and 0.36. Heights of the waveform are determined from the peak coordinate and the x-axis line, followed by expressing them as a percentage of the positive y-axis.

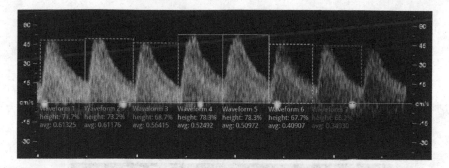

Fig. 5. Waveform clarity and height. Good clarity is indicated in green (mean intensity > 0.56), moderate in yellow, and poor in red (mean intensity < 0.36) is poor. Dotted line indicates waveforms with height less than 75%. (Color figure online)

3   Dataset

The data used for this study were gathered from a Danish national fetal ultrasound screening database containing images acquired between 2009 and 2019 as part of the standard prenatal care, with approvals from The Danish Data Protection Agency (Protocol No. P-2019-310) and by The Danish Patient Safety Authority (Protocol No. 3-3031-2915/1). In total, 657 DICOM images of Doppler ultrasound examination at the UA were retrieved from the database. From each image, two regions were cropped and exported separately: (1) the b-mode ultrasound image with color Doppler overlays (for simplicity, we will call this the color Doppler image), and (2) the pulsed Doppler spectrum image.

Subsequently, the color Doppler images were annotated by a clinician using the open-source tool LabelMe [13]. On each image, regions corresponding to the correct anatomical site (i.e. the UA) were annotated with bounding box, which was done sparsely due to the inherent difficulty in annotating all correct anatomical sites with just bounding boxes. Finally, a tangential line going in the direction of the blood vessel were added on top of each annotated bounding box to indicate the vessel's angle (see Fig. 4a).

4   Experiments and Results

4.1   Experimental Settings

The modified Faster R-CNN model was implemented in PyTorch 1.13.1 on an AlmaLinux 8.7 system. The model backbone is a ResNet50 FPN pre-trained on COCO [8] and fine-tuned on our annotated images at 80:20 train-test split with SGD optimizer, which converged after 20 epochs. The learning rate was 0.005 at the first epoch and reduced 0.1 times every 3 epochs. The batch size was set to 2. This training took less than 1 h on an NVIDIA RTX A6000 GPU. The experiments on waveform quality assessment were conducted on a server (CPU: EPYC 7252 8-Core Processor; RAM: 32 GB), using image processing algorithms implemented in Scipy 1.10.0 and Scikit-Image 0.19.3.

20   C. K. Wong et al.

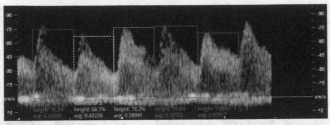

(a) Less than 3 consecutive waveforms with at least moderate clarity

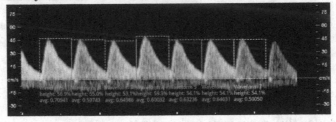

(b) Waveforms not occupying 75% of the y-axis

Fig. 6. Example spectrums not meeting the ISUOG criteria.

4.2   Results

Automatic Gate Placement. The ground-truth gate locations in our dataset are under-annotated (see Sect. 3). Hence, to better estimate the error in our angle prediction, we compared each model-suggested gate position box with the closest ground truth box, matched according to the Euclidean distance between the centroid of the two boxes. Pairs separated with a too-far distance (greater than 10 pixels; see Appendix 1) were excluded from this analysis. With a 5-fold cross validation, 85.37% (std 2.97%) of the ground truth has a matched prediction, with a mean absolute error of 19.36° (std 0.47°) in angle prediction.

Additionally, an experienced clinician was engaged to check through the model predictions on 737 test images and reject images with at least one unacceptable box prediction, giving a conservative performance estimate. This gave an acceptance rate of 68.1%.

Waveform Quality Assessment. We applied the proposed waveform quality assessment pipeline on the 657 spectrum images. Figure 6 presents two images that has failed to meet the ISUOG waveform clarity and dynamic range criteria, identified by our method. This demonstrates the promising potential of our pipeline being alternatively deployed as a retrospective waveform quality assessment tool.

5   Discussion and Conclusion

We attempted to address a real clinical problem in this paper: providing guidance to an operator on the Doppler assessment of UA, which is significant due to the shortage of skilled sonographers. We proposed a method for guiding the operator on where to place the measurement gate, which has shown promising performance on our test data. Furthermore, another method was proposed to assess the quality of the acquired spectrum, designed to be well-aligned to the criteria specified in the ISUOG guidelines. This provides a comprehensive assessment of the scan quality, ensuring compliance to criteria such as "sweep speed" and "dynamic range", which often get neglected in actual clinical practice.

In the future, we aim to extend the method for processing live video stream directly. While new challenges is foreseen with the incorporation of temporal information, better performance can be expected in multiple ways, such as an improved accuracy in differentiating between the pulsating artery and the non-pulsating vein. Overall, we have demonstrated the potential of our method in resolving the clinical problem that has motivated its development.

References

1. Aggarwal, N., Karl, W.C.: Line detection in images through regularized Hough transform. IEEE Trans. Image Process. **15**(3), 582–591 (2006)
2. Bhide, A., et al.: Isuog practice guidelines: use of doppler ultrasonography in obstetrics. Ultrasound Obstetr. Gynecol. Off. J. Int. Soc. Ultrasound Obstetr. Gynecol. **41**(2), 233–239 (2013)
3. Edvardsson, K., Ntaganira, J., Åhman, A., Sengoma, J.P.S., Small, R., Mogren, I.: Physicians' experiences and views on the role of obstetric ultrasound in rural and urban Rwanda: a qualitative study. Tropical Med. Int. Health **21**(7), 895–906 (2016)
4. Grady, L.: Random walks for image segmentation. IEEE Trans. Pattern Anal. Mach. Intell. **28**(11), 1768–1783 (2006). https://doi.org/10.1109/TPAMI.2006.233
5. Hoodbhoy, Z., Hasan, B., Jehan, F., Bijnens, B., Chowdhury, D.: Machine learning from fetal flow waveforms to predict adverse perinatal outcomes: a study protocol. Gates Open Res. **2** (2018)
6. Huang, Y.L., Chen, D.R.: Watershed segmentation for breast tumor in 2-D sonography. Ultrasound Med. Biol. **30**(5), 625–632 (2004)
7. Kennedy, A.M., Woodward, P.J.: A radiologist's guide to the performance and interpretation of obstetric doppler us. Radiographics **39**(3), 893–910 (2019)
8. Lin, T.-Y., et al.: Microsoft COCO: common objects in context. In: Fleet, D., Pajdla, T., Schiele, B., Tuytelaars, T. (eds.) ECCV 2014. LNCS, vol. 8693, pp. 740–755. Springer, Cham (2014). https://doi.org/10.1007/978-3-319-10602-1_48
9. Naftali, S., Ashkenazi, Y.N., Ratnovsky, A.: A novel approach based on machine learning analysis of flow velocity waveforms to identify unseen abnormalities of the umbilical cord. Placenta **127**, 20–28 (2022)
10. Necas, M.: Obstetric doppler ultrasound: are we performing it correctly? Aust. J. Ultrasound Med. **19**(1), 6 (2016)

11. Recker, F., Weber, E., Strizek, B., Gembruch, U., Westerway, S.C., Dietrich, C.F.: Point-of-care ultrasound in obstetrics and gynecology. Arch. Gynecol. Obstet. **303**, 871–876 (2021)
12. Ren, S., He, K., Girshick, R., Sun, J.: Faster R-CNN: towards real-time object detection with region proposal networks. In: Advances in Neural Information Processing Systems, vol. 28 (2015)
13. Wada, K.: labelme: Image polygonal annotation with Python (2018). https://github.com/wkentaro/labelme
14. Wang, S., et al.: Deep learning based fetal middle cerebral artery segmentation in large-scale ultrasound images. In: 2018 IEEE International Conference on Bioinformatics and Biomedicine (BIBM), pp. 532–539. IEEE (2018)

SonoSAM - Segment Anything on Ultrasound Images

Hariharan Ravishankar$^{(\boxtimes)}$, Rohan Patil, Vikram Melapudi,
and Pavan Annangi

GE Healthcare, Chicago, USA
hariharan.ravishankar@ge.com

Abstract. In this paper, we present SonoSAM - a promptable foundational model for segmenting objects of interest on ultrasound images. Fine-tuned exclusively on a rich, diverse set of objects from ≈ 200k ultrasound image-mask pairs, SonoSAM demonstrates state-of-the-art performance on 8 unseen ultrasound data-sets, outperforming competing methods by a significant margin on all metrics of interest. SonoSAM achieves average dice similarity score of >90% on almost all test datasets within 2–6 clicks on an average. Further, to increase practical utility of SonoSAM, we propose a two-step process of fine-tuning followed by knowledge distillation to a smaller footprint model without comprising the performance. We present detailed qualitative and quantitative comparisons of SonoSAM with state-of-the-art methods showcasing efficacy of SonoSAM as one of the first reliable, generic foundational model for ultrasound.

Keywords: Foundational model · Ultrasound · Semantic Segmentation

1 Introduction

In many of the AI-powered ultrasound imaging applications, semantic segmentation of objects is of fundamental importance. While, popular DL architectures like U-Net [1] achieve state-of-the-art (SOTA) performance, the biggest bottleneck is in getting annotated data. Obtaining exact contour markings of objects of interest in ultrasound, mandates involvement of experts with clinical knowledge, is often tedious and time-consuming. The issue is exacerbated in 3-D or 2-D+t volumes, where getting dense contour marking for multiple objects across all the frames for a subject alone is extremely challenging.

Recently, AI-powered tools have become popular for assisting object annotation in natural images. By learning on large number of image-mask pairs in the order of billions [3], these models learn the concept of "objectness" and function as generic, class-agnostic object segmentors. Models like FocalClick [2], Segment

B. Kainz et al. (Eds.): ASMUS 2023, LNCS 14337, pp. 23–33, 2023.
https://doi.org/10.1007/978-3-031-44521-7_3

anything (SAM) [3] have advanced "promptable" segmentation, where user supplies prompts and models will automatically delineate objects of interest. The different types of user prompts are scribbles [7,8], bounding box [9,10], extreme points [11], clicks (most explored owing to ease of use), texts and images [17].

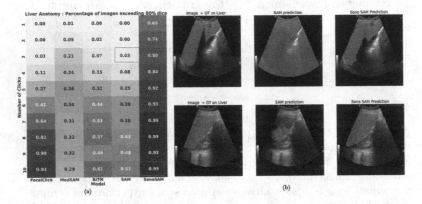

Fig. 1. a) Distribution of number of clicks versus percentage of images on which average Dice overlap exceeds 80%, b) Example images and predictions after 2 clicks for SAM and proposed method of SonoSAM.

Major breakthrough in click-based segmentation was presented in RITM [18], using iterative sampling to generate clicks during training [19]. FocalClick [2] utilized localized inference strategy to further improve accuracy. SimpleClick [23] explored the use of vision transformers for interactive segmentation. Segment anything model (SAM) [3] extended this to multiple prompts, and trained on massive data (1 billion images) to enable several mainstream applications including zero-shot segmentation. SAM has emerged as the gold standard for promptable segmentation owing to its success in multiple domains [3].

Utility of SAM [3] in medical imaging has been assessed recently in [26–28]. In an extensive experimental study [26], the authors find that while SAM obtains reasonable performance on different modalities, the performance is the poorest on ultrasound. This behavior is to be expected since ultrasound possesses unique characteristics like presence of scan cone, poor image quality and unique texture with speckles. Figure 1a shows inefficiency of SAM on liver images, where after 3 clicks, SAM achieves 80% or more dice in only 3% of images. In a more striking failure, even after 10 clicks, SAM can achieve >80% dice in roughly half the number of images. An example image shown in Fig. 1b, depicts that after two clicks, SAM segments the scan cone which is of scarce utility to the clinician.

An early attempt at developing a foundational model for medical imaging was proposed in MedSAM [27], where authors finetuned SAM on 200K image-mask pairs obtained from 11 modalities including ultrasound, using only bounding box prompts. While MedSAM outperforms SAM on first prompt, it is still extremely inadequate, fails consistently with more clicks, and is often poorer than SAM

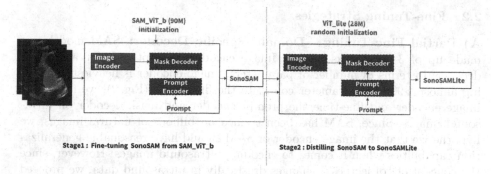

Fig. 2. Two stage process of building SonoSAM and SonoSAMLite. - Green boxes depict frozen weights and blue boxes capture fine-tuned weights. (Color figure online)

on ultrasound data. This has prompted the community to speculate that either modality-specific or organ-specific models [28] are the optimal granularity for foundation models to be of practical utility in the clinical community. With this motivation, we present SonoSAM: ultrasound modality-specific segment anything foundation model trained with a set of 200K ultrasound image-mask pairs.

The key contributions of our paper are as follows:

- a first of its kind foundational model exclusively for ultrasound images enabling promptable segmentation,
- demonstration of state-of-the-art performance on 8 unseen ultrasound datasets,
- development of a deployable low footprint model with knowledge distillation.

2   Technical Details

2.1   Architecture

For semantic segmentation, there are essentially two types of backbones in practice - 1) hierarchical backbone: predominantly CNN-based [1] which learn coefficients that exploit local image content, use downsampling layers and aggregation to capture global information. 2) Plain backbone: boosted by the success of vision transformers (ViT) in other problems, segmentation architectures without pyramidal feature aggregation architecture have become popular. In SimpleClick [4], authors proposed architecture with plain backbone of various sizes - ViT_b, ViT_l, ViT_h which correspond to base, large and huge vision transformers with 90M, 300M and 600M parameters respectively. These architectures were further used in building SAM [3] models. Owing to the success of these backbones, we fine-tuned SonoSAM models starting from ViT_b model of SAM [3].

2.2 Fine-Tuning Strategies

A) Partial Fine-Tuning - Domain Specific Decoder: SAM models are made up of 3 sub-blocks namely Image encoder, prompt encoder and mask decoder. In terms of number of parameters, image encoder is heaviest containing almost >90% of parameter count. In the first stage (Fig. 2), we freeze the image encoder and fine-tune the prompt encoder and mask decoder on ultrasound images. Since, SAM has been trained on billions of natural images, we hypothesize that the image encoder of SAM should have reasonable generalization capabilities when it comes to encoding ultrasound images. However, since the concept of "objectness" changes drastically in ultrasound data, we proceed to fine-tune the mask decoder - leading to ultrasound specific decoder which learns to produce contours of objects in ultrasound. We refer to this model as SonoSAM. We demonstrate that domain-specific decoder solution, while being practical from learning perspective, is also extremely adequate from performance perspective. SonoSAM is trained on ultrasound image-mask pairs, with DiceFocal loss proposed in [24], which is linear combination of focal loss and dice loss. We utilize Adam optimizer with initial learning rate of 1e−4 and decay of 0.5 with every 25 epochs.

B) Knowledge Distillation: To enable practical utility of SonoSAM as a general purpose segmentation model for Ultrasound applications, it is desirable to have a model of a reasonable size that can be realistically deployed on devices or scanners. However, the existing foundation models trained on billions of images consume significant amount of memory and compute. To address this, in stage 2 (Fig. 2), we use knowledge distillation [30] to build a relatively light-weight student model SonoSAMLite, with SonoSAM as the corresponding teacher. The image encoder of SonoSAMLite is a lighter ViT-based architecture, resulting in a model which is 1/3rd the size of the smallest ViT-b variant. We leverage the same architecture for the other two components - prompt encoder and mask decoder. For learning, we use a weighted combination of mask loss between student and ground truth (Eq. 1), and a distribution-based distillation loss between student and teacher predictions. We use weighted loss made up of DiceFocal loss [24] as L_{mask}, and KL-Divergence loss $L_{distill}$ for our experiments, with $\alpha = 0.1$.

$$L_{student} = (1 - \alpha) * L_{mask}(\hat{y}, y) + \alpha * L_{distill}(\hat{y}, y_{SonoSAM}) \qquad (1)$$

Similar to the teacher, the student model is also trained with an iterative training strategy (Sect. 2.3) where prompts are iteratively sampled based on the error regions of the model predictions. We employ a best-mask distillation strategy, where the output of the teacher corresponding to the iteration reporting the best mask is used for distilling the student. We hypothesize that this allows the student model to have consistent distillation targets and ground-truth targets across iterations and enables stable learning for the student.

2.3   Iterative Training Mimicking User-Interaction

Inspired by the success of training mechanisms presented in [2,3,18], we follow an iterative prompt selection strategy to simulate human interaction during training of both SonoSAM and SonoSAMLite. On every image, a foreground point or a bounding box is chosen with equal probability is chosen as the first prompt. For point prompt, a pixel with a controlled jitter around the foreground centroid is selected at random. Similarly, for a bounding box prompt, the box co-ordinates are altered on either side to make a loosely fitting bounding box. For both type of prompts, the maximum jitter added is around 20%. For the subsequent iterations, point prompts are uniformly sampled based on the error map between predicted mask and ground truth. Depending upon the dominant type of mistakes - false positive or false negative, a new negative or positive point is chosen in error region appropriately.

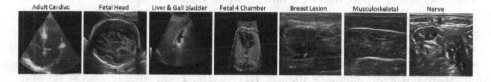

Fig. 3. Collection of images depicting variability of objects present in ultrasound.

Table 1. Left: Training data-sets; Right: Test data-sets

Training Data-set						Test Data-set				
Num	Anatomy	#Images	Objects	Probe	Device	Num	Anatomy	#Images	Objects	Probe	Device
1	Fetal Heart 4ch	2500	6	2D	Voluson E8/E10	1	Cardiac Short axis	2250	TV annulus	2D	VIVID E9/E95
2	Fetal Heart 3VT	2120	4	2D	Voluson E8/E10						
3	Fetal Thorax	8300	1	2D	Voluson E8/E10	2	Fetal Head	4786	HC	2D	Voluson E8/E10
4	Gynaecology	87000	3	3D	Voluson E10	3	Liver	95	Liver	2D	Logiq e
5	Kidney	1500	1	2D	Logiq E10	4	Breast Lesions	648	Breast lesions	3D	Public [31]
6	Liver	3700	1	2D	Logiq E10	5	Muscolo-skeletal	8000	Muscle tissue	2D	Public [34]
7	Bile Duct	150	1	2D	Logiq E10	6	Nerve	3700	Brachial Plexus	2D	Public [33]
8	Female Pelvic	682	1	4D	Voluson E10	7	Adult cardiac 4ch	10000	LV, LA	2D	Public [32]
9	Thyroid	800	3	2D	Logiq E10	8	Adult cardiac 2ch	10000	LV, LA	2D	Public [32]

3   Training Data-Sets

Ultrasound imaging poses challenges to any AI model development, specifically for foundation models due to poor SNR and CNR compared to other imaging modalities. Moreover, the concept of "objectness" do not translate well from natural images to ultrasound. As shown on few exemplar images in Fig. 3, the object boundaries are not often well defined, texture is highly varying and overall image quality has high inter-operator variability. To build generalized foundation models, training data-set has to be curated carefully to ensure sufficient diversity. We primarily utilized data from a wide variety of commercially GE HealthCare devices for training. Our training data-set (Table 1) includes almost 200k images with 1) varying echogenicity: Hyper-echogenic structures like fetal cranium, hypo-echogenic regions, anechoic and fluid filled objects like fetal cardiac, 2) varying interfaces: objects with soft tissue boundaries like kidney, bone-tissue interface in fetal thorax 3) varying texture: homogenous texture like liver, thyroid, and heterogeneous texture in uterus. 4) varying image quality: 2-D (convex/ sector/ linear) probes, 3-D mechanical probes and electronic 4-D probes. We demonstrate the value of curating such diverse data in results section.

4   Experiments and Results

We evaluate and report results of SonoSAM on 8 test datasets listed in Table 1. Note that these data-sets were chosen to test generalization capability of SonoSAM covering unseen anatomy (Adult Heart, Fetal Head, etc.), unseen pathologies (Breast Lesions, MSK pathologies), different scanners (Logiq e), public data-sets (from different challenges). We compare the performance against four state-of-the-art methods namely RITM [18], FocalClick [2], SAM [3] and MedSAM [27]. To automatically evaluate performance of these models with increasing number of user interactions, we start with centroid of the ground truth masks and add positive negative clicks depending on evolution of predictions. We note that MedSAM [27] is not trained to work with clicks and hence we start with bounding box prompt. We use Dice Similarity Coefficient (DSC) between predicted and ground truth masks as the performance metric of choice. We report on the following set of derived metrics to analyze performance.

- Distribution of DSC scores averaged across images in each data-set versus increasing number of clicks from 1 to 10.
- NoC@80, NoC@90: Number of clicks required to achieve average dice of 80% and 90% respectively.
- Failure Rate: Fraction of images where DSC score is less than 80% and 90% DSC at NoC@80 and NoC@90 respectively.
- MaxDSC: Maximum Average DSC score after 10 clicks.

4.1   Results on 2D Images

a) **SonoSAM achieves state-of-the-art performance on all test datasets:** SonoSAM achieves >90% DSC on all data-sets and comfortably surpasses competing methods by a huge margin which struggle to cross even 80% DSC. As shown in Table 2, SAM model trained on natural images, under-performs significantly on ultrasound images often being poorer than SonoSAM in range of 8–41% MaxDSC. Surprisingly, MedSAM which has been trained partly on ultrasound images is often the worst performer amongst all models, despite 3 of these datasets being 'in-domain' data-sets for MedSAM. Lack of training with clicks, severely hampers and infact deteriorates MedSAM's performance. FocalClick model, performs reasonably on two data-sets - Liver and Fetal Head but takes lot of clicks to get to meaningful results, as shown Fig. 4.

Table 2. Quantitative comparisons on SonoSAM and SonoSAMLite with SOTA methods on 8 anatomies from test data-sets

Anatomy	Fetal Head					Liver					Cardiac LV					Cardiac LA				
	NoC80	NoC90	FR80 %	FR90 %	Max DSC	NoC80	NoC90	FR80 %	FR90 %	Max DSC	NoC80	NoC90	FR80 %	FR90 %	Max DSC	NoC80	NoC90	FR80 %	FR90 %	Max DSC
RITM [18]	4.3	5.3	2.0	4.4	0.93	7.7	11.7	1.1	14.7	0.82	8.4	14.1	1.2	24.4	0.76	9.6	14.7	3.2	31.2	0.69
FocalClick [2]	3.8	4.9	1.4	2.7	0.94	6.9	9.3	0.0	2.1	0.91	11.8	14.5	11.3	21.4	0.66	11.7	14.2	13.3	24.2	0.67
MedSAM [27]	4.1	11.6	6.2	46.1	0.75	8.6	17.6	21.1	82.1	0.72	6.7	19.1	14.1	93.2	0.69	9.4	16.6	42.1	93.3	0.63
SAM [3]	5.8	9.0	4.1	11.4	0.88	9.8	14.1	16.8	37.9	0.78	9.4	14.3	14.0	40.6	0.75	13.7	16.3	40.2	58.1	0.53
SonoSAM	1.6	2.1	1.3	2.1	0.94	2.1	5.3	0.0	3.2	0.92	2.0	4.7	0.0	0.1	0.94	2.1	4.1	0.1	0.6	0.94
SonoSAMLite	1.6	2.7	1.4	2.0	0.96	3.2	7.4	1.1	8.4	0.93	2.1	3.9	0	0	0.96	2.4	5.3	0	0	0.93
Anatomy	MSK					Nerve					Breast Lesions					Cardiac SAX				
	NoC80	NoC90	FR80 %	FR90 %	Max DSC	NoC80	NoC90	FR80 %	FR90 %	Max DSC	NoC80	NoC90	FR80 %	FR90 %	Max DSC	NoC80	NoC90	FR80 %	FR90 %	Max DSC
RITM [18]	8.7	14.2	1.4	25.5	0.78	11.8	16.8	0.7	40.5	0.70	8.9	12.2	0.9	15.4	0.78	8.3	12.0	19.0	10.8	0.79
FocalClick [2]	7.7	12.6	0.1	6.9	0.86	9.2	13.4	0.6	7.2	0.82	7.3	9.6	2.2	3.7	0.96	7.6	10.8	0.0	0.4	0.88
MedSAM [27]	12.5	19.0	43.0	87.2	0.45	10.1	18.9	0.8	80.7	0.76	2.5	9.6	2.6	35.1	0.81	5.5	16.1	160.0	62.4	0.79
SAM [3]	14.2	18.9	48.0	85.9	0.65	9.6	15.4	0.7	38.9	0.72	5.0	8.9	7.1	18.6	0.86	5.2	11.3	53.0	12.6	0.88
SonoSAM	2.9	7.1	0.1	1.1	0.92	5.1	9.5	0.4	4.0	0.90	1.9	3.7	0.0	1.4	0.94	2.3	4.1	0.0	0.0	0.95
SonoSAMLite	2.4	5.8	0.2	0.8	0.94	5.2	8.3	0.1	0.4	0.95	2.5	5.6	0.5	3.2	0.93	2.1	4.19	0.0	0.5	0.95

b)SonoSAM with 2-3 clicks outperforms SAM's and MedSAM's performance with 10 clicks: Figure 4 clearly highlights the benefit of domain-specific decoder in how quickly (often 2 clicks only), SonoSAM outperforms SAM and MedSAM. As shown in Table 2, SonoSAM achieves 80% dice in less than 2 clicks (Noc@80) on all anatomies except on the most challenging nerve data where it takes 5.1 clicks. It is also impressive that to achieve 90%dice, SonoSAM often takes 2–6 clicks (Noc@90) except on nerve data-set. In other words, SonoSAM on average reaches 90% dice within 6 clicks on almost all of the data-sets. Failure rates of SAM and MedSAM illustrate the issues with using them for medical imaging further. Except on fetal head and breast lesions, SAM fails to achieve 90% dice on at least 40% of the images (FR@90) - which means that in roughly half the images, SAM will not provide satisfactory object contour even after 10 clicks. Failure rates of SonoSAM (FR@90) are often less than 1% except liver (3%) which means that it works on almost all types of images, making it as a generic, reliable tool for fast annotation on ultrasound images.

c) SonoSAM behaves predictably with user interaction. One of the complaints with SAM model is that, the mask generated with user clicks (positive or negative clicks) are unintuitive and unpredictable. As shown in Fig. 5, SAM often picks the entire FOV as the object and is unresponsive to multiple clicks. In contrast, SonoSAM's responses are predictable, as demonstrated by smooth progression of predicted contours (Fig. 5).

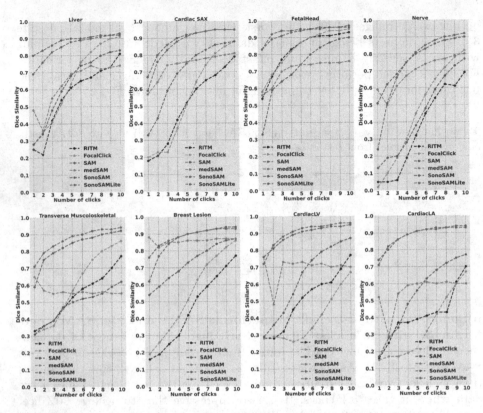

Fig. 4. Figure showing Average DSC value for SonoSAM and SonoSAMLite models along with SOTA methods for increasing number of clicks on 8 test data-sets.

4.2   Performance Comparison of SonoSAM vs SonoSAM Lite

As shown in Fig. 4, SonoSAMLite model performs very close to SonoSAM model on almost all of the 8 anatomical datasets for 1–10 clicks. For specific applications, ex. MSK and Nerve segmentation, it is quite encouraging to note that SonoSAMLite model outperforms the SonoSAM model. For a few anatomies ex. Fetal Head and Liver, the SonoSAMLite model lags slightly in the initial few clicks, however the maximum DSC at the end of 10 clicks is very similar. Likewise, as shows in Table 2, NoC80, NoC90, FR80, FR90, Max DSC for SonoSAMLite model are very similar to SonoSAM model and shows that there is no deterioration in model performance. These results are extremely encouraging, considering that the distilled model is 1/3 rd the size of the SonoSAM model (28M parameters versus 90M parameters). The distilled model with no significant reduction in performance can have significant clinical impact and makes the usability of our work much more practical.

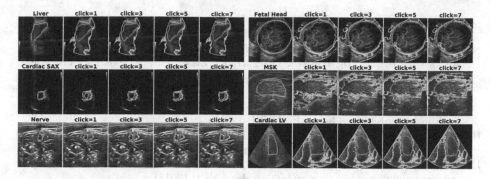

Fig. 5. Evolution of segmentation predictions for clicks - *1,3,5,7* on 6 anatomies from test data-set. Legend - Red: SAM prediction, Green: SonoSAM, Cyan: GT (Color figure online)

5   Conclusion

In this work, we present SonoSAM - a breakthrough foundational model for ultrasound which for the first time - achieves performance on ultrasound images on-par with vision models in natural images. We demonstrate that by carefully curating training data-set of sufficient diversity, images in order of $200k$ is sufficient to get SOTA results. We illustrate that partial fine-tuning of large vision models - building domain-specific decoder is tractable and promising solution for ultrasound images. While success in computer vision has been achieved with humungous models, we show that with knowledge distillation, SonoSAMLite model of meager $30M$ parameters can perform as good as, if not outperform large models. In our future research, we plan to analyze failure modes in detail, explore full fine-tuning, anatomy-specific smaller models, adding text prompts and finally zero-shot segmentation.

References

1. Falk, T., et al.: U-net: deep learning for cell counting, detection, and morphometry. Nat. Methods **16**(1), 67–70 (2019)
2. Chen, X., Zhao, Z., Zhang, Y., Duan, M., Qi, D., Zhao, H.: FocalClick: towards practical interactive image segmentation. In: CVPR (2022)
3. Kirillov, A., et al.: Segment anything. arXiv preprint arXiv:2304.02643 (2023)
4. Liu, Q., Xu, Z., Bertasius, G., Niethammer, M.: SimpleClick: interactive image segmentation with simple vision transformers. arXiv preprint arXiv:2210.11006 (2022)
5. Author, A.-B.: Contribution title. In: 9th International Proceedings on Proceedings, pp. 1–2. Publisher, Location (2010)
6. LNCS Homepage. http://www.springer.com/lncs. Accessed 4 Oct 2017

7. Bai, J., Wu, X.: Error-tolerant scribbles based interactive image segmentation. In: CVPR (2014)
8. Kim, T.H., Lee, K.M., Lee, S.U.: Generative image segmentation using random walks with restart. In: Forsyth, D., Torr, P., Zisserman, A. (eds.) ECCV 2008. LNCS, vol. 5304, pp. 264–275. Springer, Heidelberg (2008). https://doi.org/10.1007/978-3-540-88690-7_20
9. Zhang, S., Liew, J.H., Wei, Y., Wei, S., Zhao, Y.: Interactive object segmentation with inside-outside guidance. In: CVPR (2020)
10. Wu, J., Zhao, Y., Zhu, J.-Y., Luo, S., Tu, Z.: MILCut: a sweeping line multiple instance learning paradigm for interactive image segmentation. In: CVPR (2014)
11. Maninis, K.-K., Caelles, S., Pont-Tuset, J., Gool, L.V.: Deep extreme cut: from extreme points to object segmentation. In: CVPR (2018)
12. Rother, C., Kolmogorov, V., Blake, A.: "GrabCut": interactive foreground extraction using iterated graph cuts. ACM Trans. Graph. **23** (2004)
13. Boykov, Y., Jolly, M.-P.: Interactive graph cuts for optimal boundary and region segmentation of objects in n-d images. In: ICCV (2001)
14. Grady, L.: Random walks for image segmentation. IEEE Trans. PAMI **28** (2006)
15. Gulshan, V., Rother, C., Criminisi, A., Blake, A., Zisserman, A.: Geodesic star convexity for interactive image segmentation. In: CVPR (2010)
16. Xu, N., Price, B., Cohen, S., Yang, J., Huang, T.: Deep interactive object selection. In: CVPR (2016)
17. Radford, A., et al.: Learning transferable visual models from natural language supervision. In: ICML (2021)
18. Sofiiuk, K., Petrov, I.A., Konushin, A.: Reviving iterative training with mask guidance for interactive segmentation. arXiv:2102.06583 (2021)
19. Mahadevan, S., Voigtlaender, P., Leibe, B.: Iteratively trained interactive segmentation. In: BMVC (2018)
20. Forte, M., Price, B., Cohen, S., Xu, N., Pitié, F.: Getting to 99% accuracy in interactive segmentation. arXiv:2003.07932 (2020)
21. Jang, W.-D., Kim, C.-S.: Interactive image segmentation via backpropagating refinement scheme. In: CVPR (2019)
22. Sofiiuk, K., Petrov, I., Barinova, O., Konushin, A.: f-BRS: rethinking backpropagating refinement for interactive segmentation. In: CVPR (2020)
23. Liu, Q., Xu, Z., Bertasius, G., Niethammer, M.: SimpleClick: interactive image segmentation with simple vision transformers. arXiv:2210.11006 (2022)
24. Carion, N., Massa, F., Synnaeve, G., Usunier, N., Kirillov, A., Zagoruyko, S.: End-to-end object detection with transformers. In: Vedaldi, A., Bischof, H., Brox, T., Frahm, J.-M. (eds.) ECCV 2020. LNCS, vol. 12346, pp. 213–229. Springer, Cham (2020). https://doi.org/10.1007/978-3-030-58452-8_13
25. Hu, E.J., et al.: Lora: low-rank adaptation of large language models. arXiv preprint arXiv:2106.09685 (2021)
26. Mazurowski, M.A., et al.: Segment anything model for medical image analysis: an experimental study. arXiv preprint arXiv:2304.10517 (2023)
27. Ma, J., Wang, B.: Segment anything in medical images. arXiv preprint arXiv:2304.12306 (2023)
28. Zhang, S., Metaxas, D.: On the challenges and perspectives of foundation models for medical image analysis. arXiv preprint arXiv:2306.05705 (2023)
29. Zhang, K., Liu, D.: Customized segment anything model for medical image segmentation. arXiv preprint arXiv:2304.13785 (2023)
30. Hinton, G., Vinyals, O., Dean, J.: Distilling the knowledge in a neural network. arXiv preprint arXiv:1503.02531 (2015)

31. Al-Dhabyani, W., Gomaa, M., Khaled, H., Fahmy, A.: Dataset of breast ultrasound images. Data Brief **28**, 104863 (2020). https://doi.org/10.1016/j.dib.2019.104863
32. Leclerc, S., Smistad, E., Pedrosa, J., Ostvik, A., et al.: Deep learning for segmentation using an open large-scale dataset in 2D echocardiography. IEEE Trans. Med. Imaging **38**(9), 2198–2210 (2019). https://doi.org/10.1109/TMI.2019.2900516
33. Montoya, H.: kaggle446, shirzad, Will Cukierski, yffud, ultrasound-nerve-segmentation, Kaggle (2016). https://kaggle.com/competitions/ultrasound-nerve-segmentation
34. Marzola, F., van Alfen, N., Doorduin, J., Meiburger, K.M.: Deep learning segmentation of transverse musculoskeletal ultrasound images for neuromuscular disease assessment. Comput. Biol. Med. 104623 (2021). ISSN 0010-4825, https://doi.org/10.1016/j.compbiomed.2021.104623

Echo from Noise: Synthetic Ultrasound Image Generation Using Diffusion Models for Real Image Segmentation

David Stojanovski[1]([✉])[iD], Uxio Hermida[1][iD], Pablo Lamata[1][iD],
Arian Beqiri[1,2][iD], and Alberto Gomez[1,2][iD]

[1] School of Biomedical Engineering and Imaging Sciences, King's College London,
London SE1 7EU, UK
{david.stojanovski,uxio.hermida,pablo.lamata,arian.beqiri,
alberto.gomez}@kcl.ac.uk
[2] Ultromics Ltd., Oxford OX4 2SU, UK
{arian.beqiri,alberto.gomez}@ultromics.com

Abstract. We propose a novel pipeline for the generation of synthetic ultrasound images via Denoising Diffusion Probabilistic Models (DDPMs) guided by cardiac semantic label maps. We show that these synthetic images can serve as a viable substitute for real data in the training of deep-learning models for ultrasound image analysis tasks such as cardiac segmentation. To demonstrate the effectiveness of this approach, we generated synthetic 2D echocardiograms and trained a neural network for segmenting the left ventricle and left atrium. The performance of the network trained on exclusively synthetic images was evaluated on an unseen dataset of real images and yielded mean Dice scores of 88.6 ± 4.91, 91.9 ± 4.22, $85.2 \pm 4.83\%$ for left ventricular endocardium, epicardium and left atrial segmentation respectively. This represents a relative increase of 9.2, 3.3 and 13.9% in Dice scores compared to the previous state-of-the-art. The proposed pipeline has potential for application to a wide range of other tasks across various medical imaging modalities.

Keywords: Diffusion Models · Image synthesis · Ultrasound

1 Introduction

1.1 Background and Motivation

Echocardiography (echo) is the most widely used method for evaluating the heart, because it is more cost-effective and safer than other imaging modalities,

This work was supported by the Wellcome/EPSRC Centre for Medical Engineering [WT203148/Z/16/Z] and by the National Institute for Health Research (NIHR) Biomedical Research Centre at Guy's and St Thomas' NHS Foundation Trust and King's College London. The views expressed are those of the author(s) and not necessarily those of the NHS, the NIHR or the Department of Health.

Supplementary Information The online version contains supplementary material available at https://doi.org/10.1007/978-3-031-44521-7_4.

B. Kainz et al. (Eds.): ASMUS 2023, LNCS 14337, pp. 34–43, 2023.
https://doi.org/10.1007/978-3-031-44521-7_4

while providing high resolution images in real-time. However, a major drawback of echo is its heavy dependence on operators' expertise to obtain high-quality images and associated anatomical and functional measurements.

Convolutional neural networks (CNNs) have shown great potential for automating medical image analysis tasks and are capable of accurately learning complex relevant features from large sets of data. A major challenge in the use of CNNs for medical imaging tasks is the need for labelling such large sets of data for model training. Further, CNN accuracy can be limited by the quality of the labels used during training, particularly in the presence of noise or other artefacts that can lead to inter-observer errors. Experienced cardiologists have been shown to have inter-observer errors up to 22% when labelling common measurements in echo [2].

Previous research has shown the feasibility of generating realistic natural and medical images [1,5,21]. Until recently, the state-of-the-art (SOTA) results were achieved with Generative Adversarial Networks (GANs) and CycleGANs. GANs are known to be notoriously difficult to train, due to training instability as the generator and discriminator are trained simultaneously, and the loss function can be highly non-convex, making it challenging to find the global minimum. Additionally, GANs can suffer from vanishing gradients, which can lead to slow or non-existent convergence. This often leads to failed training runs and great difficulty in reproducing results. GANs are also prone to mode collapse, where the generator learns to produce a limited set of outputs, which can be repeated instead of generating diverse samples [4]. This can happen when the discriminator is too strong in comparison to the generator, and rejects any samples that do not match the training data, forcing the generator to produce only a limited set of outputs. When using a guide image for synthetic image synthesis (e.g., to generate a synthetic medical image guided by an anatomical representation), CycleGANs have been the go-to technique of choice, but typically fail to reproduce the anatomy under large transformations of the guide images and collapse to anatomy seen in the training set, as illustrated later in this paper.

Denoising Diffusion Probabilistic models (DDPMs) are more recent generative models that are far less susceptible to the pitfalls of GAN based methods [10]. However, limited research has been performed on medical images, with a few notable examples [9,14]. No prior research studies have explored their use in semantically guided image synthesis, or to ultrasound imaging at all. In this paper, we use DDPMs to generate synthetic echo images and train a segmentation model.

1.2 Related Works

The two primary Deep Learning (DL) techniques for generating synthetic images are GANs and DDPMs.

Generative Adversarial Networks: GANs and the CycleGAN subclass have shown success in generating synthetic medical images. Examples include Cycle-MedGAN [1] that achieved 0.91 Structural Similarity Index Measure (SSIM) in a Positron Emission Tomography to Computed Tomography (CT) unsupervised translation task. The SOTA in segmentation is presented by Gilbert et al. who used a CycleGAN architecture to generate images for training a network to segment an unseen real cardiac ultrasound test set. They achieved 79.4, 88.6 and 71.3% mean Dice scores on the left ventricle endocardium, left ventricle epicardium and left atrium respectively [6].

Diffusion Models: Sohl-Dickstein et al. initially proposed DDPMs [18], which have been used successfully for unsupervised image-to-image translation in both the natural and medical image domains. Pinaya et al. achieved a Fréchet inception distance (FID) of 7.8×10^{-3} for brain Magnetic Resonance Imaging (MRI) generation versus an FID of 5×10^{-4} for real brain MRI [14]. Lyu et al. achieved > 0.85 SSIM score for their conversion of CT to MRI images [9].

These works relate to the problem of image-to-image domain adaption. Instead, we use diffusion models to address the issue of limited labelled training data in echo image segmentation, by using a semantically guided network that receives an anatomical semantic label map to generate conditional synthetic echo images which adhere to the anatomy. Our work aims to combine the benefits of DDPMs with semantically guided medical imaging to synthetically increase dataset size and enable the creation of out-of-distribution images.

1.3   Contributions of This Study

This is the first work to utilize DDPMs for generating medical images using semantic label maps as a source image for conditioning the generated image. To summarize our contributions, we: 1) Demonstrate that a semantic label map guided diffusion model can be trained to synthesize cardiac ultrasound images and matching semantic labels that can be used to train a segmentation model that then performs to high accuracy on real echo data, and 2) Release the generated datasets, as well as the code, for public usage.

The code is available at https://github.com/david-stojanovski/echo_from_noise. The generated diffusion model dataset, as described in Sect. 2.1 is available at https://zenodo.org/record/7921055#.ZGYS_9LMLmE.

2   Methods

As an overview, our image synthesis pipeline implements the Semantic Diffusion Model (SDM) proposed by Wang et al. [20], the details of which are described in Sect. 2.1. Subsequently, these generated images are used to train and validate a segmentation model. This model is then tested on an unseen dataset of real echocardiographic images, as described in Sect. 2.2. An overview of the pipeline is given in Fig. 1.

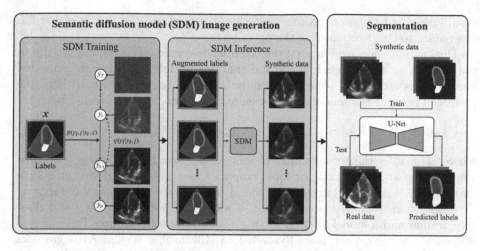

Fig. 1. Pipeline for generating synthetic ultrasound images from a semantic diffusion model (SDM), to be used in segmentation training and testing on real data. **SDM Training**: The SDM is trained to transform the noise to the realistic image through an iterative denoising process. **SDM inference**: The trained SDM is inferenced on augmented labels to generate corresponding realistic synthetic ultrasound images. **Segmentation**: The set of generated synthetic ultrasound images are used to train a segmentation network. The segmentation performance is tested on real data. x denotes the semantic label map; y_t denotes the noisy image at each time step t.

2.1 Synthetic Ultrasound Generation: Semantic Diffusion Model

Data: We used the CAMUS echocardiography dataset [8] which contains 500 patients in total with semantically segmented left ventricle myocardium, endocardium, and left atrial surface for 4 chamber and 2 chamber images at both end-diastole (ED) and end-systole (ES) frames. The official test subset, of 50 patients, was reserved for testing segmentation networks. We used the remaining 450 patients for training and validating the generative models, by splitting them into 400 training and 50 validation. Note that only the ED frames were used for training and validating the two diffusion models (2C and 4C), totaling 400 training + 50 validation frames used to train each model.

An additional label was added to the label maps to describe the ultrasound sector (see Fig. 1), by applying a simple thresholding to the ultrasound images.

Proposed Model: We made a few notable modifications to the Semantic Diffusion Model (SDM), including some best practices proposed by Nichol et al. [11].

Firstly we used a cosine noise schedule, instead of a linear schedule, to reduce the rate at which noise is added, thus increasing the contribution of the noise in later steps of the forward process. Secondly, the objective function being optimized is the summation of the predicted noise given an input label map at each time point and the Kullback-Leibler (KL) divergence between the estimated distribution and diffusion process posterior. We modified the weight of the KL divergence to 0.001 to stabilize the optimization.

During inference, we removed the classifier-free guidance sampling for disentanglement, as it was found to add minimal perceptible difference to generated images. This allowed us to approximately halve the inference time. Briefly, the predicted noise of the model from a semantic label map is represented by:

$$\hat{\epsilon}_\theta(y_t|x) = \epsilon_\theta(y_t|x) + s \cdot (\epsilon_\theta(y_t|x) - \epsilon_\theta(y_t|\emptyset)) \tag{1}$$

where $\hat{\epsilon}_\theta(y_t|x)$ is the total-estimated noise in a ground truth image y at time step t, given an input semantic label map x, s is a user-defined guidance scale and $\epsilon_\theta(y_t|\emptyset)$ is estimated noise in a ground truth image given a null input, $\emptyset$.

Two separate models were trained, a model on 4 chamber (4C) end diastolic frames and a model on 2 chamber (2C) end diastolic frames. Training and inference was performed using Pytorch 1.13 [13] on 8 × Nvidia A100 graphics processing units for 50,000 steps using an annealing learning rate and a batch size of 12.

2.2 Segmentation

Data: From the 400+50 CAMUS patient images used to build the diffusion models, we took the semantic maps (4 per patient: 2C and 4C both ED and ES) to produce four synthetic datasets: 2CED, 2CES, 4CED and 4CES. For each dataset, we took the 400+50 semantic maps and applied five random transformations (each being a combination of random affine and elastic deformation), to produce a total of 2000 (training) + 250 (validation) semantic maps per dataset. Affine transformation ranges for rotation degrees, translate, scale and shear were: $(-5, 5)°$, $(0, 0.05)$, $(0.8, 1.05)$ and $5°$ respectively. The number of control points and max displacement were $(10, 10, 4)$ and $(0, 30, 30)$. The corresponding echo images were generated by using the previously trained SDMs (the same SDM was used for ED and ES frames from a given view). A fifth dataset is built by aggregating the other four.

The exact generated datasets constituency is shown in Fig. 2. The results given for the segmentation tasks are the values from testing on the official test split of the CAMUS dataset.

Model: We implemented an 8 layer U-Net model [16], identical to the one in [5] for fair comparison. Five instances of this model were trained with the 5 aforementioned datasets. Segmentation accuracy was assessed using the 2D Dice score [17]. The segmentation model was an in-house implementation of the standard U-Net using MONAI [3], adapted for multiple labels and image resolution of (256, 256) as input. The network contains 8 layers (L) with 2^L channels in each layer and was trained for 300 epochs with the Adam optimizer and a learning rate of 1×10^{-3}, β_1 of 0.9 and β_2 of 0.999. These hyperparameters were chosen based on best practices proposed in literature [7].

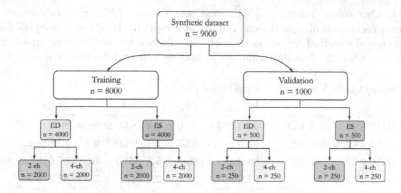

Fig. 2. Flow chart of semantic diffusion model dataset design. ED: end diastolic frames, ES: end systolic frames, 2-ch: echo 2 chamber images, 4-ch: echo 4 chamber images.

2.3   Baseline CycleGAN Model and Data

The CycleGAN network from [5] was used as a benchmark for the SDM ultrasound image generation. The CycleGAN was trained with 2C and 4C slices from a public dataset of 1000 synthetic cardiac meshes [15]. Data was divided into a 70/15/15% train/validation/test split and trained for 200 epochs. The training procedure was implemented as described in [19]. The Dice score comparisons were made with the originally published results by Gilbert et al. [6].

3   Experiments and Results

The final Dice scores on the unseen CAMUS test set of 50 patients are shown in Table 1. Example images generated with the SDMs in all frames for a single patient are shown in Fig. 3. We also present extreme augmentations in Fig. 4 to illustrate the robustness of the SDM model to inputs that would be out of the distribution of the training set. Figure 5 shows a comparison of our SDM model against a CycleGAN model for inferencing across a range of augmentations.

Using the CAMUS pretrained *All SDM frames* model and performing testing on the EchoNet-Dynamic Atrial 4 Chamber at End Diastole dataset [12], the model achieved $87.83 \pm 7.21\%$ vs $85.6 \pm 7.0\%$ obtained by *Gilbert et al.* when training a dataset-specific CycleGAN model.

Qualitatively, our results suggest that our SDMs are able to generate ultrasound images with superior overall image realism and propensity for adhering to anatomical input constraints, as well as the ability to generate images from extreme out-of-distribution semantic label maps. Representative examples of generated images are shown in Fig. 3, 4 and 5.

An example of our model vs CycleGAN (previous SOTA) is shown in Fig. 5. Columns 2 and 3 represent examples of CycleGAN's limited ability to generate anatomically realistic images, even with a realistic anatomical guiding image. CycleGAN outputs show atrial walls merging, hallucinated septal wall thickening, or complete collapse of the ventricle.

Table 1. Dice scores for the CAMUS test set. LV_{endo}, LV_{epi} and LA denote left ventricular endocardium, epicardium and atrium respectively. Rows stating *all frames* show mean and standard deviation for each label from a network trained on all views. *All frames* refers to 2CH and 4CH images at both systole and diastole (4 images total).

Train/Validation Data	Dice Score (%)			
	LV_{endo}	LV_{epi}	LA	$Mean$
SDM 4 Chamber ED	91.3 ± 4.4	94.0 ± 3.2	82.6 ± 16.9	89.3 ± 4.9
SDM 4 Chamber ES	87.8 ± 5.5	92.7 ± 2.7	88.0 ± 5.3	89.5 ± 2.3
SDM 2 Chamber ED	88.0 ± 4.9	89.3 ± 5.5	77.5 ± 16.8	85.0 ± 5.3
SDM 2 Chamber ES	87.0 ± 5.7	92.9 ± 2.4	87.9 ± 7.3	89.3 ± 2.6
All SDM frames	**88.6**±5.8	**91.9**±4.2	**85.2**±13.2	**88.6**±2.7
CycleGAN [6] all frames	79.4 ± 9.9	88.6 ± 5.4	71.3 ± 23.7	79.7±7.1
All real CAMUS frames	87.8 ± 6.8	90.9 ± 5.4	82.6 ± 14.4	87.1±3.4

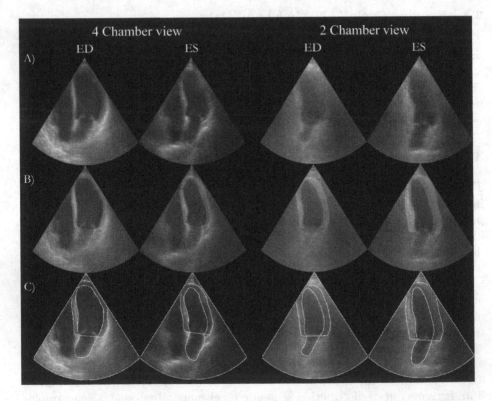

Fig. 3. Example images generated from our trained SDM networks. A) SDM synthetic images; B) SDM synthetic images overlaid with input semantic label map; C) Synthetic image with contour of input semantic label map. ED: End diastole; ES: End systole.

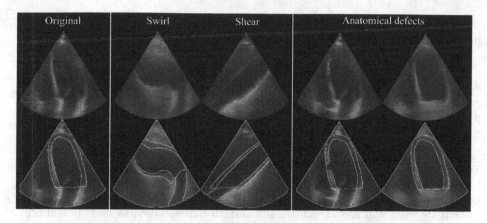

Fig. 4. Example images generated from extreme semantic map distortions. Top row: Synthetic images; Bottom row: Synthetic images with semantic label map contours. Anatomical defects: a hand-crafted septal defect (left), and missing left atrium (right).

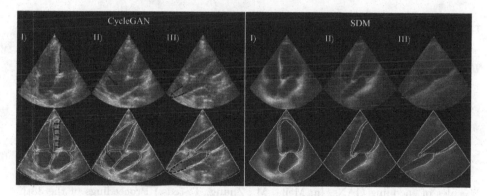

Fig. 5. Comparison of generated images from the SDM and our CycleGAN network. Top row: Generated synthetic images, bottom row: Overlay of the corresponding label map. Red dashed lines and arrows point to anatomical features missed or wrongly predicted by the CycleGAN model. Green dashed lines and arrows point to anatomical features correctly predicted by the SDM model. (Color figure online)

4   Discussion and Conclusions

Our anatomy-guided diffusion models generate realistic echo images that, compared to SOTA methods, adhere better to the anatomical constraints of a given label map, even when the prescribed anatomy is very different from the training set. Indeed, While CycleGAN can generate realistic ultrasound images, we observed that their ability to reproduce the anatomy under large deformation of the guide images is limited. Further, the anatomically accurate synthetic data generated with our model significantly improves the performance of the segmentation model on real images, showing the potential to address challenges involving rare medical conditions, data privacy, or limited data availability.

A segmentation network trained on the SDM-generated synthetic data significantly outperformed SOTA methods, and even training on the original real data, in segmentation of real 2 and 4 chamber ultrasound images. The LV endocardium, epicardium, and atrium were segmented with high accuracy (88.6 ± 5.8, 91.9 ± 4.2, $85.2 \pm 13.2\%$ Dice score respectively). These results represent an 11.6, 3.7 and 19.5% improvement in relation to previous SOTA results. Moreover, our results showed reduced standard deviation for all labels, suggesting our model yields realistic images more consistently, leading to less variation in segmentation performance. These results also highlight the adaptability of SDMs for generating new data.

Future work will include addressing variation across devices and clinical centers and investigating temporal aspects of synthetic data generation. The results presented in this paper show promise for synthetic data generation that can be used to train deep neural networks to high performance, addressing a crucial problem in medical imaging such as the availability of expert-labeled data.

References

1. Armanious, K., Jiang, C., Abdulatif, S., Küstner, T., Gatidis, S., Yang, B.: Unsupervised medical image translation using cycle-medGAN (2019). http://arxiv.org/abs/1903.03374, https://doi.org/10.23919/EUSIPCO.2019.8902799

2. Armstrong, A.C., et al.: Quality control and reproducibility in m-mode, two-dimensional, and speckle tracking echocardiography acquisition and analysis: the cardia study, year 25 examination experience. Echocardiography **32**, 1233–1240 (2015). https://doi.org/10.1111/echo.12832

3. Consortium, T.M.: Project Monai (2020). https://doi.org/10.5281/zenodo.4323059

4. Feng, R., Lin, Z., Zhu, J., Zhao, D., Zhou, J., Zha, Z.J.: Uncertainty principles of encoding GANs. In: Meila, M., Zhang, T. (eds.) Proceedings of the 38th International Conference on Machine Learning. Proceedings of Machine Learning Research, vol. 139, pp. 3240–3251. PMLR, 18–24 July 2021. https://proceedings.mlr.press/v139/feng21c.html

5. Gilbert, A., Marciniak, M., Rodero, C., Lamata, P., Samset, E., McLeod, K.: Generating synthetic labeled data from existing anatomical models: an example with echocardiography segmentation. IEEE Trans. Med. Imaging **40**, 2783–2794 (10 2021). https://doi.org/10.1109/TMI.2021.3051806

6. Gilbert, A., Marciniak, M., Rodero, C., Lamata, P., Samset, E., McLeod, K.: Supplementary materials for generating synthetic labeled data from existing anatomical models: an example with echocardiography segmentation. https://github.com/adgilbert/data-generation/blob/main/SupplementaryMaterial.pdf

7. Kingma, D.P., Ba, J.L.: Adam: a method for stochastic optimization. In: 3rd International Conference on Learning Representations, ICLR 2015 - Conference Track Proceedings, pp. 1–15 (2015)

8. Leclerc, S., et al.: Deep learning for segmentation using an open large-scale dataset in 2D echocardiography. IEEE Trans. Med. Imaging **38**(9), 2198–2210 (2019)

9. Lyu, Q., Wang, G.: Conversion between CT and MRI images using diffusion and score-matching models (2022). http://arxiv.org/abs/2209.12104

10. Müller-Franzes, G., et al.: Diffusion probabilistic models beat GANs on medical images (2022). http://arxiv.org/abs/2212.07501
11. Nichol, A., Dhariwal, P.: Improved denoising diffusion probabilistic models (2021). http://arxiv.org/abs/2102.09672
12. Ouyang, D., et al.: Video-based AI for beat-to-beat assessment of cardiac function. Nature **580**(7802), 252–256 (2020). https://doi.org/10.1038/s41586-020-2145-8
13. Paszke, A., et al.: PyTorch: an imperative style, high-performance deep learning library. In: Advances in Neural Information Processing Systems, vol. 32 (NeurIPS) (2019)
14. Pinaya, W.H.L., et al.: Brain imaging generation with latent diffusion models (2022). http://arxiv.org/abs/2209.07162
15. Rodero, C., et al.: Linking statistical shape models and simulated function in the healthy adult human heart. PLoS Comput. Biol. **17**(4), 1–28 (2021). https://dx.doi.org/10.1371/journal.pcbi.1008851
16. Ronneberger, O., Fischer, P., Brox, T.: U-net: convolutional networks for biomedical image segmentation (2015). http://arxiv.org/abs/1505.04597
17. Skrifter, B., Ind, B.V., Thorvald, B.S., København, R.: Det kongelige danske videnskabernes selskab a method of establish in g groups of equal amplitude in plant sociology based on similarity of species content and its application to analyses of the vegetation on Danish commons
18. Sohl-Dickstein, J., Weiss, E.A., Maheswaranathan, N., Ganguli, S., Edu, S.: Deep unsupervised learning using nonequilibrium thermodynamics (2015)
19. Stojanovski, D., Hermida, U., Muffoletto, M., Lamata, P., Beqiri, A., Gomez, A.: Efficient pix2vox++ for 3D cardiac reconstruction from 2d echo views. In: Aylward, S., Noble, J.A., Hu, Y., Lee, S.L., Baum, Z., Min, Z. (eds.) ASMUS 2022. LNCS, vol. 13565, pp. 86–95. Springer, Cham (2022). https://doi.org/10.1007/978-3-031-16902-1_9
20. Wang, W., et al.: Semantic image synthesis via diffusion models (2022). http://arxiv.org/abs/2207.00050
21. Zhu, J.Y., Park, T., Isola, P., Efros, A.A.: Unpaired image-to-image translation using cycle-consistent adversarial networks (2017). http://arxiv.org/abs/1703.10593

Graph Convolutional Neural Networks for Automated Echocardiography View Recognition: A Holistic Approach

Sarina Thomas[1]($\boxtimes$), Cristiana Tiago[2], Børge Solli Andreassen[1],
Svein-Arne Aase[2], Jurica Šprem[2], Erik Steen[2], Anne Solberg[1],
and Guy Ben-Yosef[3]

[1] Division of Digital Signal and image processing, University of Oslo, Oslo, Norway
sarinat@uio.no
[2] GE Vingmed Ultrasound, GE Healthcare, Horten, Norway
[3] GE Research, Niskayuna, NY, USA

Abstract. To facilitate diagnosis on cardiac ultrasound (US), clinical practice has established several standard views of the heart, which serve as reference points for diagnostic measurements and define viewports from which images are acquired. Automatic view recognition involves grouping those images into classes of standard views. Although deep learning techniques have been successful in achieving this, they still struggle with fully verifying the suitability of an image for specific measurements due to factors like the correct location, pose, and potential occlusions of cardiac structures. Our approach goes beyond view classification and incorporates a 3D mesh reconstruction of the heart that enables several more downstream tasks, like segmentation and pose estimation. In this work, we explore learning 3D heart meshes via graph convolutions, using similar techniques to learn 3D meshes in natural images, such as human pose estimation. As the availability of fully annotated 3D images is limited, we generate synthetic US images from 3D meshes by training an adversarial denoising diffusion model. Experiments were conducted on synthetic and clinical cases for view recognition and structure detection. The approach yielded good performance on synthetic images and, despite being exclusively trained on synthetic data, it already showed potential when applied to clinical images. With this proof-of-concept, we aim to demonstrate the benefits of graphs to improve cardiac view recognition that can ultimately lead to better efficiency in cardiac diagnosis.

Keywords: Graph convolutional networks · Detection · Diffusion models · View recognition · Mesh reconstruction · Echocardiography

---

Supplementary Information The online version contains supplementary material available at https://doi.org/10.1007/978-3-031-44521-7_5.

B. Kainz et al. (Eds.): ASMUS 2023, LNCS 14337, pp. 44–54, 2023.
https://doi.org/10.1007/978-3-031-44521-7_5

1   Introduction

In the field of diagnosing heart diseases, cardiovascular ultrasound—also known as echocardiography—is the most commonly used technique due to its accessibility, instantaneous results, and lack of ionizing radiation. Cardiac diagnosis includes the collection of multiple ultrasound (US) images of the heart to identify possible pathologies. In these images, measurements of anatomical structures are obtained to identify pathological deviations from standard norms. The accuracy of measurements is heavily dependent on the quality of the image. The American Society of Echocardiography (ASE) guidelines [11] recommend obtaining specific standardized views to ensure quality. These views ideally show all the required anatomical landmarks. However, anatomical variations, for example, the body mass index, can complicate the obtaining of correct views, leading to multiple attempts and non-standard views. Diagnostic measurements are time-consuming as clinical experts must carefully identify suitable images. One solution to speed up this process is to employ machine learning methods to automatically select appropriate views, called automatic view recognition. State-of-the-art methods utilize deep learning techniques, which involve training convolutional neural networks (CNNs) on large datasets to directly classify view labels. However, an automated selection may not result in a suitable image. Several factors come into play, such as whether structures of interest are fully visible. These factors vary for each view and measurement following the guidelines [11]. We propose a holistic measurement-centric approach to assess the suitability of images for diagnosis beyond selecting the correct view. Our approach addresses multiple tasks relevant to echocardiography quality control: By estimating the 3D heart pose in relation to the US probe, it becomes possible to select the correct view, localize chambers, and identify any issues such as sector intersections, misalignment, or occlusions, consequently aiding in discarding unsuitable images. Our contribution includes: (1) a **graph convolutional neural network for pose regression** of the US plane w.r.t. a 3D mesh, (2) a multi-structure graph for **localizing all chambers and ventricles**, and (3) exploring a **diffusion-based approach** to overcome the lack of 3D annotations. To our knowledge, this is the first work to apply a graph approach to 2D-3D reconstruction in echocardiography, demonstrating simultaneous localization of chambers and view prediction.

2   Related Work

Although our work is geared toward automatic view recognition, it touches on a variety of research fields. Therefore, this chapter reviews view recognition approaches but also the current state-of-the-art in graph neural networks (GNN) for medical image segmentation and 2D-3D reconstruction. In the literature, automatic view recognition is mainly regarded a classification problem that predicts a view label defined by the ASE. Various CNN architectures have been explored, including different variations based on ResNet [24], Inception-Net [21] and VGG [25]. The studies vary in the number of training samples and

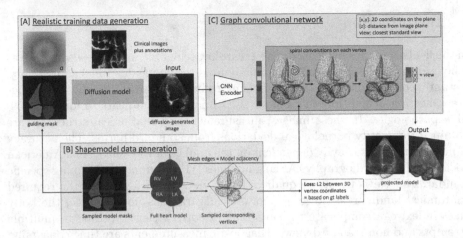

Fig. 1. Pipeline overview: A) A diffusion model is trained with real US images and segmentations to generate synthetic images guided by the segmentations of the 3D mesh. B) Synthetic segmentations are sampled from 3D heart meshes along with the 3D coordinates of the model and the view. C) A GCN uses the 3D mesh vertices as nodes and predicts the 3D vertex positions on the 2D image.

view classes. More recent approaches also include contrastive learning and incorporate contrast-enhanced US images [2]. All aforementioned approaches have in common that they only output a label without indicating how close the view is in relation to the corresponding standard view. Paseloup et al. [17] estimate probe rotation and tilt by formulating view recognition as a regression problem. Their approach provides the relative probe rotation along with the view; however, it does not include the probe translation. Due to their strong ability to model spatial relations, GNNs have been successfully applied to various tasks in medical imaging, demonstrating their potential in segmenting structures in X-Rays [3] and in spatio-temporal US [22]. Kong et al. [10] were the first to propose a GNN approach to create a 3D representation of the entire heart given a 3D CT or MR scan. Stojanovski et al. [20] use a Pix2Vox++ model to predict a 3D voxel representation from multiple 2D US images but without aligning the images to the resulting volume. Our research is founded on the notion of 3D mesh models, which have been derived from natural images such as a human body [9], face [14] and hand mesh [13], and more recently, X-Ray images [15]. In the proposed work, dense graph convolutions are applied in various training methods together with 3D parametric models. Our aim is to expand existing methods and integrate them with generative models [7] to create synthetic training data.

3 Method

The proposed pipeline aims to provide additional information on whether an image is suitable for diagnostic measurement. Instead of simply classifying the view label, we want to answer whether 1) relevant structures exist in the image, 2) those structures are fully visible, and 3) the image is taken from a view suitable for the measurement. All these questions can be answered by predicting the 3D position of a cutplane within a virtual shape model. The core of the method, illustrated in Fig. 1C, consists of a graph neural network that receives a single US image as input and predicts 3D coordinates of a 4-chamber heart model aligned with this US plane. Training the network in a supervised manner requires images with corresponding 3D coordinates. The following sections introduce the 3D model definition and training data generation. For this work, no annotated clinical 3D data was available. Therefore, a diffusion model was used to create synthetic US images given a guiding segmentation provided by the 3D mesh.

3.1 Model Embedding

The backbone of the pipeline is a 3D model (Fig. 1B) that can be aligned to the image. An anatomical structure can be represented as a closed mesh i.e. generated from a binary voxel representation. A mesh comprises 3D vertices and connecting edges. In this study, publically available patient heart meshes from [19] with multiple structures are utilized. Four structures are extracted, namely, left ventricle (LV), right ventricle (RV), left atrium (LA) and right atrium (RA). Fine-grained meshes are already registered, but their vertices do not correspond. One important feature in the model design is estimating the correspondences to build a relation between the meshes. Thus, a single template mesh is selected to define initial correspondences, and all other meshes are registered and sampled at vertices with the closest distance to the template. Consequently, all meshes share the same number of vertices where anatomical landmarks are roughly aligned. For efficiency, the meshes are down-sampled. In this work, original patient meshes are used, but in general, their corresponding vertices can also be used to build a statistical shape model that allows the generation of arbitrary meshes.

3.2 Data Generation

A 2D US image displays a cutplane through the heart depending on the 3D pose of the US probe. The pipeline introduced by Gilbert et al. [4] was extended to generate ground truth annotations. The aim is to sample 2D images from the 3D mesh that mimic realistic views obtained by a cardiologist. Alignment of the model towards specific standard views can be achieved using anatomical landmarks. For example, the apical 4 chamber view (a4ch) cuts the heart along a virtual axis built between the LV apex perpendicular to the midpoint between the mitral and tricuspid valve. Note that this only serves as a reference and can be highly patient-specific in clinical practice. After defining those standard planes, arbitrary other planes can be sampled by varying scaling, rotation, and translation of the 3D mesh which is aligned to the coordinate system built by the landmarks, e.g., the a4ch view origin (0,0,0) is set to the intersection between the mitral valve and tricuspid valve. With this, planes reflect the natural acquisition variability, and a cut through the mesh results in a 2D multi-label segmentation.

Segments are further concatenated with randomly sampled black cones to mimic the sector around a typical US image. For further details on the pipeline, the reader is referred to [4]. Unlike the original pipeline, the output mesh is defined in the plane coordinate system; x and y coordinates are translations on the image plane, and z represents the depth. In addition to generated segmentation, 3D vertices and the closest standard view are stored.

3.3   Diffusion Model Data Generation

Different echocardiography datasets have been published [1,12,16]. However, no dataset with all the four chambers is available, which would be required to train the GCN in a supervised manner. Labeling 3D US images is time-consuming and challenging due to their varying quality. Instead, a diffusion model is used to generate realistic US images based on the segmentations from Sect. 3.2. Diffusion models [7] have shown promising results in generating realistic and diverse images, including medical images. These models iteratively transform sampled noise into a more complex, realistic image. The training involves a forward path with multiple diffusion steps, where noise is increasingly added to the training image, and a reverse path to gradually denoise the noise source to generate a sample. Since the diffusion process aims to model the gradual transition from the initial noise source to the target image distribution, these models generate high-quality samples that progressively become more realistic. Building on the research of Tiago et al. [23], an adversarial denoising diffusion model is combined with a generative adversarial network (GAN) to learn the reverse denoising process, which combines the advantages of two generative models. The GAN attempts to create realistic image samples, whose statistical distribution is similar to the original, utilizing an extra label, particularly a segmentation mask, to simplify the image generation process. Using the segmentation masks described in Sect. 3.2, the goal is for the generated images to look like clinical images and align with the cardiac structures, so that they can be used as training data for the graph neural network.

3.4   Graph Neural Network

A 3D mesh can be defined by a graph $G = (V, E)$ in which nodes $V = \{v_i | i = 1, ..., N\}$ represent vertices and E represent edges of the surface faces. Unlike CNNs, graph neural networks (GCNs) allow for operating on arbitrary non-Euclidean structured data by aggregating the information of neighboring nodes using the edges and a weighting term. Spatial changes of a vertex likely affect neighboring vertices, but may also affect other vertices that are not in direct spatial proximity. There are different ways to define edge relations in an adjacency matrix. Gong et al. [5] propose using spiral convolutions on a closed surface. This operator enforces a fixed ordering of neighboring nodes during message passing to compute node updates with $x_i^k = \gamma^k \left(\|_{j \in S(i,l)} x_j^{k-1} \right)$ where $S(i, l)$ is the fixed spiral concatenation of indices of neighboring vertices x_j and γ is a multi-layer perceptron. Here, we extend the work in [22] to model a 3D heart mesh. An adjacency matrix is built for each structure and is concatenated. Similarly to the 2D approach, each graph node is assigned with a feature vector as the initial input. For this purpose, a CNN (ResNet50 [6]) predicts a feature representation from the input image. The GCN decoder is equipped with an initial dense layer to compress the input features, followed by four spiral layers, and complemented by an exponential linear activation unit. The last GCN layer outputs a 3D vector for each node and represents a mesh aligned with the image. The network is optimized using an L2 loss between the predicted and ground truth vertices.

4   Experiments and Results

The proposed GCN generates a 3D mesh from an US image. The performance can be evaluated on multiple downstream tasks important for clinical workflow optimization, such as segmentation of anatomical structures, view recognition, and foreshortening detection. In this proof of concept, experiments focused on view recognition and structure localization to answer the following questions:

Q1. Can the GCN be used to predict a 3D representation from a 2D image?
Q2. Trained solely on synthetic data, can the GCN predict a view label from a synthetic and a clinical US image?
Q3. Can the GCN accurately localize the four different chambers in the image?

Data and Implementation: Different data sources were used for the experiments. 4258 synthetic segmentations were sampled from 20 patient meshes processed by the data generation pipeline following [4]. All meshes were downsampled to a total of 2008 vertices. Based on the four standard views, 4-chamber ($a4ch$), 2-chamber ($a2ch$), 5-chamber ($a5ch$), and apical long axis ($aplax$), variations of the target planes were augmented by applying rotation, translation and scaling parameters sampled from a uniform distribution. Distribution limits were chosen for each view to reflect clinical variation. For training the diffusion model, an internal 2D echocardiography dataset was used since there was no public dataset with 4 chambers. This dataset consists of 1318 training and 248 test images from multiple sites and US probes and the aforementioned four standard views for which two timesteps, namely end-diastole (ED) and end-systole (ES), were labeled by experienced cardiologists. Labeled structures include ventricles LV and RV and atriums LA and RA. The diffusion model was applied to the synthetic segmentations to create 4258 synthetic US images. All datasets were divided into training, validation and test. Different appearance-based augmentations (CLAHE, gamma, multiplicative and Gaussian noise) were applied. The network was trained with a batchsize of 32 and optimized with a learning rate of 4e-4 using ADAM [8] until convergence.

View Recognition: Four standard views are encoded in the template mesh by computing the cutplane and identifying all vertices close to that plane. Those corresponding vertices can be used to transfer the ground truth plane to the predicted mesh and compare it to the plane spanned by the predicted vertices that

Table 1. Quantitative results for the task of view recognition evaluated on 480 synthetic and 248 clinical test cases. 'syn' refers to the images created by the diffusion model and 'real' refers to clinical cases. The method is compared to a standard classification network (ResNet50) based on accuracy, precision, and recall.

Method	Data		weighted avg	a2ch		aplax		a5ch		a4ch	
	Train	Test	view acc.	prec.	recall	prec.	recall	prec.	recall	prec	recall
ResNet50	syn	syn	0.88	1.00	1.00	0.60	0.78	0.88	0.76	1.00	0.99
ResNet50	syn	real	0.46	0.89	0.53	0.02	1.00	0.92	0.19	0.12	0.87
3DGCN	syn	syn	0.93	1.00	1.00	0.99	1.00	0.87	0.87	0.84	0.84
3DGCN	syn	real	0.75	0.97	0.59	0.63	1.00	0.69	0.64	0.74	0.82

Table 2. Quantitative results for the task of structure localization evaluated on 480 synthetic and 248 clinical test cases based on the bounding box mIoU of different structures and the mean 3D keypoints error. 'segm' refers to the segmentations, 'syn' refers to the images created by the diffusion model and 'real' refers to clinical cases.

Method	Data		mIoU				mkptsErr [%]
	Train	Test	LV	LA	RV	RA	
3DGCN	segm	segm	0.97	0.96	0.93	0.83	2.16 ± 0.74
3DGCN	syn	syn	0.96	0.96	0.89	0.79	2.68 ± 1.13
3DGCN	syn	real	0.88	0.88	0.82	0.87	N/A

intersect with the image plane. Results are shown in Table 1 and Fig. 2. In most synthetic test cases, the model successfully derived the correct label. However, when applied to clinical cases, the model struggled to differentiate between *a5ch* and *a4ch* and between *aplax* and *a2ch*. To benchmark this performance drop, a ResNet classifier was trained as a reference in addition to the 3DGCN using the same pipeline. The implementation included a ResNet50 backbone pre-trained on ImageNet with similar data and augmentation. The 3DGCN was able to outperform the ResNet, although it should be noted that training conditions were not specifically targeted towards the ResNet. The results show that the domain gap between synthetic and clinical images is present for the ResNet, with an even larger performance drop. The observed domain gap could be attributed to differences in how chambers are labeled in clinical images. In particular the LVOT, which was not included in the clinical annotations, is among the main distinguishable features of the *a5ch* and *aplax* view. This might have adversely affected the synthetic image generation that in return lead to inaccuracies in the view prediction. Regardless of the model, distinguishing between *a4ch* and *a5ch* views seems to be most challenging as those two only differ by a tilt of approx. 10-20° around the LV apex, which can be difficult to discern.

2D/3D Reconstruction: This experiment can only be evaluated on the synthetic and segmentation datasets as no ground truth coordinates are available

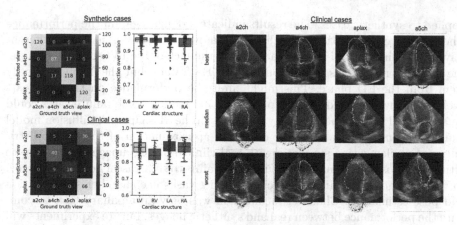

Fig. 2. Left: Confusion matrix of the view prediction and bounding box IoU for 480 synthetic and 248 clinical test cases. Right: Qualitative examples of the projected 3D GCN output applied to clinical cases (best, median, worst based on mIoU). The larger dots indicate where the mesh intersects the image plane (see example in suppl. video).

for clinical cases. Here, *segmentation* refers to the original segmentations, which should be a simple task for the graph. The mean 3D coordinate error (mkptsErr) is measured between the ground truth and the prediction and averaged over all 3D points. Since synthetic images do not have absolute pixel values, we computed the error in relation to the image size. As shown in Table 2, the kpts error is higher for synthetic US images, likely caused by the distribution shift between the segmentation masks and the synthetic data created by the diffusion model, as the latter could introduce unnatural appearance variations or inaccuracies.

Structure Localization: Intersecting the 3D mesh with the image plane leads to multiple 2D contours that allow semantic segmentation. However, a direct comparison is unfeasible due to structural differences between synthetic and clinical segmentations. Instead, bounding boxes are analyzed, and the mean Intersection over Union (mIoU) is computed at box level rather than pixel level. For the bounding box, points are considered that lie closer than 5% of the image size. The results presented in Fig. 2 and Table 2 demonstrate good performance on synthetic data but also a noticeable performance drop on clinical data.

5   Discussion and Conclusion

We present a novel approach solving cardiac view recognition. Based on a US image, a GCN reconstructs a 3D mesh to extract the contours of four chambers and to estimate the pose and view. To tackle the lack of 3D ground truth annotations, a diffusion model was employed to generate realistic US images based on binary masks. The GCN was solely trained on those images demonstrating promising potential for both view recognition and structure detection when applied to synthetic cases. The results indicate a domain gap in the performance when testing on synthetic versus clinical data, possibly attributed to the different ways of labeling clinical cases—particularly the lack of the LVOT. Furthermore, the diffusion model was trained on ED and ES frames, but the 3D meshes only stem from the ED phase. This might limit the performance on the full heart cycle and may be solved by incorporating a 4D model. Some failure cases could be attributed to low image quality and unusual heart shapes. A diffusion model trained on limited data can only create an approximation of the target distribution. Supplementing synthetic with real clinical 3D US images could help to ultimately close the domain gap. This study aims to showcase a holistic approach to view recognition, which can facilitate other tasks like chamber segmentation and pose estimation. Chamber localization was only an auxiliary task to compare the performance between real and synthetic images. Future experiments will assess the segmentation quality directly as soon as the LVOT is annotated. Still, chamber localization can serve as a feature for automatic image quality control. With the resulting 3D mesh, an intersection of structures with the US sector and foreshortening could potentially be detected which needs to be verified in the future. Since the 3D mesh includes more anatomical structures, their relative location encoded in the mesh can also be estimated as opposed to semantic segmentation. The 3DGCN can handle occlusions (illustrated in Fig. 2), both within and outside the image plane and can be trained on multiple views, eliminating the need for view-specific keypoints, which are required for the 2DGCN [22]. In the future, the GCN can be extended to fuse several views to refine the 3D mesh further. Using the original patient meshes from [19], we aimed to provide the diffusion model with shapes close to the training distribution. In the future, we plan to add a statistical shape model as described in [18]. While the full potential has not yet been fully demonstrated in clinical cases, this approach stands out from other black-box view recognition methods by providing direct visual feedback, thereby increasing explainability in failure cases. In conclusion, the concept of applying GCNs to view recognition seems to be promising as it combines different tasks relevant to assist the cardiologist in quality control.

Acknowledgment:. We thank Anna Novikova and Daria Kulikova for their valuable clinical consultation and for annotating the training data.

References

1. Bernard, O., et al.: Challenge on endocardial three-dimensional ultrasound segmentation. CREATIS, The MIDAS Journal (2014). https://doi.org/10.54294/j78w0v
2. Cheng, L.H., Sun, X., van der Geest, R.J.: Contrastive learning for echocardiographic view integration. In: Wang, L., Dou, Q., Fletcher, P.T., Speidel, S., Li, S. (eds.) MICCAI 2022. LNCS, vol. 13434, pp. 340–349. Springer, Cham (2022). https://doi.org/10.1007/978-3-031-16440-8_33
3. Gaggion, N., Mansilla, L., Milone, D.H., Ferrante, E.: Hybrid graph convolutional neural networks for landmark-based anatomical segmentation. In: de Bruijne, M., et al. (eds.) MICCAI 2021. LNCS, vol. 12901, pp. 600–610. Springer, Cham (2021). https://doi.org/10.1007/978-3-030-87193-2_57

4. Gilbert, A., Marciniak, M., Rodero, C., Lamata, P., Samset, E., McLeod, K.: Generating synthetic labeled data from existing anatomical models: an example with echocardiography segmentation. IEEE Trans. Med. Imaging, 2783–2794 (2021). https://doi.org/10.1109/TMI.2021.3051806

5. Gong, S., Chen, L., Bronstein, M., Zafeiriou, S.: Spiralnet++: a fast and highly efficient mesh convolution operator. In: Proceedings of the IEEE International Conference on Computer Vision Workshops (CVPR) (2019)

6. He, K., Zhang, X., Ren, S., Sun, J.: Deep residual learning for image recognition. In: Proceedings of the IEEE Conference on Computer Vision and Pattern Recognition, pp. 770–778 (2016). https://doi.org/10.1109/CVPR.2016.90

7. Ho, J., Jain, A., Abbeel, P.: Denoising diffusion probabilistic models. CoRR abs/2006.11239 (2020). https://arxiv.org/abs/2006.11239

8. Kingma, D., Ba, J.: Adam: a method for stochastic optimization. arXiv:1412.6980 (2014)

9. Kolotouros, N., Pavlakos, G., Daniilidis, K.: Convolutional mesh regression for single-image human shape reconstruction. In: 2019 IEEE/CVF Conference on Computer Vision and Pattern Recognition (CVPR), pp. 4496–4505 (2019). https://doi.org/10.1109/CVPR.2019.00463

10. Kong, F., Wilson, N., Shadden, S.: A deep-learning approach for direct whole-heart mesh reconstruction. Med. Image Anal. **74**, 102222 (2021). https://doi.org/10.1016/j.media.2021.102222

11. Lang, R., et al.: Recommendations for cardiac chamber quantification by echocardiography in adults: an update from the American society of echocardiography and the European association of cardiovascular imaging, **16**(3), 233–270 (2015). https://doi.org/10.1093/ehjci/jev014

12. Leclerc, S., et al.: Deep learning for segmentation using an open large-scale dataset in 2D echocardiography. IEEE Trans. Med. Imaging **38**(9), 2198–2210 (2019)

13. Li, M., et al.: Interacting attention graph for single image two-hand reconstruction. In: Proceedings of the IEEE/CVF Conference on Computer Vision and Pattern Recognition, pp. 2761–2770 (2022)

14. Lin, J., Yuan, Y., Shao, T., Zhou, K.: Towards high-fidelity 3D face reconstruction from in-the-wild images using graph convolutional networks. In: Proceedings of the IEEE/CVF Conference on Computer Vision and Pattern Recognition (CVPR), June 2020

15. Nakao, M., Nakamura, M., Matsuda, T.: Image-to-graph convolutional network for 2D/3D deformable model registration of low-contrast organs. IEEE Trans. Med. Imaging **41**(12), 3747–3761 (2022). https://doi.org/10.1109/TMI.2022.3194517

16. Ouyang, D., et al.: Interpretable AI for beat-to-beat cardiac function assessment. Nature (2020). https://doi.org/10.1038/s41586-020-2145-8

17. Pasdeloup, D., et al.: Real-time echocardiography guidance for optimized apical standard views. Ultrasound Med. Biol. **49**(1), 333–346 (2023). https://doi.org/10.1016/j.ultrasmedbio.2022.09.006

18. Rodero, C., et al.: Virtual cohort of 1000 synthetic heart meshes from adult human healthy population (2021). https://doi.org/10.5281/zenodo.4506930

19. Rodero, C., et al.: Virtual cohort of adult healthy four-chamber heart meshes from CT images (2021). https://doi.org/10.5281/zenodo.4590294

20. Stojanovski, D., Hermida, U., Muffoletto, M., Lamata, P., Beqiri, A., Gomez, A.: Efficient pix2vox++ for 3D cardiac reconstruction from 2d echo views. In: Aylward, S., Noble, J.A., Hu, Y., Lee, S.L., Baum, Z., Min, Z. (eds.) ASMUS 2022. LNCS, vol. 13565, pp. 86–95. Springer, Cham (2022). https://doi.org/10.1007/978-3-031-16902-1_9

21. Østvik, A., Smistad, E., Aase, S.A., Haugen, B.O., Lovstakken, L.: Real-time standard view classification in transthoracic echocardiography using convolutional neural networks. Ultrasound Med. Biol. **45**(2), 374–384 (2019). https://doi.org/10.1016/j.ultrasmedbio.2018.07.024

22. Thomas, S., Gilbert, A., Ben-Yosef, G.: Light-weight spatio-temporal graphs for segmentation and ejection fraction prediction in cardiac ultrasound, 380–390 (2022). https://doi.org/10.1007/978303116440837

23. Tiago, C., Snare, S.R., Šprem, J., McLeod, K.: A domain translation framework with an adversarial denoising diffusion model to generate synthetic datasets of echocardiography images. IEEE Access **11**, 17594–17602 (2023). https://doi.org/10.1109/ACCESS.2023.3246762

24. Wu, L., et al.: Standard echocardiographic view recognition in diagnosis of congenital heart defects in children using deep learning based on knowledge distillation. Front. Pediatrics **9** (2022). https://doi.org/10.3389/fped.2021.770182

25. Zhang, J., et al.: Fully automated echocardiogram interpretation in clinical practice. Circulation **138**(16), 1623–1635 (2018). https://doi.org/10.1161/CIRCULATIONAHA.118.034338

Predictive Analysis, Learning, and Classification

Leveraging Shape and Spatial Information for Spontaneous Preterm Birth Prediction

Paraskevas Pegios[1]([✉])(iD), Emilie Pi Fogtmann Sejer[2](iD), Manxi Lin[1](iD),
Zahra Bashir[3](iD), Morten Bo Søndergaard Svendsen[2,4](iD), Mads Nielsen[4](iD),
Eike Petersen[1](iD), Anders Nymark Christensen[1](iD), Martin Tolsgaard[2](iD),
and Aasa Feragen[1](iD)

[1] Technical University of Denmark, Kongens Lyngby, Denmark
{ppar,afhar}@dtu.dk
[2] Region Hovedstaden Hospital, Copenhagen, Denmark
[3] Slagelse Hospital, Copenhagen, Denmark
[4] University of Copenhagen, Copenhagen, Denmark

Abstract. Spontaneous preterm birth prediction from transvaginal ultrasound images is a challenging task of profound interest in gynecological obstetrics. Existing works are often validated on small datasets and may lack validation of model calibration and interpretation. In this paper, we present a comprehensive study of methods for predicting preterm birth from transvaginal ultrasound using a large clinical dataset. We propose a shape- and spatially-aware network that leverages segmentation predictions and pixel spacing information as additional input to enhance predictions. Our model demonstrates competitive performance on our benchmark, providing additional interpretation and achieving the highest performance across both clinical and machine learning baselines. Through our evaluation, we provide additional insights which we hope may lead to more accurate predictions of preterm births going forwards.

Keywords: Spontaneous Preterm Birth · Transvaginal Ultrasound · Transparency

1 Introduction

Spontaneous preterm birth (sPTB), usually defined as birth occurring before 37 weeks of gestation, is considered a pressing challenge, with substantial health, societal, and financial implications. Affecting millions of cases annually it is the key factor causing neonatal morbidity [24], as premature infants are vulnerable to several complications. These risks often necessitate prolonged hospitalization in neonatal intensive care units, with potentially adverse outcomes [13]. The ability to accurately predict sPTB is of paramount importance in the prevention of neonatal mortality and morbidity. By identifying pregnancies at risk, healthcare professionals can provide support to the affected infants and their families. Despite considerable efforts, predicting sPTB remains an open problem.

© The Author(s), under exclusive license to Springer Nature Switzerland AG 2023
B. Kainz et al. (Eds.): ASMUS 2023, LNCS 14337, pp. 57–67, 2023.
https://doi.org/10.1007/978-3-031-44521-7_6

Cervical length (CL) measurements obtained from cervical ultrasound images currently serve as the clinical gold standard for sPTB prediction, with a threshold usually of CL < 25 mm indicating an increased risk [7]. The success of machine learning opened up new opportunities [2,26] by analyzing ultrasound images, electronic health data, and electrohysterogram signals, and emerging imaging modalities [20]. With the rise of deep learning, U-Net-based methods [25,27] have demonstrated state-of-the-art results using ultrasound images. Yet, existing methods may suffer from potential risk of bias [28] due to their small effective sample size, and their lack of model transparency, and calibration evaluation for assessing the reliability of individual confidences.

We present a comprehensive analysis of methods that seek to predict sPTB using a class-balanced dataset of 7862 transvaginal ultrasound images. We argue that the shape, spatial, and textural information of the cervix are strong candidates for predicting sPTB. To this end, we leverage DTU-Net [16] for measuring CL, utilizing its ability to segment curvilinear structures. From this, we build a shape- and spatially-aware SA-SonoNet classifier, based on the SonoNet architecture [4], which uses predicted segmentations to enhance predictions following [15]. In summary, we contribute 1) an extensive evaluation of both clinical and machine learning baselines on a large clinical dataset and 2) a new method that outperforms existing approaches while providing additional explainability.

2   Related Work

Sonographic assessment of CL is considered the most accessible and accurate predictor for sPTB [7]. Nevertheless, improving population-wide screening for low-risk cases requires addressing the challenges of low sensitivity and prevalence of CL [23]. Thus, measurements of the uterocervical angle (UCA), i.e., the angle between the uterine wall and the cervical canal, have been explored [9,10] or combined with CL [17,21] as an additional biomarker, along with wall thickness measurements of the upper and lower uterine segment [1]. However, these approaches rely on the skills of the sonographer to measure biomarkers or require specialized protocols for data collection. We provide a) a method to automate CL measurements, and b) a second method to automatically predict sPTB directly from transvaginal ultrasound, simultaneously improving performance, speeding up the data collection, and reducing the demand on the clinician's competences.

Another branch of work [3,6,11] focuses on the analysis of cervical texture. In clinically hypothesized regions of interest (ROIs) hand-crafted textural features are extracted and used in conjunction with standard machine learning techniques. While these have shown promise, especially combined with CL [5], they are often hard to reproduce [2], and evaluated on small and highly class-unbalanced datasets with very few cases, and of higher image quality than the clinical standard. In this study, we implement and integrate a texture-based baseline into our analysis, evaluated on a large, class-balanced clinical dataset.

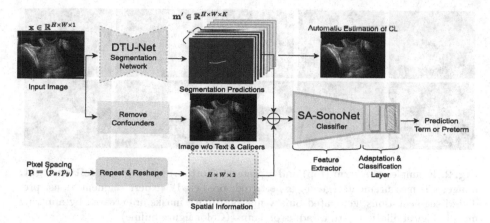

Fig. 1. Overview of the proposed method.

Recently, deep learning methods have been used to recognize cervical anatomy and interrogate sPTB predictions. In [27], a segmentation model predicts a binary mask around the cervical canal, and then CL and UCA are estimated and serve as inputs for standard statistical methods. As an alternative to the binary mask, [8,29] use multiple cervical coarse ROIs in order to provide feedback to clinicians. In [25], a multi-task framework is used both for classification and segmentation of the ROI surrounding the cervical canal. Although existing methods provide valuable information to clinicians, their utility in predicting sPTB is yet to be explored. In this work, we employ a DTU-Net [16] for recognizing cervical structures and leverage its predictions as additional inputs for our classification model, while we further inject it using spatial information.

3   Method

We summarize the architecture of our proposed method in Fig. 1. First, we use a DTU-Net [16] to automatically measure CL by detecting curvilinear structures in cervix images. Next, we introduce SA-SonoNet, a shape- and spatially-aware SonoNet [4] for predicting sPTB, which enhances performance by concatenating input images, segmentation predictions, and pixel spacing information.

3.1   Estimating Cervical Length from Curvilinear Segmentation

We quantify CL using a DTU-Net [16] that segments the curvilinear structures of the cervical canal (CC), inner boundary (IB) and outer boundary (OB), and the volumetric structure of the bladder (BL), from background. From the CC segmentation, CL is measured via its left and right-most points (see Fig. 1). Robust binary masks covering the area near the CC, as utilized in [25,27], can be created by applying morphological dilation to the CC predictions (see Fig. 2).

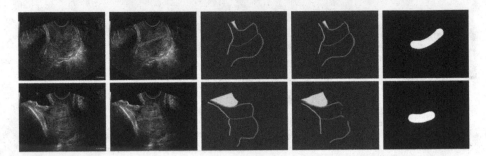

Fig. 2. Examples of a term (top) and a preterm (bottom) birth. **From left to right:** image, CL measurements (green: expert, red: predicted), expert segmentations, predicted segmentations, generated binary masks. Binary masks are created by applying morphological dilation with a radius of 4 mm. (Color figure online)

3.2 Injecting Shape and Spatial Information into SonoNet

We hypothesize that the shape, size, and texture of the cervix are predictive of sPTB. Recognizing the inherent texture bias [14] of convolutional neural networks (CNNs), we inject shape and spatial information into SonoNet [4], a state-of-the-art CNN for ultrasound standard plane classification. As classification of standard plane quality benefits from combining images with predicted segmentations in [15], we similarly include the cervical shape information. As sonographers adjust image resolution during examinations, and we expect cervix size and texture to depend on resolution, we include pixel spacing as an input feature.

Let $\mathbf{x} \in \mathbb{R}^{H \times W \times 1}$ be a grayscale image with height H and width W, with pixel spacing information $\mathbf{p} = (p_x, p_y)$ representing the physical distance between the centers of each 2D pixel. We assume that we have access to a trained segmentation network g – in our experiments, the DTU-Net discussed in Sect. 3.1. During inference, g predicts a segmentation map $g(\mathbf{x}) = \mathbf{m} \in \mathbb{R}^{H \times W \times L}$, where L is the number of segmentation labels and $\mathbf{m}_{x,y}$ represents the probability distribution for the pixel at position (x, y) across the set of learned segmentation labels. We keep only the K segmentation predictions, that are relevant to the classification task, i.e., $\mathbf{m}' \in \mathbb{R}^{H \times W \times K}$. In our experiments, $K = 5$. Our goal is to learn a mapping $f(\mathbf{x}, \mathbf{m}', \mathbf{p}) \mapsto y$ where y indicates a predicted target and f is a SonoNet classifier. In practice, the pixel-spacing values (p_x, p_y) are repeated and reshaped to the image dimension $H \times W$, resulting in input channels with the same value at each position for each direction. These are concatenated together with the segmentation predictions $\mathbf{m}'$ and the corresponding image $\mathbf{x}$. We refer to our architecture as SA-SonoNet, a shape- and spatially-aware SonoNet.

Clinical ultrasound images have embedded text and calipers. While these do not impact segmentation performance, they can introduce confounding factors when training a classification model [18]. To reduce their effect on generalization, cofounders are removed by applying thresholding in hue space to identify text and using the telea inpainting method [22] to eliminate calipers from the input image $\mathbf{x}$ before feeding it into our model. Our framework is summarized in Fig. 1.

4 Experiments

Existing work often faces evaluation limitations, such as small datasets and lack of method comparison, calibration evaluation, and model transparency [28]. In this section, we address these issues by conducting a comprehensive comparison of the proposed method with current approaches on a large dataset.

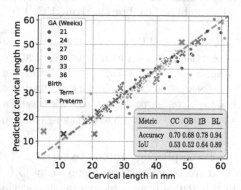

Fig. 3. CL estimates from segmentation. The table shows DTU-Net's segmentation performance in detecting the four cervical structures, CC, OB, IB, and BL (K = 5, including background). Note that while accuracy and IoU are naturally low for thin curvilinear structures, the CL mean absolute error of 1.79 mm indicates that the CC segmentations are indeed appropriate for robustly estimating CL.

Dataset. Our main dataset comprises 7862 transvaginal ultrasound images extracted from a national fetal ultrasound screening database (ANONYMIZED). The original images have different resolutions with the same physical pixel distance in each direction which varies in the range $[0.037, 0.276]$ with a mean of 0.116 mm and standard deviation of 0.027 mm. The samples cover a range of gestational age (GA) at scan time ranging from week 19 to 32, with equal representation of preterm/term births per GA week. To ensure robust evaluation, we employ a 5-fold stratified cross-validation strategy, where folds have non-overlapping patients and evenly sampled term/preterm births per GA week. Furthermore, we divide (using the same strategy) each fold into equal-size validation and test sets and swap them during assessment, resulting in 10 splits with 6290/786/786 samples for training/validation/test sets.

DTU-Net is trained and tested on an external multi-class segmentation dataset with $L = 14$ structures which includes 908/155 cervix images for training/test and additional standard planes (1481/271 head, 892/240 abdomen, 639/129 femur).

Validation of DTU-Net and CL Estimates. As Fig. 3 illustrates, DTU-Net accurately identifies the CL. Evaluation against expert CL measurements on 155 test images shows a mean absolute error of 1.79 mm, and CL predictions are robust across scan time gestational ages (GAs). Example expert annotations, DTU-Net predictions, and CL estimations are shown in Fig. 2.

Baselines. We benchmark our model against 4 baseline methods, including the current clinical standard which defines sPTB when CL < 25 mm. To measure

Table 1. Classification results averaged across 10 balanced test splits. Reported metrics are area under the curve (AUC), accuracy (ACC), sensitivity (SEN), specificity (SPE), and an unbiased calibration error (UCE) [19].

Method	AUC ↑	ACC ↑	SEN ↑	SPE ↑	UCE ↓
CL < 25 mm	0.673 ± 0.032	0.626 ± 0.026	0.406 ± 0.043	**0.846 ± 0.018**	–
TextureNet	0.685 ± 0.025	0.642 ± 0.025	0.545 ± 0.037	0.740 ± 0.027	**0.015 ± 0.016**
MT U-Net [25]	0.700 ± 0.020	0.645 ± 0.019	0.558 ± 0.043	0.732 ± 0.023	0.079 ± 0.024
SonoNet w/PS	0.700 ± 0.032	0.645 ± 0.030	0.590 ± 0.048	0.700 ± 0.021	0.021 ± 0.024
SA-SonoNet	**0.750 ± 0.034**	**0.686 ± 0.033**	**0.629 ± 0.037**	0.743 ± 0.041	0.035 ± 0.021

CL, we employ our automated strategy, (Sect. 3.1). Additionally, we implement a texture-based method inspired by [3, 6, 11]. We extract 102 hand-crafted textural features from a binary mask covering the area near the cervical canal (see Fig. 2) and apply principal component analysis (PCA) maintaining 97% of the information, i.e., 32 PCA features, which are used to train a two-layer multi-layer perceptron (MLP) called TextureNet. Furthermore, we compare our results with a multi-task U-Net (MT U-Net) [25], trained both for classification and segmentation of the same binary mask. Finally, we include as a baseline, a pre-trained SonoNet-32 [4] injected only with pixel spacing information (SonoNet /w PS).

Implementation Details. All models were trained using binary cross-entropy loss, except MT U-Net, which followed the multitask loss defined in [25]. We used SGD optimizer with a momentum of 0.9 and batch size of 64, while we decayed the initial learning rate of 10^{-3} by a factor of 75% when the validation loss plateaued for 10 epochs. We applied an L2-regularization of 10^{-4} and saved models with the best validation loss for evaluation. TextureNet was implemented with a two-layer MLP with 128 and 64 neurons including batch normalization and drop-out layers. We used pyfeats [12] to extract early and late texture features. Our model was based on pre-trained SonoNet-32 [4], with modifications to the first layer to match the input channel size. The images were resized to

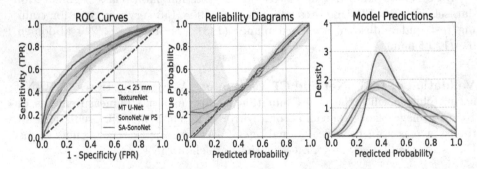

Fig. 4. From left to right: ROC curves, loess-based reliability diagrams, and model predictions. Uncertainty is estimated with a 95% confidence interval.

Table 2. SA-SonoNet performance when removing or modifying parts of the inputs; image (IM), cervical canal (CC), outer boundary (OB), inner boundary (IB), bladder (BL), background (BG) defined as the image with all segmented structures subtracted, and pixel spacing (PS). R stands for replacing the original PS by random sampling from pixel spacing distributions, and B stands for blacking out from the image the pixels surrounding the cervix.

IM	CC	OB	IB	BL	BG	PS	AUC	ACC	SEN	SPE
✓	✓	✓	✓	✓	✓	✓	**0.750 ± 0.034**	**0.686 ± 0.033**	0.629 ± 0.037	0.743 ± 0.041
✓						✓	0.514 ± 0.038	0.505 ± 0.023	0.771 ± 0.199	0.232 ± 0.212
✓	✓					✓	0.514 ± 0.038	0.507 ± 0.031	0.788 ± 0.190	0.220 ± 0.209
✓		✓				✓	0.549 ± 0.033	0.527 ± 0.023	0.744 ± 0.216	0.304 ± 0.249
✓			✓			✓	0.582 ± 0.048	0.539 ± 0.031	0.696 ± 0.198	0.376 ± 0.239
✓				✓		✓	0.512 ± 0.038	0.503 ± 0.025	0.780 ± 0.192	0.220 ± 0.204
✓					✓	✓	0.629 ± 0.025	0.531 ± 0.028	**0.917 ± 0.052**	0.114 ± 0.096
✓	✓				✓	✓	0.663 ± 0.015	0.576 ± 0.032	0.831 ± 0.057	0.320 ± 0.114
✓		✓			✓	✓	0.684 ± 0.021	0.615 ± 0.025	0.717 ± 0.062	0.513 ± 0.108
✓			✓		✓	✓	0.705 ± 0.041	0.611 ± 0.044	0.820 ± 0.036	0.401 ± 0.106
✓				✓	✓	✓	0.633 ± 0.027	0.537 ± 0.030	0.911 ± 0.051	0.163 ± 0.100
✓	✓	✓	✓	✓	✓		0.542 ± 0.076	0.507 ± 0.037	0.831 ± 0.173	0.185 ± 0.185
✓	✓	✓	✓	✓	✓	R	0.681 ± 0.021	0.629 ± 0.025	0.498 ± 0.096	**0.758 ± 0.060**
	✓	✓	✓	✓	✓	✓	0.705 ± 0.028	0.642 ± 0.032	0.677 ± 0.071	0.605 ± 0.104
B	✓	✓	✓	✓	✓	✓	0.733 ± 0.027	0.663 ± 0.027	0.649 ± 0.091	0.676 ± 0.103

224×288, pixel intensity was normalized to $[-1, 1]$, pixel spacing was calculated for the resized images, and injected in mm. During training, we applied standard data augmentation such as random flipping, rotations, contrast, and brightness. Source code will be available at https://github.com/ppegiosk/SA-SonoNet-sPTB.

Results. We evaluate all methods across 10 test splits in terms of area under the curve (AUC), accuracy (ACC), sensitivity (SEN), specificity (SPE), and an unbiased calibration error (UCE) [19]. Results are found in Table 1. We also provide receiver operating characteristic (ROC) curves, loess-based reliability diagrams and distribution of model predictions in Fig. 4. Our model demonstrates competitive performance across metrics while being well-calibrated.

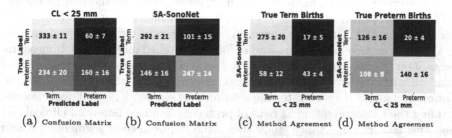

(a) Confusion Matrix   (b) Confusion Matrix   (c) Method Agreement   (d) Method Agreement

Fig. 5. Confusion and method (dis-)agreement matrices across 10 test splits.

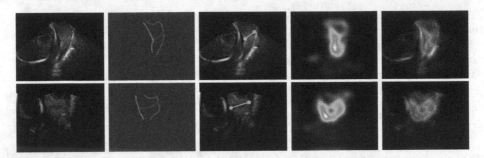

Fig. 6. Examples of high-confidence preterm birth correct predictions for a short, CL = 19.8 mm, (top) and a larger, CL = 30.1 mm, (bottom) cervix. **From left to right:** image without cofounders, DTU-Net's segmentation predictions, automatic CL measurements, saliency maps, saliency maps on top of the input image.

Feature Relevance. We assess feature relevance of different inputs of our model by evaluating model performance when removing or modifying parts of the input channels at test time. Results are found in Table 2.

Model Interpretation. Since our model is well-calibrated and performs well, confidence scores can be interpreted as risk of preterm birth. Moreover, our feature importance study brings insight into the driving features of our predictions.

For additional insight into how the model differs from the clinical standard, we provide confusion matrices for CL-based predictions in Fig. 5a and our model in Fig. 5b. Moreover, (dis)-agreement matrices between the two approaches for term and preterm births are shown in Fig. 5c and Fig. 5d, respectively.

Finally, we leverage the explainability of SonoNet [4], which is a fully CNN architecture replacing standard fully-connected layers with 1×1 convolutions. This modification maintains the correspondence between class score maps and input images, enabling the extraction of class-specific saliency maps. Examples of high-confidence predictions are shown in Fig. 6.

5   Discussion and Conclusion

The experimental results highlight the effectiveness of our method for predicting sPTB by incorporating cervical shape and spatial information into our model. Our automated CL estimation approach achieves similar predictive performance for sPTB prediction as previous studies [5,6] that relied on manual CL measurements. Our model achieves the highest specificity beyond the current clinical standard while maintaining the highest sensitivity among all methods. The calibration evaluation demonstrates the reliability of our model's confidence scores, enabling their interpretation as risks of preterm birth in a potential clinical setting. Our feature importance study shows the importance of segmentation and pixel spacing inputs in driving model predictions, enhancing transparency. Furthermore, Fig. 5d shows that our model identifies pregnancies at risk in cases of

CL > 25 mm where the current clinical standard falls short. Leveraging its inherent architecture, we generate saliency maps that enhance model interpretability.

Limitations. Our model assumes a well-trained segmentation model. Obtaining expert annotations for segmentation models can pose a practical constraint. However, we show the feasibility of using a DTU-Net [16] trained for general multi-class segmentation tasks and more standard planes than the cervix.

Summary. In this paper, we propose SA-SonoNet, a shape- and spatially-aware network for predicting sPTB. Differing from existing methods, SA-SonoNet leverages segmentation predictions and pixel spacing as additional information. We validated our model on a large class-balanced clinical dataset consisting of 7862 images, where the proposed method surpasses baselines considerably.

Acknowledgments. This work was supported by the Pioneer Centre for AI (DNRF grant nr P1), the DIREC project EXPLAIN-ME (9142-00001B), and the Novo Nordisk Foundation through the Center for Basic Machine Learning Research in Life Science (NNF20OC0062606).

References

1. Ahmed, W.S., Madny, E., Habash, Y., Ibrahim, Z., Morsy, A., Said, M.: Ultrasonographic wall thickness measurement of the upper and lower uterine segments in the prediction of the progress of preterm labour. Clin. Exp. Obstetr. Gynecol. **42**(3), 331–335 (2015)
2. Akazawa, M., Hashimoto, K.: Prediction of preterm birth using artificial intelligence: a systematic review. J. Obstetr. Gynaecol. **42**(6), 1662–1668 (2022)
3. Baños, N., et al.: Quantitative analysis of cervical texture by ultrasound in mid-pregnancy and association with spontaneous preterm birth. Ultrasound Obstetr. Gynecol. **51**(5), 637–643 (2018)
4. Baumgartner, C.F., et al.: SonoNet: real-time detection and localisation of fetal standard scan planes in freehand ultrasound. IEEE TMI **36**(11) (2017)
5. Burgos-Artizzu, X.P., et al.: Mid-trimester prediction of spontaneous preterm birth with automated cervical quantitative ultrasound texture analysis and cervical length: a prospective study. Sci. Rep. **11**(1), 1–7 (2021)
6. Bustamante, D., et al.: Cervix ultrasound texture analysis to differentiate between term and preterm birth pregnancy: a machine learning approach. In: IEEE IUS, pp. 1–4. IEEE IUS (2022)
7. Coutinho, C., et al.: Isuog practice guidelines: role of ultrasound in the prediction of spontaneous preterm birth. Ultrasound Obstetr. Gynecol. Off. J. Int. Soc. Ultrasound Obstetr. Gynecol. **60**(3), 435–456 (2022)
8. Dagle, A.B., et al.: Automated segmentation of cervical anatomy to interrogate preterm birth. In: Licandro, R., Melbourne, A., Abaci Turk, E., Macgowan, C., Hutter, J. (eds.) PIPPI 2022. LNCS, vol. 13575, pp. 48–59. Springer, Cham (2022). https://doi.org/10.1007/978-3-031-17117-8_5

9. Dziadosz, M., et al.: Uterocervical angle: a novel ultrasound screening tool to predict spontaneous preterm birth. Am. J. Obstetr. Gynecol. **215**(3) (2016)
10. Farràs Llobet, A., et al.: The uterocervical angle and its relationship with preterm birth. J. Maternal-Fetal Neonatal Med. **31**(14), 1881–1884 (2018)
11. Fiset, S., Martel, A., Glanc, P., Barrett, J., Melamed, N.: Prediction of spontaneous preterm birth among twin gestations using machine learning and texture analysis of cervical ultrasound images. U Toronto Med. J. **96**(1) (2019)
12. Giakoumoglou, N.: Pyfeats (2021). https://doi.org/10.5281/zenodo.6783286
13. Hemming, V.G., Overall, J.C., Jr., Britt, M.R.: Nosocomial infections in a newborn intensive-care unit: results of forty-one months of surveillance. N. Engl. J. Med. **294**(24), 1310–1316 (1976)
14. Hermann, K., Chen, T., Kornblith, S.: The origins and prevalence of texture bias in convolutional neural networks. In: NeurIPS, vol. 33, pp. 19000–19015 (2020)
15. Lin, M., Feragen, A., Bashir, Z., Tolsgaard, M.G., Christensen, A.N.: I saw, I conceived, I concluded: progressive concepts as bottlenecks. arXiv:2211.10630 (2022)
16. Lin, M., et al.: DTU-net: learning topological similarity for curvilinear structure segmentation. In: Frangi, A., de Bruijne, M., Wassermann, D., Navab, N. (eds.) IPMI 2023. LNCS, vol. 13939, pp. 654–666. Springer, Cham (2023). https://doi.org/10.1007/978-3-031-34048-2_50
17. Luechathananon, S., Songthamwat, M., Chaiyarach, S.: Uterocervical angle and cervical length as a tool to predict preterm birth in threatened preterm labor. Int. J. Women's Health, 153–159 (2021)
18. Mikolaj, K., et al.: Removing confounding information from fetal ultrasound images. arXiv:2303.13918 (2023)
19. Petersen, E., Ganz, M., Holm, S., Feragen, A.: On (assessing) the fairness of risk score models. In: FAccT, pp. 817–829 (2023)
20. Pizzella, S., El Helou, N., Chubiz, J., Wang, L.V., Tuuli, M.G., England, S.K., Stout, M.J.: Evolving cervical imaging technologies to predict preterm birth. Seminars Immunopathol. **42**, 385–396 (2020). Springer
21. Sepúlveda-Martínez, A., Diaz, F., Muñoz, H., Valdés, E., Parra-Cordero, M.: Second-trimester anterior cervical angle in a low-risk population as a marker for spontaneous preterm delivery. Fetal Diagn. Ther. **41**(3), 220–225 (2017)
22. Telea, A.: An image inpainting technique based on the fast marching method. J. Graph. Tools **9**(1), 23–34 (2004)
23. Ven, V.D., et al.: The capacity of mid-pregnancy cervical length to predict preterm birth in low-risk women: a national cohort study. Acta Obstet. Gynecol. Scand. **94**(11), 1223–1234 (2015)
24. Vogel, J.P., Chawanpaiboon, S., Moller, A.B., Watananirun, K., Bonet, M., Lumbiganon, P.: The global epidemiology of preterm birth. Best Pract. Res. Clin. Obstetr. Gynaecol. **52**, 3–12 (2018)
25. Włodarczyk, T., et al.: Spontaneous preterm birth prediction using convolutional neural networks. In: Hu, Y., et al. (eds.) ASMUS/PIPPI -2020. LNCS, vol. 12437, pp. 274–283. Springer, Cham (2020). https://doi.org/10.1007/978-3-030-60334-2_27
26. Włodarczyk, T., et al.: Machine learning methods for preterm birth prediction: a review. Electronics **10**(5), 586 (2021)
27. Włodarczyk, T., et al.: Estimation of preterm birth markers with U-net segmentation network. In: Wang, Q., et al. (eds.) PIPPI/SUSI -2019. LNCS, vol. 11798, pp. 95–103. Springer, Cham (2019). https://doi.org/10.1007/978-3-030-32875-7_11

28. Yang, Q., et al.: Reporting and risk of bias of prediction models based on machine learning methods in preterm birth: a systematic review. Acta Obstet. Gynecol. Scand. **102**(1), 7–14 (2023)
29. Zuo, J., McFarlin, B.L., Simpson, D.G., O'Brien, W.D., Han, A.: Automated region of interest placement on cervical ultrasound images for assessing preterm birth risk. J. Acoust. Soc. Am. **153**(3), A352–A352 (2023)

Leveraging Self-supervised Learning for Fetal Cardiac Planes Classification Using Ultrasound Scan Videos

Joseph Geo Benjamin[1][✉][iD], Mothilal Asokan[1][iD], Amna Alhosani[1][iD],
Hussain Alasmawi[1][iD], Werner Gerhard Diehl[2], Leanne Bricker[2],
Karthik Nandakumar[1][iD], and Mohammad Yaqub[1][iD]

[1] Mohamed bin Zayed University of Artificial Intelligence,
Abu Dhabi, United Arab Emirates
{joseph.benjamin,mothilal.asokan,amna.alhosani,hussain.alasmawi,
karthik.nandakumar,mohammad.yaqub}@mbzuai.ac.ae
[2] Abu Dhabi Health Services Company (SEHA), Abu Dhabi, United Arab Emirates
{wernerd,LeanneB}@seha.ae

Abstract. Self-supervised learning (SSL) methods are popular since they can address situations with limited annotated data by directly utilising the underlying data distribution. However, adoption of such methods is not explored enough in ultrasound (US) imaging, especially for fetal assessment. We investigate the potential of dual-encoder SSL in utilizing unlabelled US video data to improve the performance of challenging downstream Standard Fetal Cardiac Planes (SFCP) classification using limited labelled 2D US images. We study 7 SSL approaches based on reconstruction, contrastive loss, distillation and information theory, and evaluate them extensively on a large private US dataset. Our observations and finding are consolidated from more than 500 downstream training experiments under different settings. Our primary observation shows that for SSL training, the variance of the dataset is more crucial than its size because it allows the model to learn generalisable representations which improve the performance of downstream tasks. Overall, the BarlowTwins method shows robust performance irrespective of the training settings and data variations, when used as an initialisation for downstream tasks. Notably, full fine-tuning with 1% of labelled data outperforms ImageNet initialisation by 12% in F1-score and outperforms other SSL initialisations by at least 4% in F1-score, thus making it a promising candidate for transfer learning from US video to image data. Our code is available at https://github.com/BioMedIA-MBZUAI/Ultrasound-SSL-FetalCardiacPlanes.

Keywords: Ultrasound Scan Videos · Standard Fetal Cardiac Planes · Self-supervised Learning

---

J.G. Benjamin and M. Asokan—Contributed equally.

© The Author(s), under exclusive license to Springer Nature Switzerland AG 2023
B. Kainz et al. (Eds.): ASMUS 2023, LNCS 14337, pp. 68–78, 2023.
https://doi.org/10.1007/978-3-031-44521-7_7

1   Introduction

Fetal sonography is used to assess the growth and well-being of the fetus. The ISUOG[1] guidelines [3] and the FASP[2] handbook [17] recommend the acquisition and use of standardised planes for fetus abnormality and growth assessment which is done manually by sonographers. In practice, a well-trained sonographer should account for variations caused by fetal movement & position, maternal body habitus, probe placement angle, etc. At the device level, even calibration and manufacturing differences can produce variations in image quality and measurements. This makes it hard to acquire Standard Fetal Planes (SFP) consistently and even more complicated for Standard Fetal Cardiac Planes (SFCP) which is critical in assessing conditions such as congenital heart diseases and intrauterine growth restrictions. Building automated systems to tackle aforementioned issues faces challenges due to large intra-class variations and inter-class similarities among the anatomical structures. This becomes even more challenging for SFCP, with fast motion due to heartbeats, leading to many misclassifications.

A myriad of work exists to solve the automated FSP classification using data-driven approaches like supervised machine learning [25] and deep learning (DL) [2,24] with fetal ultrasound (US) images. But labelling large amounts of data that can help capture class variability and distribution shifts is expensive. In addition, unlike natural images, the existence of large public datasets is also hindered by privacy concerns. In most healthcare facilities, large volumes of unlabelled data will be found in isolation, which could neither be shared publicly nor be labelled to utilise privately. Recent Self-supervised learning (SSL) techniques mitigate the requirement of large labelled datasets to train good DL models. Although SSL methods have been applied on US imaging analysis especially echocardiography [12,19], it is understudied in the fetal image analysis field. Since US scanning involves the recording of fetal scans as videos alongside the acquisition of 2D images, it can be leveraged for data-hungry self-supervision methods and thus can be utilised on private data available at healthcare facilities to create/improve AI systems.

In this work, we aim to clarify the following two questions regarding the dual-encoder SSL methods. *How does SSL pretraining on US video data impact downstream SFCP classification with limited labelled data? Which SSL method is effective in utilizing US video data?*

We believe that answering these questions will facilitate practical decision-making in a broad scope and easier adoption of leveraging real-world healthcare data instead of relying on complex engineering techniques to achieve good performance. This work does not intend to provide a new technical addition to the deep learning community. The research contribution of this work is to provide a thorough analysis of a set of well-established SSL methods, that strictly do not require labelled data, for the problem of fetal US image classification. We conduct several ablations for SSL training with different frame sampling, amount

---

[1] International Society of Ultrasound in Obstetrics and Gynecology.
[2] Fetal Anomaly Screening Programme NHS UK.

of data and seed weights which leads to some interesting implications that are important to disseminate to the research community and help make better use of unlabelled fetal US videos.

2   Related Work

SSL methods have been explored for utilizing fetal US videos with pretext tasks such as correcting reordered frames and predicting geometric transformations [14] or restoring altered images [4] to learn transferable representations for downstream tasks. More recently, SSL has moved towards dual-encoder architectures [1, 5, 10, 11, 26] (similar to siamese network) which rely on the distribution of data itself to learn meaningful representations rather than crafting pretext tasks that suit specific problems/data of interest. This line of SSL methods has not gained much focus for applications utilizing US video. A comprehensive survey by Fiorentino et al. [8] studies DL methods in fetal sonography and highlights recent trends and challenges. This shows a gap in the adoption of SSL, especially dual-encoder methods for US videos. Benchmark analysis by Taher et al. [13] shows the effective transferability of Self-supervised pretraining over supervised pretraining using ImageNet [7] dataset for a variety of medical imaging tasks.

The work by Fu et al. [9] incorporates a contrastive SSL approach with anatomical information by utilising labels. Zhang et al. [27] proposed hierarchical semantic level alignments for US videos using contrastive learning with labels through a smoothing strategy to improve the transferability. Different from these works, our study focuses on leveraging medical data itself i.e. US scan videos for SSL with no annotation information. A survey by Schiappa et al. [20] provides a detailed review and comparison of SSL techniques including dual-encoder using contrastive methods in the natural video domain.

3   Methodology

3.1   Data and Preprocessing

We perform our experiments on a large private fetal US scan data. This dataset consists of two modalities, labelled images of SFP and unlabelled videos (mainly SFCP and a few other views) collected from pregnant patients during their second trimester screening. The data is gathered over one calendar year and across different machine types (Voluson E8/E10/P8/S10-Expert/V830). For classification (Cls), we use four classes corresponding to the following standard cardiac planes: 3 Vessels View/3 Vessels Trachea view (3VV/3VT), 4 Chamber view (4CH), Left Ventricular Outflow Tract view (LVOT), and Right Ventricular Outflow Tract view (RVOT) and sample few non-heart SFP and create a 5th class corresponding to a non-heart view. Table 1 shows the distribution of images and patients in the dataset. The datasets are split at the patient level to avoid any information leakage about the classification test set, even patients in the validation/test set were removed from US videos used for SSL training.

Table 1. Subtable.1 indicates the classwise imbalance both in terms of the images and patients, Subtable.2 shows different sampling frequency and frame count (images) used for SSL training and Subtable.3 shows the statistics of Video.

Class	Images			Patients			Sampling Freq	V.Frame Count
	Train	Valid	Test	Train	Valid	Test		
3VV/3VT	1703	170	580	1013	96	342	All frames	405363
4CH	2699	307	876	1317	155	438	Every 5th	81556
LVOT	4371	464	1439	2017	228	663	Every 35th	12217
RVOT	4036	442	1306	1974	222	650	Every 70th	6464
Non-Heart	4400	462	1441	2434	254	754	1 per video	1349
Total	17209	1845	5642	3198	359	1033	**Patients Count:**	**575**

Video Stat.	mean	std	median	min	max
Frame Rate	70	27	69	11	123
Frame Count	456	245	358	3	800

Preprocessing: We filter out videos that have Doppler & split views or any other artifacts. To prevent any shortcut learning, we perform inpainting following the approach described in [6] on videos/images thereby removing any inframe marking or annotations done by sonographers. We further verify the cleanness of preprocessing by training a ResNet-18 classifier with processed data and applying Grad-CAM [21] on a random test subset. we observe that the network focuses on heart features rather than inpainted regions.

3.2   Self-supervision Procedure

To study the benefits of various SSL methods adopted for pretraining, we select methods belonging to different strategies
   *(a) **Reconstruction*** - AutoEncoder [16], Inpainting [18]
   *(b) **Contrastive Loss*** - SimCLR-v2 [5], MoCo-v2 [11]
   *(c) **Distillation-based*** - BYOL [10]
   *(d) **Information theory*** - VICReg [1], BarlowTwins [26]
   These methods do not explicitly require labelled data which is a critical consideration as we use unlabelled scan videos. We use ResNet-50 as the backbone network along with the appropriate projector network as mentioned in the literature for each dual-encoder method and a convolutional decoder network to output an image plane for reconstruction methods.

Weight Initialisation: We study the effect of weight initialisation on SSL training by comparing ImageNet classification pretrained weights and random weights initialisation, both as available in PyTorch.

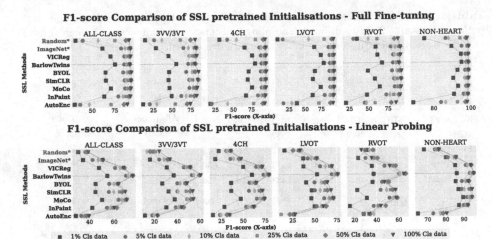

Fig. 1. BarlowTwins performs consistently better even for challenging views. ∗ indicates Non-SSL initilisations.

Hyperparameters: We follow optimal hyperparameters, optimizer settings, and augmentations as suggested in the respective literature of all the dual-encoder SSL methods[1,5,10,11,26]. We intend to identify the approach that works consistently without dataset specific tweaks or grid searches, as it would be infeasible or compute expensive in many real-world deployments. For AutoEncoder and Inpainting training, we use AdamW optimizer with a learning rate of 10^{-3}, a weight decay of 10^{-6}, a StepLR scheduler with stepsize 50, and a gamma 0.5624. All the methods are trained for 1000 epochs.

Batch Size: Training SSL with larger batch sizes is known to yield better performance in final downstream tasks. But we use a batch size of 256 to make fair comparisons under a practical setting because many facilities might not have IT infrastructure that supports the large batch sizes recommended by the original works. The chosen size could be fit in a single NVIDIA A100-SXM4-40 GB machine without memory overflows for SSL training.

Video Frame Sampling Frequency: We conduct experiments using data created by sampling every 5th frame from each video by default and to study the effect of sampling, we conduct a separate experiment with varying sampling frequency for SSL training as shown in Table 1. Though sampled at a fixed frequency, the difference in frame rate and frame count in each video produces the effect of sampling at different time intervals for each video ensuring variance in data distribution. Irrespective of sampling frequency, 1st frame of a video is always included in training data. This is to make sure that at least one frame of each video is included in SSL training even with a larger sampling frequency.

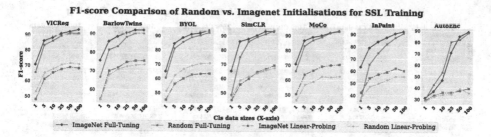

Fig. 2. Linear probing shows a different trend than full fine-tuning in random *vs.* Imagenet initialisation for some SSL training.

3.3 Classification Procedure

We use a network initialised with different SSL pretrained weights *(SSL-weight)* as the feature extractor and attach a linear classifier layer on top to train for downstream tasks. We perform full network fine-tuning to gauge the adaptability of pretrained weights to the downstream task. We also perform linear probing to understand the linear separable quality of the representations learned during SSL training. We freeze the entire backbone network, attach the BatchNorm layer with $(\gamma = 1\ \beta = 0)$ and fine-tune only the linear classifier layer. Along with *SSL-weights*, we run classification training with random (Kaiming) and ImageNet pretrained weights for comparison.

Hyperparameters: We use AdamW optimiser with a learning rate of 10^{-3}, a weight decay of 10^{-6} without any scheduler, and a batch size of 128. We run the experiments for 100 epochs and select the model at an epoch with the best F1-score in the validation set.

Labelled Data Size: From the entire (100%) classifier training data we obtain $50\%, 25\%, 10\%, 5\%, 1\%$ of data using a stratified sampling technique and run classification experiments on each of them separately. The sample images in each split are kept the same for all the experiments. The F1-score is reported for a fixed number of test samples. This setup enables us to understand the data efficiency achieved by different SSL methods.

4 Results and Discussions

How Do SSL Pretrained Models Perform on Different Data Sizes? Under full fine-tuning, the SSL pretrained weights *(SSL-weight)* perform better than the de facto ImageNet initialisation when the annotated data size is low. But as the annotated data size increases, the gains diminish and for 100% of the data to fine-tune on, the difference becomes marginal. Even randomly initialised weights for classification show comparable results in larger data setting. F1-Scores for different *SSL-weights* across different data sizes are shown in Fig. 1.

Since we train SSL on video data and train the downstream classification on a different set of 2D image data, the aforementioned observation could be

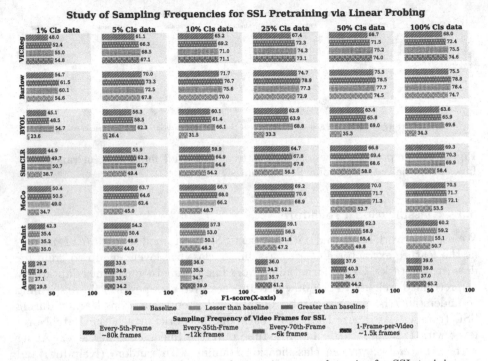

Fig. 3. Results show trade-off between data variance *vs.* data size for SSL trainings.

because of the following reasons: (a) the data available for SSL training is not very representative of the entire distribution which can lead to limited generalisation, or (b) gain of transfer learning diminishes as the amount of labelled data is more [15] although it might help in faster convergence of the models. Generative methods perform poorly compared to other SSL methods, notoriously AutoEncoders only learn to memorize the input and reconstruct without learning any contextual information. Amongst the SSL methods, BarlowTwins gives a significant gain performance followed by MoCo and VICReg. It is observed that these methods that reduce the contrastive loss or maximize the statistical variance within a batch, underperform BarlowTwins which only decorrelates the representation space. We conduct linear probing of *SSL-weights* to understand the quality of representations learned across models and classes. We observe that outcomes of BarlowTwins followed by MoCo and VICReg are consistently better.

What is the Effect of Random *vs.* Imagenet Initialisation During SSL Training? We observe that ImageNet weight initialisation at the beginning of SSL training *(Imnet-setting)* yields a noticeable gain in accuracy during the full fine-tuning of the downstream task compared to the random initialization *(Rand-setting)*. The results are compared in Fig. 2. We concur that ImageNet initialisation gives better generalisation capability by converging weights to a

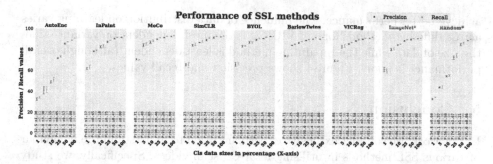

Fig. 4. Mean & SD obtained by training with 3 different sampling of labelled data and seed values.

better representational function during SSL training. Surprisingly, when evaluated with linear probing, we observe *Rand-setting* outperforms *Imnet-setting* for SSL methods such as BYOL, VICReg and marginally in SimCLR. This indicates that representations learnt by these methods under *Rand-setting* are inherently better than *Imnet-setting*. Yet for the same SSL methods during full fine-tuning *Imnet-setting* is better. We reason that certain inductive biases encoded in Imagenet weights that help in generalization, might not be sufficiently adapted for the US dataset during the SSL training phase of these methods. Whereas in *Rand-setting* model has to learn US data-specific cues during SSL training to converge from a random state. Thus, *Imnet-setting* performs poorly in linear probing. But inductive biases kick in during full fine-tuning of *Imnet-setting*, aiding in generalization which leads to better results. Interestingly BarlowTwins and MoCo consistently perform better in both full fine-tuning and linear probing, which could mean that they leverage ImageNet specific biases effectively during SSL training itself. This could also be the reason for relatively superior performance compared to other methods that follow a similar SSL training strategy (BarlowTwins *vs.* VICReg and MoCo *vs.* SimCLR/BYOL).

Does Sampling More Frames from Videos Help Improve SSL Training?
We train *SSL-weight* with different video frame sampling frequencies, such that a higher sampling frequency leads to a lower frame count for training. We conduct linear probing to understand the quality of representations learned. We make an interesting observation in Fig. 3 that for many cases, as we use lesser frames per video (high sampling frequency) for SSL pretraining, the accuracy increases. This might be counterintuitive to the generally held notion that a larger dataset can enhance SSL performance. Though the number of frames per video increases, the variance of samples in a batch throughout the training decreases. As many of these SSL methods directly or indirectly rely on batch variance for learning good representations [22], batches with lesser variance seem to impact learning. In such cases, highly redundant mutual information also hurts SSL training [23]. But this trend breaks as soon as SSL data size decreases drastically, indicating that there should be an ideal balance between the amount of data and its variance to

achieve better performance. The influence of data distribution on learning varies across different methods for e.g. VICReg is the most dependent on variance than the size of data while the Inpainting method is least dependent (although overall performance is poor). Figure 4 shows precision and recall values.

5   Conclusion

In this work, we conduct extensive experimentation to understand the behaviour of various SSL methods in utilising fetal US scan videos. Specifically, we study their empirical value in Cardiac Planes (SFCP) classification under real-world medical constraints. Our observations show that SSL methods give a boost in performance under limited annotated data. We found that BarlowTwins is most robust to variations in data distribution/size and training settings and gives consistent performance. In the scope of this study, we do not consider different backbones or methods that leverage label information during SSL training, since our motive is to evaluate the utility of SSL methods requiring no labels. However, our findings could be further extended with different backbones or methods leveraging labels during SSL training. We believe that our findings will lay a firm foundation for future works focused on recent forms of SSL methods for the US domain, especially in leveraging video data.

References

1. Bardes, A., Ponce, J., LeCun, Y.: VICReg: variance-invariance-covariance regularization for self-supervised learning. In: International Conference on Learning Representations (2022). https://openreview.net/forum?id=xm6YD62D1Ub
2. Baumgartner, C.F., et al.: Sononet: real-time detection and localisation of fetal standard scan planes in freehand ultrasound. IEEE Trans. Med. Imaging **36**(11), 2204–2215 (2017). https://doi.org/10.1109/TMI.2017.2712367
3. Carvalho, J.S., et al.: Isuog practice guidelines (updated): fetal cardiac screening. Ultrasound Obstetr. Gynecol. **61**(6), 788–803 (2023). https://doi.org/10.1002/uog.26224
4. Chen, L., Bentley, P., Mori, K., Misawa, K., Fujiwara, M., Rueckert, D.: Self-supervised learning for medical image analysis using image context restoration. Med. Image Anal. **58**, 101539 (2019). https://doi.org/10.1016/j.media.2019.101539
5. Chen, T., Kornblith, S., Norouzi, M., Hinton, G.: A simple framework for contrastive learning of visual representations. In: Proceedings of the 37th International Conference on Machine Learning. ICML'20. JMLR.org (2020). https://dl.acm.org/doi/abs/10.5555/3524938.3525087
6. Dadoun, H., Delingette, H., Rousseau, A.L., Kerviler, E.d., Ayache, N.: Combining Bayesian and deep learning methods for the delineation of the fan in ultrasound images. In: 2021 IEEE 18th International Symposium on Biomedical Imaging (ISBI), pp. 743–747 (2021). https://doi.org/10.1109/ISBI48211.2021.9434112
7. Deng, J., Dong, W., Socher, R., Li, L.J., Li, K., Fei-Fei, L.: Imagenet: a large-scale hierarchical image database. In: 2009 IEEE Conference on Computer Vision and Pattern Recognition, pp. 248–255 (2009). https://doi.org/10.1109/CVPR.2009.5206848

8. Fiorentino, M.C., Villani, F.P., Di Cosmo, M., Frontoni, E., Moccia, S.: A review on deep-learning algorithms for fetal ultrasound-image analysis. Med. Image Anal. 83, 102629 (2023). https://doi.org/10.1016/j.media.2022.102629

9. Fu, Z., Jiao, J., Yasrab, R., Drukker, L., Papageorghiou, A.T., Noble, J.A.: Anatomy-aware contrastive representation learning for fetal ultrasound. In: Karlinsky, L., Michaeli, T., Nishino, K. (eds.) ECCV 2022. LNCS, vol. 13803, pp. 422–436. Springer, Cham (2023). https://doi.org/10.1007/978-3-031-25066-8_23

10. Grill, J.B., et al.: Bootstrap your own latent a new approach to self-supervised learning. In: Proceedings of the 34th International Conference on Neural Information Processing Systems. NIPS'20. Curran Associates Inc., Red Hook (2020). https://dl.acm.org/doi/abs/10.5555/3495724.3497510

11. He, K., Fan, H., Wu, Y., Xie, S., Girshick, R.: Momentum contrast for unsupervised visual representation learning. In: 2020 IEEE/CVF Conference on Computer Vision and Pattern Recognition (CVPR), pp. 9726–9735 (2020). https://doi.org/10.1109/CVPR42600.2020.00975

12. Holste, G., Oikonomou, E.K., Mortazavi, B.J., Wang, Z., Khera, R.: Self-supervised learning of echocardiogram videos enables data-efficient clinical diagnosis. arXiv abs/2207.11581 (2022). https://api.semanticscholar.org/CorpusID:251040927

13. Hosseinzadeh Taher, M.R., Haghighi, F., Feng, R., Gotway, M.B., Liang, J.: A systematic benchmarking analysis of transfer learning for medical image analysis. In: Albarqouni, S., et al. (eds.) DART/FAIR -2021. LNCS, vol. 12968, pp. 3–13. Springer, Cham (2021). https://doi.org/10.1007/978-3-030-87722-4_1

14. Jiao, J., Droste, R., Drukker, L., Papageorghiou, A.T., Noble, J.A.: Self-supervised representation learning for ultrasound video. In: 2020 IEEE 17th International Symposium on Biomedical Imaging (ISBI), pp. 1847–1850 (2020). https://doi.org/10.1109/ISBI45749.2020.9098666

15. Kornblith, S., Shlens, J., Le, Q.V.: Do better imagenet models transfer better? In: 2019 IEEE/CVF Conference on Computer Vision and Pattern Recognition (CVPR), pp. 2656–2666. IEEE Computer Society, Los Alamitos, CA, USA (2019). https://doi.org/10.1109/CVPR.2019.00277

16. Masci, J., Meier, U., Cireşan, D., Schmidhuber, J.: Stacked convolutional autoencoders for hierarchical feature extraction. In: Honkela, T., Duch, W., Girolami, M., Kaski, S. (eds.) ICANN 2011. LNCS, vol. 6791, pp. 52–59. Springer, Heidelberg (2011). https://doi.org/10.1007/978-3-642-21735-7_7

17. NHS-England: Fetal anomaly screening programme handbook: 20-week screening scan, 4 May 2023. https://www.gov.uk/government/publications/fetal-anomaly-screening-programme-handbook/20-week-screening-scan

18. Pathak, D., Krähenbühl, P., Donahue, J., Darrell, T., Efros, A.A.: Context encoders: Feature learning by inpainting. In: 2016 IEEE Conference on Computer Vision and Pattern Recognition (CVPR), pp. 2536–2544 (2016). https://doi.org/10.1109/CVPR.2016.278

19. Saeed, M., Muhtaseb, R., Yaqub, M.: Contrastive pretraining for echocardiography segmentation with limited data. In: Yang, G., Aviles-Rivero, A., Roberts, M., Schönlieb, C.B. (eds.) MIUA 2022. LNCS, vol. 13413, pp. 680–691. Springer, Cham (2022). https://doi.org/10.1007/978-3-031-12053-4_50

20. Schiappa, M.C., Rawat, Y.S., Shah, M.: Self-supervised learning for videos: a survey. ACM Comput. Surv. 55(13s) (2023). https://doi.org/10.1145/3577925

21. Selvaraju, R.R., Cogswell, M., Das, A., Vedantam, R., Parikh, D., Batra, D.: Grad-CAM: visual explanations from deep networks via gradient-based localization. In: 2017 IEEE International Conference on Computer Vision (ICCV), pp. 618–626 (2017). https://doi.org/10.1109/ICCV.2017.74

22. Shwartz-Ziv, R., Balestriero, R., LeCun, Y.: What do we maximize in self-supervised learning? In: First Workshop on Pre-training: Perspectives, Pitfalls, and Paths Forward at ICML 2022 (2022). https://openreview.net/forum?id=FChTGTaVcc

23. Tian, Y., Sun, C., Poole, B., Krishnan, D., Schmid, C., Isola, P.: What makes for good views for contrastive learning? In: Proceedings of the 34th International Conference on Neural Information Processing Systems. NIPS'20. Curran Associates Inc., Red Hook, NY, USA (2020). https://dl.acm.org/doi/10.5555/3495724.3496297

24. Wu, L., Cheng, J.Z., Li, S., Lei, B., Wang, T., Ni, D.: Fuiqa: fetal ultrasound image quality assessment with deep convolutional networks. IEEE Trans. Cybern. 47(5), 1336–1349 (2017). https://doi.org/10.1109/TCYB.2017.2671898

25. Yaqub, M., Kelly, B., Papageorghiou, A.T., Noble, J.A.: Guided random forests for identification of key fetal anatomy and image categorization in ultrasound scans. In: Navab, N., Hornegger, J., Wells, W.M., Frangi, A.F. (eds.) MICCAI 2015. LNCS, vol. 9351, pp. 687–694. Springer, Cham (2015). https://doi.org/10.1007/978-3-319-24574-4_82

26. Zbontar, J., Jing, L., Misra, I., LeCun, Y., Deny, S.: Barlow twins: self-supervised learning via redundancy reduction. In: Proceedings of the 38th International Conference on Machine Learning. Proceedings of Machine Learning Research, vol. 139, pp. 12310–12320. PMLR, 18–24 July 2021. https://proceedings.mlr.press/v139/zbontar21a.html

27. Zhang, C., Chen, Y., Liu, L., Liu, Q., Zhou, X.: Hico: hierarchical contrastive learning for ultrasound video model pretraining. In: Wang, L., Gall, J., Chin, T.J., Sato, I., Chellappa, R. (eds.) ACCV 2022. LNCS, vol. 13846, pp. 3–20. Springer, Cham (2023). https://doi.org/10.1007/978-3-031-26351-4_1

Self-Supervised Learning to More Efficiently Generate Segmentation Masks for Wrist Ultrasound

Yuyue Zhou[1(✉)], Jessica Knight[1], Banafshe Felfeliyan[1], Shrimanti Ghosh[1],
Fatima Alves-Pereira[1], Christopher Keen[2],
Abhilash Rakkunedeth Hareendranathan[1], and Jacob L. Jaremko[1]

[1] Department of Radiology and Diagnostic Image, University of Alberta,
Edmonton, Canada
yuyue2@ualberta.ca
[2] Department of Biomedical Engineering, University of Alberta, Edmonton, Canada

Abstract. Deep learning automation of medical image analysis is highly desirable for purposes including organ/tissue segmentation and disease detection. However, deep learning traditionally relies on supervised training methods, while medical images are far more expensive to label than natural images. Self-supervised learning (SSL) has been gaining attention as a technique that allows strong model performance with only a small amount of labeled data. This would be particularly useful in ultrasound (US) imaging, which can involve hundreds of images per video sweep, saving time and money for labeling.

In this paper, we proposed a new SSL-based image segmentation technique that can be applied to bone segmentation in wrist US. This is the first use of the classification models SSL pretraining method SimMIM in wrist US. We modified the SimMIM SSL pretraining architecture, used a speckle noise masking policy to generate noise artifacts similar to those seen in US, changed the loss function, and analyzed how they influenced the downstream segmentation tasks.

Using modified SimMIM, our approach surpassed the performance of state-of-the-art fully supervised models on wrist bony region segmentation by up to 3.2% higher Dice score and up to 4.5% higher Jaccard index, using an extremely small labeled dataset with only 187/935 images and generated labels visually consistent with human labeling on the test set of 3822 images. The SSL pretrained models were also robust on the test set annotated by different medical experts.

Keywords: Wrist ultrasound · Self-supervised learning · Segmentation · Deep learning

Supplementary Information The online version contains supplementary material available at https://doi.org/10.1007/978-3-031-44521-7_8.

1   Introduction

Precise segmentation of anatomical structures plays a crucial role in disease diagnosis, disease severity evaluation, and treatment planning. Deep learning (DL) based segmentation models have made great strides in the field of medical image segmentation, enabling accurate and efficient segmentation of various anatomical structures [20]. Traditional DL segmentation models including convolutional neural network (CNN) [18] based U-Net [25] and ViT [7] backbone TransUNet [4] heavily rely on the labeled dataset size. Unlike natural image labeling, medical image labeling is far more expensive and scarce as it requires medical experts. Pixelwise labeling of ultrasound (US) data is impractical and especially time and money-consuming as a single video can contain as many as 300–800 frames. Finding a way to use less labeled dataset for training has a far-reaching meaning in US image analysis.

Wrist injuries are common in young children [15,21] often resulting in pain, swelling, and movement restrictions. Treatment procedure depends on the extent of the injury and currently, these are examined using the unportable heavy machine X-ray [15,21]. US is shown to be equivalent to X-ray in terms of diagnostic sensitivity [17,30] and is increasingly seen as a less expensive, safer and more easily portable alternative. Deep learning-based automatic bone segmentation methods using US have been proven to be successful [23] in areas including computer-assisted orthopedic surgery [10], knee osteoarthritis [27], and developmental dysplasia of the hip [16]. Nevertheless, detection of wrist fractures from US is relatively sparse [3] and especially new with DL tools. Unsurprisingly, there is a paucity of large labeled datasets which makes it an ideal use case for self-supervised learning (SSL).

In this study, we proposed a new domain-specific SSL approach that used the removal of speckle noise and masked region reconstruction as the pretext task. This task mimics noise artifacts that are commonly seen in US videos. We adapted the SimMIM SSL, designed for classification models SSL, for image segmentation. We embedded two popular segmentation models, U-Net and TransUNet, into this framework. We validated the approach by segmenting various bony regions from wrist US data on different medical experts' labelings.

2   Related Work

SSL aims to train DL models with only a small number of labels. The general idea of SSL is that models are pretrained with proxy tasks on the unlabeled dataset to learn the data representation and then fine-tuned on a small labeled dataset for downstream tasks. SSL approaches can be broadly categorized into generative, contrastive, and generative-contrastive [19]. Contrastive pretraining use negative or positive image pairs [5,6,12,14] or image clustering [2] to learn the data distribution. This is inherently different from segmentation tasks that require a dense data representation. Generative-contrastive approaches like GAN [11], have been used for image-translation.

Generative methods, such as gray-scale image colorization [31], inpainting (Context Encoders [24]) and masked feature predictions (MaskFeat [28]), are better suited for SSL segmentation pretraining since they use pretext tasks that are more similar to segmentation, and they have been successfully applied in medical image segmentation [22,26]. SimMIM [29] is a masked region reconstruction-based SSL method. Images are split into patches and randomly masked. A model with encoder-prediction head architecture is trained to restore masked areas as a proxy task. Unlike another masked region reconstruction SSL method Masked Autoencoder [13] which only processed the unmasked embedding sequences as input, SimMIM uses all masked and unmasked areas as input, making it suitable for both ViT backbone and CNN backbone models. The authors claimed that a lightweight prediction head or even a linear layer achieved similar performance on image reconstruction and generated fine-tuning results as good as a heavy-weight prediction head with several layers. It was first designed for classification tasks and has been shown to be successful in ImageNet-1K dataset top-1 classification with Transformer-based models and CNN-based models. Almalki et al. [1] transferred the pretrained Swin Transformer weights to the backbone of Cascade Mask R-CNN, for instance, segmentation in dental panoramic radiographs. Extending these techniques to US data is non-trivial mainly due to the unique nature of noise artifacts seen in US.

3 Methods

3.1 Data Collection

Data was collected prospectively at Stollery Children's Hospital emergency department with institutional ethics approval. We scanned 118 children aged 0–17 years using a Philips Lumify probe. Images were manually segmented by a musculoskeletal sonographer with 10 years of experience (expert A) and a trained radiology fellow (expert B) using the medical image segmentation software ITK-Snap. Data was anonymized and split into training/validation/test sets based on patient study ID to avoid any data leakage. US videos were converted into a sequence of single frames. We used frames with distinct and clear views of pathology. As US images are highly similar and redundant and some researchers found that a large dataset is necessary for SSL pretraining using denoising autoencoder [8], to determine the necessary number of images for our pretraining task, we did prescreen experiments and evaluated model performance with weights pretrained on 50% and 10% of the training set using the SimMIM technique. We found that the number decreasing of SSL pretraining images did not lead to an obvious performance drop in the downstream segmentation task. Therefore, we decided to use 1/10 training images for SSL pretraining. Subsequently, 10% and 50% of the SSL 1870 pretraining images were randomly selected for segmentation fine-tuning (Table 1).

3.2 Self-supervised Pretraining

We built our pretraining pipeline on the SimMIM architecture using randomly and partially masked images for reconstruction (Fig. 1): (1) Unlabeled images

Table 1. Dataset details

	SSL pretraining	Segmentation fine-tuning: bony region vs background				
	Training set (10%)	Training set (1%)	Training set (5%)	Validation set	Test set	Test set
# of patients	83	81	83	17	18	18
# of sweep videos	415	185	401	84	89	65
# of images	1870	187	935	4215	3822	2821
Expert segmentation	No	Expert A	Expert A	Expert A	Expert A	Expert B

were split into patch sizes of 32 * 32 and patches randomly added masks with a ratio of 0.6. The masked regions were represented by zeros. We changed the original SimMIM masking policy to mask+speckle noise. (2) All regions including unmasked patches, masked patches, and patches with speckle noise were used as input for the SimMIM pretraining network. (3) The SimMIM default encoder and prediction head architecture were accommodated by U-Net or TransUNet models for image reconstruction. Output channel was set as 3. (4) Loss was computed over reconstructed regions of masked/speckle noise patches. Inspired by Felfeliyan's work [9], the default mean absolute error (MAE) loss was replaced by root mean squared error (RMSE) loss + MAE loss. Details of SSL pretraining settings can be found in Table 2.

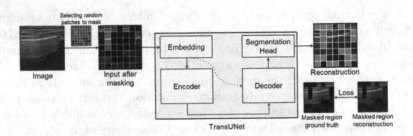

Fig. 1. SSL pretraining of TransUNet. U-Net architecture is similar as TransUNet except it does not have Embedding and features are passed from encoder to decoder through skip-connections.

Table 2. SSL pretraining settings

Model name	A	B	C	D	E
Initialized with ImageNet	No	Yes	No	No	No
Mask/speckle noise ratio	0.6/0	0.6/0	0.48/0.12	0.3/0.3	0.6/0
Loss function	MAE	MAE	MAE	MAE	MAE + RMSE

3.3   Segmentation Fine-Tuning

Models were loaded with weights pretrained with SSL. We explored model performance on (embedding+)encoder or (embedding+)encoder-decoder initialized with pretrained weights, since the embedding exists in TransUNet but not in U-Net. The lightweight segmentation head of TransUNet and U-Net, an analogy to the lightweight prediction head for image reconstruction in Xie's SimMIM work, was not initialized with pretrained weights. TransUNet and U-Net pretrained on ImageNet were set as a baseline model for comparison on the same training sets. We used sigmoid as the activation function in the segmentation head and BCE+Dice loss as the loss function. The model with the smallest validation loss was saved as the best model and tested on the test set. We set the segmentation threshold based on the validation set probability map using Otsu's method, minimizing intra-class intensity variance and maximizing inter-class variance.

3.4   Implementation Details and Evaluation Metrics

The proposed method was developed based on the TransUNet from Chen's [4] work. ResNet34 backbone U-Net with a depth of 5 was used in our study.

For all experiments, images were read as grayscale 3-channel images, padding to squares, resized to $224 * 224$, and normalized before being fed into the network.

For SSL pretraining, input images were passed through random horizontal flips. We selected AdamW as the optimizer, consistent with the SimMIM paper. Weights were initialized randomly. After hyperparameter tuning, we set 64 as batch size, 0.05 as weight decay, and 0.0005 as learning rate. The training time was about 27 h for 1200 epochs.

For segmentation fine-tuning, we use unmasked images with 16 as batch size. SGD was used as the optimizer with a learning rate of 0.002, and momentum of 0.99 for both models, weight decay of 0.05 for TransUNet and weight decay of 0.02 for U-Net after hyperparameter tuning, with training time of 10 and 6 h respectively for 187 training images for 200 epochs, and 935 training images for 100 epochs. All models were implemented in PyTorch and trained on V100 GPU.

Dice score, Jaccard index, Matthews correlation coefficient (MCC), and Hausdorff distance were used as the evaluation metrics for segmentation. For all these metrics except Hausdorff distance, a higher value indicates better performance.

4   Results

4.1   SSL Pretraining - Image Reconstruction

Figure 2 shows the SSL reconstruction results. TransUNet and U-Net successfully restored the masked region of the original image. However, the unmasked region reconstruction was less successful compared to the masked regions, which is the same as Xie's SimMIM work [29]. Dense image representation and global and local information in the unmasked regions were learned during the pretraining process.

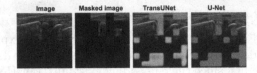

Fig. 2. Masked image reconstruction with modified SimMIM SSL training.

4.2 Bony Region Segmentation

Table 3 shows the statistical results of model performances on expert A labeled test set: baseline models and model with SSL pretraining. The encoder/encoder-decoder indicated that models initialized (embedding+)encoder/(embedding+) encoder-decoder weights pretrained with SSL. For each SSL setting, we showed the best model with encoder or encoder-decoder pretrained weights. Full results can be found in supplementary materials.

There are obvious and solid increases of Dice score, Jaccard index, and MCC in models with SSL pretraining compared to the baseline model pretrained on ImageNet only, and the increased values were up to 0.032, 0.045 and 0.034 for TransUNet and up to 0.017, 0.024 and 0.019 for U-Net respectively. We performed the student's t-test of Dice score, the most commonly used evaluation metrics for medical image segmentation, between SSL-pretrained models and baseline models and found that most of the SSL-pretrained models have a statistically highly significant increase compared to baseline models. Adding SSL pretraining did not decrease the Hausdorff distance, which reflects the marginal segmentation. Some of the models with SSL pretraining on 1% training set outperforming the baseline models on 5% training set, together with the full results in supplemental materials, further demonstrate the value of masked image reconstruction SSL pretraining on downstream fine-tuning task.

Figure 3 shows the bony region segmentation visualization results. All models generated visually satisfying results. However, the baseline segmentation results had some problems: they missed part of the bony region shown in the yellow rectangle or wrongly segmented the non-bony regions shown in red rectangles. SSL pretraining not only helped segmentation models remove the non-bony region but also filled in the incomplete prediction, indicating its great performance in wrist US segmentation.

In order to see how human labeling could potentially influence model results, we evaluated the model performance of bony region segmentation on the test set segmented by medical expert B/the union of experts A and B. We evaluated the performances of baseline models and the best model with SSL pretraining based on the Dice score and Jaccard index, and the full table can be found in supplemental materials. In most cases, models with SSL pretraining surpassed the baseline model, especially on Dice score, Jaccard index, and MCC, up to 0.032, 0.036, and 0.036 respectively on expert B labeling, and up to 0.036, 0.050, 0.037 respectively on the union of expert A and B labeling. The results of different

Table 3. TransUNet and U-Net bony region segmentation results

Model	# of training images (% of training set)	Dice	Jaccard	MCC	Hausdorff distance
Baseline TransUNet	187(1%)	0.805	0.681	0.797	27.41
TransUNet-A, encoder		**0.837****	0.725	0.823	**25.28**
TransUNet-B, encoder-decoder		0.833**	0.720	0.826	24.37
TransUNet-C, encoder		**0.837****	**0.726**	**0.831**	28.47
TransUNet-D, encoder		0.836**	0.724	0.829	25.34
TransUNet-E, encoder-decoder		0.834**	0.722	0.827	24.43
Baseline TransUNet	935(5%)	0.833	0.722	0.827	24.61
TransUNet-A, encoder		0.841**	0.732	0.834	22.87
TransUNet-B, encoder-decoder		**0.843****	**0.735**	**0.836**	**21.55**
TransUNet-C, encoder		0.840**	0.730	0.833	23.01
TransUNet-D, encoder-decoder		0.840**	0.731	0.834	24.09
TransUNet-E, encoder		0.842**	0.733	0.835	25.35
Baseline U-Net	187(1%)	0.821	0.704	0.813	28.36
U-Net-A, encoder		0.828**	0.712	0.821	30.14
U-Net-B, encoder		0.826**	0.711	0.819	28.91
U-Net-C, encoder		0.836**	0.725	**0.829**	29.18
U-Net-D, encoder		**0.838****	**0.728**	**0.832**	**23.72**
U-Net-E, encoder-decoder		0.835**	0.723	0.828	26.32
Baseline U-Net	935(5%)	0.835	0.725	0.828	23.31
U-Net-A, encoder		**0.852****	**0.749**	**0.847**	20.44
U-Net-B, encoder-decoder		0.848**	0.741	0.841	**19.54**
U-Net-C, encoder		0.849**	0.742	0.842	20.62
U-Net-D, encoder		0.851**	0.746	0.845	20.96
U-Net-E, encoder		0.844**	0.737	0.838	23.90

Models were evaluated on the test set annotated by expert A. Student's t-test of Dice score was performed between baseline and SSL models. **: p value<0.01.

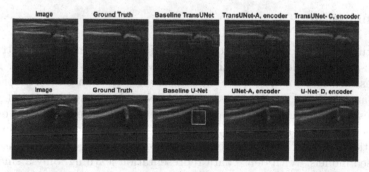

Fig. 3. TransUNet and U-Net bony region segmentation results. The result of segmentation without SSL where the model missed part of bony region (yellow box in row 2, missed part of metaphysis) or wrongly segmented non-bony region(red box in row 1, connected metaphysis and epiphysis; red boxes in row 1 and 2, incorrectly segments muscle tissue that appear similar to bone). Columns 4–5 show the segmentations with SSL that are almost identical to ground truth. (Color figure online)

human experts' labelings indicate the robust performance improvement of SSL methods.

5   Discussion

We adapted the masked image reconstruction self-supervised learning pretraining method SimMIM to segmentation models in US images. With our changes including masking, our results show that we performed a successful adaptation of this natural image classification SSL method to medical image segmentation pretraining, on both CNN-based U-Net and ViT-backbone TransUNet models. The SSL pretraining loss was calculated only on masked regions, leading to insufficient learning and less successful reconstruction on unmasked regions. Changing the SSL random masking policy to random masking+noise or changing the loss function had a similar effect on downstream tasks, demonstrating the broad applicability of image reconstruction-based SSL pretraining.

Unlike other medical imaging such as X-rays or CT which have a clear distinction between bones and muscles, both the bony regions and muscle regions in US images are bright. Some muscle regions even look like bony regions with thin, bright areas and distinct boundaries, therefore models could easily segment non-bony regions. The dense data representation learned during SSL pretraining enables downstream segmentation improvement, by shrinking the wrong segmentation regions and fulfilling the incomplete predictions, leading to the increase of Dice score, Jaccard index, and MCC.

Hausdorff distance can be an indicator for estimating the non-bony region prediction. We will extend the research on the algorithm to optimize the model with less non-bony region prediction in the future.

6   Conclusion

In this study, we performed the adaptation of a masked image reconstruction-based self-supervised learning method SimMIM, originally designed for natural image classification, to wrist US bony region segmentation on a ViT backbone model TransUNet and a CNN-based model U-Net. We changed the masking policy and loss function and found that they achieved similar performance on minimal dataset segmentation. We showed that SSL-pretrained models outperformed the traditional ImageNet pretrained supervised models in both ViT-based and CNN-based models. With dense data representation learning, only a small fraction of images used in SSL pretraining can have a great positive impact on the downstream task. Image reconstruction self-supervised learning methods can be a good choice for segmentation tasks, especially on datasets with limited annotation.

References

1. Almalki, A., Latecki, L.J.: Self-supervised learning with masked image modeling for teeth numbering, detection of dental restorations, and instance segmentation in dental panoramic radiographs. In: 2023 IEEE/CVF Winter Conference on Applications of Computer Vision (WACV), pp. 5583–5592. IEEE (2023)
2. Caron, M., Misra, I., Mairal, J., Goyal, P., Bojanowski, P., Joulin, A.: Unsupervised Learning of Visual Features by Contrasting Cluster Assignments, June 2020. https://doi.org/10.48550/arXiv.2006.09882
3. Champagne, N., Eadie, L., Regan, L., Wilson, P.: The effectiveness of ultrasound in the detection of fractures in adults with suspected upper or lower limb injury: a systematic review and subgroup meta-analysis. BMC Emergency Med. **19**(1), 17 (2019)
4. Chen, J., et al.: TransUNet: Transformers Make Strong Encoders for Medical Image Segmentation, February 2021. https://doi.org/10.48550/arXiv.2102.04306, arXiv:2102.04306 [cs]
5. Chen, T., Kornblith, S., Norouzi, M., Hinton, G.: A Simple Framework for Contrastive Learning of Visual Representations, February 2020. https://doi.org/10.48550/arXiv.2002.05709
6. Chen, X., He, K.: Exploring Simple Siamese Representation Learning, November 2020. https://doi.org/10.48550/arXiv.2011.10566
7. Dosovitskiy, A., et al.: An Image is Worth 16x16 Words: Transformers for Image Recognition at Scale, October 2020. https://doi.org/10.48550/arXiv.2010.11929
8. El-Nouby, A., Izacard, G., Touvron, H., Laptev, I., Jegou, H., Grave, E.: Are Large-scale Datasets Necessary for Self-Supervised Pre-training? https://doi.org/10.48550/arXiv.2112.10740
9. Felfeliyan, B., et al.: Self-Supervised-RCNN for Medical Image Segmentation with Limited Data Annotation, July 2022. https://doi.org/10.48550/arXiv.2207.11191
10. Gebhardt, C., et al.: Femur reconstruction in 3D ultrasound for orthopedic surgery planning, **18**(6), 1001–1008. https://doi.org/10.1007/s11548-023-02868-4
11. Goodfellow, I.J., et al.: Generative Adversarial Networks, June 2014. https://doi.org/10.48550/arXiv.1406.2661
12. Grill, J.B., et al. : Bootstrap your own latent: a new approach to self-supervised Learning, June 2020. https://doi.org/10.48550/arXiv.2006.07733
13. He, K., Chen, X., Xie, S., Li, Y., Dollár, P., Girshick, R.: Masked Autoencoders Are Scalable Vision Learners, November 2021. https://doi.org/10.48550/arXiv.2111.06377
14. He, K., Fan, H., Wu, Y., Xie, S., Girshick, R.: Momentum contrast for unsupervised visual representation learning. In: 2020 IEEE/CVF Conference on Computer Vision and Pattern Recognition (CVPR), pp. 9726–9735. IEEE, Seattle, WA, USA (2020)
15. Hedström, E.M., Svensson, O., Bergström, U., Michno, P.: Epidemiology of fractures in children and adolescents: increased incidence over the past decade: a population-based study from northern Sweden. Acta Orthop. **81**(1), 148–153 (2010)
16. Jaremko, J.L., Hareendranathan, A., Bolouri, S.E.S., Frey, R.F., Dulai, S., Bailey, A.L.: AI aided workflow for hip dysplasia screening using ultrasound in primary care clinics, **13**(1), 9224. https://doi.org/10.1038/s41598-023-35603-9
17. Knight, J., et al.: 2D/3D ultrasound diagnosis of pediatric distal radius fractures by human readers vs artificial intelligence. Sci. Rep. **13**, 14535 (2023). https://doi.org/10.1038/s41598-023-41807-w

18. LeCun, Y., et al.: Handwritten digit recognition with a back-propagation network. In: Advances in Neural Information Processing Systems, vol. 2. Morgan-Kaufmann (1989)
19. Liu, X., et al.: Self-supervised learning: generative or contrastive, **35**(1), 857–876 (2021)
20. Malhotra, P., Gupta, S., Koundal, D., Zaguia, A., Enbeyle, W.: Deep neural networks for medical image segmentation. J. Healthc. Eng. **2022**, 9580991 (2022)
21. Meena, S., Sharma, P., Sambharia, A.K., Dawar, A.: Fractures of distal radius: an overview. J. Family Med. Primary Care **3**(4), 325 (2014)
22. Ouyang, C., Biffi, C., Chen, C., Kart, T., Qiu, H., Rueckert, D.: Self-supervised learning for few-shot medical image segmentation, **41**(7), 1837–1848 (2022)
23. Pandey, P.U., Quader, N., Guy, P., Garbi, R., Hodgson, A.J.: Ultrasound bone segmentation: a scoping review of techniques and validation practices, **46**(4), 921–935 (2020)
24. Pathak, D., Krahenbuhl, P., Donahue, J., Darrell, T., Efros, A.A.: Context encoders: feature learning by inpainting. In: 2016 IEEE Conference on Computer Vision and Pattern Recognition (CVPR), pp. 2536–2544. IEEE, Las Vegas, NV, USA, June 2016
25. Ronneberger, O., Fischer, P., Brox, T.: U-Net: Convolutional Networks for Biomedical Image Segmentation, May 2015. arXiv:1505.04597 [cs]
26. Tang, Y., et al.: Self-supervised pre-training of swin transformers for 3D medical image analysis, pp. 20730–20740 (2022)
27. du Toit, C., Orlando, N., Papernick, S., Dima, R., Gyacskov, I., Fenster, A.: Automatic femoral articular cartilage segmentation using deep learning in three-dimensional ultrasound images of the knee, **4**(3), 100290. https://doi.org/10.1016/j.ocarto.2022.100290
28. Wei, C., Fan, H., Xie, S., Wu, C.Y., Yuille, A., Feichtenhofer, C.: Masked Feature Prediction for Self-Supervised Visual Pre-Training. pp. 14668–14678
29. Xie, Z., et al.: SimMIM: A Simple Framework for Masked Image Modeling, November 2021. https://doi.org/10.48550/arXiv.2111.09886
30. Zhang, J., Boora, N., Melendez, S., Rakkunedeth Hareendranathan, A., Jaremko, J.: Diagnostic accuracy of 3D ultrasound and artificial intelligence for detection of pediatric wrist injuries. Children (Basel, Switzerland) **8**(6), 431 (2021)
31. Zhang, R., Isola, P., Efros, A.A.: Colorful image colorization. In: Leibe, B., Matas, J., Sebe, N., Welling, M. (eds.) ECCV 2016. LNCS, vol. 9907, pp. 649–666. Springer, Cham (2016). https://doi.org/10.1007/978-3-319-46487-9_40

Synthetic Boost: Leveraging Synthetic Data for Enhanced Vision-Language Segmentation in Echocardiography

Rabin Adhikari[ID], Manish Dhakal[ID], Safal Thapaliya[ID], Kanchan Poudel[ID], Prasiddha Bhandari[ID], and Bishesh Khanal[✉][ID]

Nepal Applied Mathematics and Informatics Institute for research (NAAMII),
Lalitpur, Nepal
{rabin.adhikari,manish.dhakal,safal.thapaliya,kanchan.poudel,
prasiddha.bhandari,bishesh.khanal}@naamii.org.np

Abstract. Accurate segmentation is essential for echocardiography-based assessment of cardiovascular diseases (CVDs). However, the variability among sonographers and the inherent challenges of ultrasound images hinder precise segmentation. By leveraging the joint representation of image and text modalities, Vision-Language Segmentation Models (VLSMs) can incorporate rich contextual information, potentially aiding in accurate and explainable segmentation. However, the lack of readily available data in echocardiography hampers the training of VLSMs. In this study, we explore using synthetic datasets from Semantic Diffusion Models (SDMs) to enhance VLSMs for echocardiography segmentation. We evaluate results for two popular VLSMs (CLIPSeg and CRIS) using seven different kinds of language prompts derived from several attributes, automatically extracted from echocardiography images, segmentation masks, and their metadata. Our results show improved metrics and faster convergence when pretraining VLSMs on SDM-generated synthetic images before finetuning on real images. The code, configs, and prompts are available at https://github.com/naamiinepal/synthetic-boost.

Keywords: Vision-Language Models · Vision-Language Segmentation Models · Echocardiography · Synthetic Data

1 Introduction

Echocardiography (heart ultrasound) is an integral diagnostic tool for several cardiovascular diseases (CVDs). It is widely used because it is cheap, portable, has no harmful radiation, and has a high temporal resolution (the ability to see high-definition images in real-time). Accurately estimating clinically relevant quantitative measures in echocardiography images, such as cardiac substructure volumes and Ejection Fraction (EF), requires reliable segmentation algorithms. However,

---

R. Adhikari, M. Dhakal and S. Thapaliya—Equal Contribution.

B. Kainz et al. (Eds.): ASMUS 2023, LNCS 14337, pp. 89–99, 2023.
https://doi.org/10.1007/978-3-031-44521-7_9

segmenting various parts of the heart is challenging as the same standard plane image can have diverse appearances depending on the operator, and the presence of shadows, speckles, strong attenuation, and low contrast difference among areas of interest in ultrasound images [1]. Different CNN- and ViT-based [3] U-Net-like models [2,6,9,21] are the state-of-the-art segmentation models that rely on supervised training with a relatively large set of annotated echocardiography images. These segmentation models, however, must be trained on predefined classes that necessitate retraining or architecture changes (in the final layer) when new classes are required. It is also challenging to manually intervene in or inject specific conditioning and make them explicitly benefit from the spatiotemporal relationships of different foreground structures. Besides, they lack explainability and are not resilient to distribution shifts.

Recently, Vision-Language Models (VLMs) have been proposed that learn a joint representation of image and language [4,8,10,13,19,22,29]. VLMs extract rich supplementary information via image and language prompt pairs, potentially aiding deep learning models to benefit from the richer information. VLMs have one encoder each for image and language inputs, and the encoders are trained together to optimize a joint representation using losses such as contrastive loss. Vision-Language Segmentation Models (VLSMs) are adapted from VLMs where a decoder is added and trained on top of pretrained VLMs to segment the input image while leveraging information provided by language prompts [16,20,26]. However, almost all VLMs are trained using a large set of natural images, and no VLSMs are trained on an extensive collection of ultrasound datasets. Although some recent methods show that VLMs and VLSMs could be finetuned on limited medical data [18], the performance of these VLSMs is still below the supervised segmentation networks trained and optimized for specific datasets and foreground masks.

One major challenge to improving VLSMs for ultrasound images is the lack of large language-image paired datasets. To address the limited data problem, generative models like GANs [5] and diffusion models [7] could generate images with a distribution closer to the real-world samples. Stojanovski et al. [23] trained Semantic Diffusion Models (SDMs) [25] on the CAMUS dataset [12] to generate synthetic cardiac ultrasound images and showed that the segmentation model trained exclusively on a generated dataset results in a test dice score of 89.0 ± 2.5 in the CAMUS dataset. The use of synthetic images has not been explored for VLSMs. In this work, we explore whether the synthetic images from SDMs can improve the performance of VLSMs in echocardiography images.

Our primary contributions are as follows.

1. We show that the VLSMs, pretrained on natural images, generalize to the real dataset (CAMUS) when finetuned on SDM-generated echocardiography images.
2. We show that although numerous synthetic samples alone are not as good as a small number of real annotated data, the model finetuned on synthetic data is a good starting point for VLSMs to further finetune on real datasets.

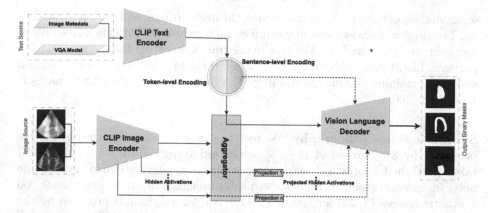

Fig. 1. The basic architecture of CRIS and CLIPSeg VLSMs. The key components in the architecture are a *Text Encoder*, an *Image Encoder*, a *Vision-Language Decoder (VLD)*, and an *Aggregator*. The images and the corresponding prompts are passed to the CLIP image and text encoders, respectively. The Aggregator generates intermediate representations utilizing image-level, sentence-level, or word-level representations to feed to the VLD. The VLD outputs a binary segmentation mask for an image-text pair.

2   Methodology

2.1   Vision-Language Segmentation Models (VLSMs)

CLIP [19] is a widely used VLM that jointly trains an image encoder and a text encoder to project semantically similar image-text pairs closer together and semantically disjoint image-text pairs farther apart. As shown in Fig. 1, the contrastive feature representation obtained from the two encoders of CLIP is fed to a vision-language decoder which generates a binary segmentation mask. We investigate CLIPSeg [16] and CRIS [26], two state-of-the-art VLSMs for natural images, with various combinations of language prompts, real images, and synthetic images.

We use the publicly accessible CLIPSeg and CRIS weights learned during pretraining on natural image-text pairings [11, 28]. The two VLSMs are finetuned on echocardiography datasets, starting from their publicly available pretrained weights. The two echocardiography datasets are: (**i**) CAMUS [12], and (**ii**) SDM CAMUS [23]. To test if pretraining with synthetic data boosts the segmentation performance on the real data, natural images pretrained VLSMs are further trained on extensive synthetic data and then finetuned on a smaller CAMUS dataset.

2.2   Datasets

CAMUS. CAMUS [12] is a cardiac segmentation dataset containing 2D apical two-chamber (2C) and four-chamber (4C) views from 500 patients at both end-diastole (ED) and end-systole (ES) cycles. The dataset contains the semantic segmentation of the left ventricular cavity, the myocardium, and the left atrial cavity. The original dataset randomly sampled images from 50 patients as the official test split, and the remaining 450 kept in the train split. From those remaining 450 patients, like Stojanovski et al. [23], we selected the first 50 patients for validation and the remaining 400 for the training. The number of train/val/test images is 1, 600/400/200.

Synthetic Echocardiography. We use the synthetic echocardiography images proposed by Stojanovski et al. [23], generated using SDMs [25]. This model takes perturbed anatomical masks as conditioning information to denoise the noisy images and generates echocardiographic images. Our experiments use 9, 000 synthetic images (8, 000 for training and 1, 000 for validation) provided by the authors, the same splits they used to train and validate a vanilla U-Net [21] model.

2.3   Prompt Engineering

Prompts for CAMUS. For our experiments, prompts, images, and masks are needed as triplets but are unavailable in the CAMUS dataset. Finding the best prompt for the task is challenging, and creating the prompts manually for each image and mask pair is tedious and not scalable when the dataset size increases. Also, the choice of prompts seems to significantly affect the performance of the VLMs in the medical domain [18].

   We follow Poudel et al. [17] to generate automatic prompts adapted for the CAMUS dataset to explore if specific image features could be aligned to language prompts explaining those features. The foreground cardiac structure's size and shape depend on the subjects' age, sex, and cardiac cycle phase. Similarly, image quality information may help models adapt accordingly. As shown in Table 1, various language prompts are designed by including words corresponding to the target structure name, its shape, the information about apical views, cardiac cycle phase, the subject's sex, the subject's age, and image quality (labeled by an expert within

Table 1. The description of the attribute and its possible values. The prompt number aside shows the prompt in which the attribute is introduced.

	Description	Possible Values
P0	Empty String	
P1	Target Structure	left ventricular cavity, myocardium, or left atrium cavity
P2	Apical View	two-chamber view or four-chamber view
P3	Cardiac Cycle	end of systole or diastole cycle
P4	Patient's Sex	male or female
P5	Patient's Age	all ages
P6	Image Quality	good, medium, or poor
P7	Structure's Shape	circle, triangle, oval, square, or rectangle

the CAMUS dataset). There are 7 attributes generated for the CAMUS dataset and 7 prompts (**P1–P7**) from the attributes, each added incrementally. **P0** is an empty string. The attributes in **P1–P7** are ordered in descending order of the attribute's perceived importance (**P1** being the most important).

The sources of the attributes are listed below.

1. **Image Filename**: We parse the images' filenames and masks to get the anatomical structure to segment, apical view, and cardiac cycle.
2. **Image Metadata**: We parse the official metadata provided with the images and masks to get patients' sex, age, and image quality.
3. **VQA Model**: We use OFA (One For All) VQA [24] to get target structures' shapes. The VQA model is presented with the question, *What is the shape of the* <structure> *in the green box?*. Here, the green box is the boundary of the target structure extracted from its mask.

One example prompt **P7** with seven attributes: ***Left ventricular cavity*** of **oval shape** in **two-chamber view** in the cardiac ultrasound at the end of the **diastole cycle** of a **40-year-old female** with **poor image quality**.

Prompts for SDM CAMUS. We did not use the image quality attribute in SDM CAMUS dataset as the synthetic images' quality is not annotated. When synthesizing the prompts, we used the SDM CAMUS dataset's values derived from the original dataset for all other attributes: patient id, view information, and cardiac cycle. One example prompt **P6** for the SDM CAMUS dataset: ***Left ventricular cavity*** of **oval shape** in **two-chamber view** in the cardiac ultrasound at the end of the **diastole cycle** of a **40-year-old female**.

3   Experimental Settings

Unless specified, the VLSM's hyperparameters are the same as mentioned in the original implementation by the respective authors for all experiments. The models are finetuned and inferred in NVIDIA GeForce RTX 3090, Titan Xp, and V100 GPUs. We use float-16 mixed-precision training for models with different batch sizes of 32 and 128 for CRIS and CLIPSeg, respectively. The batch sizes were chosen to utilize the full memory of the GPUs (maximum 24GB); since CRIS has a greater memory footprint than CLIPSeg, we reduced the former's batch size.

We use AdamW [15] optimizer with the weight decay of 10^{-3} and an initial learning rate of 2×10^{-3} and 2×10^{-5} for CLIPSeg and CRIS, respectively. The learning rate is reduced by a factor of 10 if validation loss does not decrease for 5 consecutive epochs[1].

Three different strategies are employed to train the models: (**i**) training only on real data from the CAMUS dataset (*real*), (**ii**) training only on synthetic data generated from the SDM model (*synthetic*), and (**iii**) first training the

---

[1] https://pytorch.org/docs/stable/generated/torch.optim.lr_scheduler.ReduceLROn Plateau.html.

model on the synthetic data, then finetuning on the real data (*synth-PT:real-FT*). CLIPSeg and CRIS resize the input images to 416×416 and 352×352, respectively. We normalize the resized images with the means and standard deviations provided by the respective models. No augmentation and further post-processing are done to assess the models' raw performance.

We used the weighted sum of soft Dice and Binary Cross Entropy losses with weights 1 and 0.2, respectively. All the dice scores are computed at 512×512 (nearly the median width of the dataset), resizing the model's output when required. For each experiment, the metrics reported are for the model with the best dice score on the validation set, across the epochs, with an output threshold of 0.5 on the predicted binary segmentation map.

To study the ability of the VLSMs to represent the alignment of image-text pairs, we perform two experiments: (**i**) freezing the VLM encoders of CRIS and CLIPSeg, and (**ii**) unfreezing the VLM encoders during finetuning on all datasets. The dice score for the unfrozen encoders is shown in the Table 2 whereas that of the frozen ones is demonstrated in Table 3.

4 Results

4.1 Synthetic Data is Better Than No Data

Table 2 shows that while the VLSMs pretrained on natural images perform very poorly on ultrasound images in zero-shot segmentation, models trained on synthetic data provide much better results in real ultrasound images.

4.2 Real Data is Better Than Synthetic Data

Figure 2 shows that VLSMs have better dice scores when finetuned in real data than finetuning only in synthetic data. When comparing the best dice scores for both strategies, the models trained on the synthetic dataset have a lower dice score (-5.19), which is statistically highly significant by the Wilcoxon signed-rank test [27] with a p-value of 8.8×10^{-73}, on the official test split of real images.

Table 2. The dice score (mean $\pm$ std) of models trained and validated using various strategies and evaluated on the CAMUS's official test split when the encoders of the VLMs are unfrozen. The zero-shot performance of the models is extracted from Poudel et al. [17] for comparison.

Strategy	Prompt → Model ↓	P0	P1	P2	P3	P4	P5	P6	P7
zeroshot	CLIPSeg	0.00±0.0	0.00±0.0	0.21±1.8	0.16±1.9	0.19±2.1	0.51±3.7	0.46±3.1	1.81±6.6
	CRIS	23.53±12.0	9.04±13.9	8.36±13.2	8.24±13.2	8.24±13.2	8.24±13.2	8.24±13.2	5.45±10.4
synthetic	CLIPSeg	45.69±13.2	84.24±12.0	84.87±10.9	85.27±9.7	84.38±11.0	83.18±12.8	83.32±12.5	N/A
	CRIS	42.29±17.6	84.72±11.9	84.72±10.5	85.48±10.2	85.12±11.2	85.84±10.0	84.35±13.3	N/A
real	CLIPSeg	46.52±13.3	88.53±7.2	88.81±7.2	88.77±7.2	88.58±7.7	88.27±7.4	88.45±7.5	88.16±8.0
	CRIS	46.46±13.1	91.00±6.3	91.03±6.2	89.9±7.6	90.94±6.6	90.87±6.4	90.79±7.1	90.99±6.3
synth-PT: real-FT	CLIPSeg	46.26±13.2	88.56±7.5	89.44±6.9	89.8±6.8	88.68±7.5	88.55±7.4	89.36±6.6	89.53±6.6
	CRIS	41.09±18.6	91.26±6.1	91.39±5.9	91.12±6.3	91.04±7.2	91.23±6.4	91.11±6.8	91.08±6.6

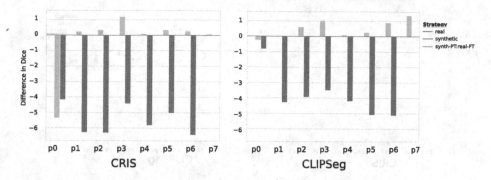

Fig. 2. Difference in mean dice scores between different training strategies for CLIPSeg and CRIS for different prompts, relative to real. Pretraining on synthetic data before finetuning them on real data helps to improve the performance of VLSMs.

4.3 Pretraining on Synthetic Data Helps in Finetuning on Real Data

In both CRIS and CLIPSeg, the pretraining on synthetic data and then finetuning on real data (*synth-PT:real-FT* strategy) performs better than the experiments trained with either real or artificial images as illustrated in Fig. 2. This second stage pretraining strategy has a higher dice score (+0.34), which is statistically significant by the Wilcoxon signed-rank test [27] with a p-value of 8.3×10^{-6}, than the models that haven't seen synthetic data.

4.4 Unfreezing VLM Encoders During Finetuning Affects Models Differently

For **P0** (empty prompt), the output class is ambiguous for the models. From Table 3, we can infer that CLIPSeg dealt with this obscurity by predicting a segmentation map of a union of all the classes, while CRIS chose just noise (all zeros in the case of the last strategy).

Figure 3 shows that CRIS's performance improves when encoders are not frozen during finetuning. In contrast, CLIPSeg's performance degrades when the encoders are unfrozen for the CAMUS dataset (real one), which seems to have improved when synthetic data is introduced.

Table 3. The dice score (mean ± std) on the CAMUS's official test split when the encoders of the VLMs are frozen.

Strategy	Prompt → Model ↓	P0	P1	P2	P3	P4	P5	P6	P7
synthetic	CLIPSeg	45.71±13.6	84.08±11.1	84.01±10.5	84.48±11.0	84.02±11.0	84.47±10.7	85.47±9.3	N/A
	CRIS	35.13±19.5	84.19±13.0	84.02±12.2	84.62±11.9	84.94±11.5	84.23±12.3	80.70±17.0	N/A
real	CLIPSeg	46.52±13.2	88.81±7.2	89.04±7.0	88.65±7.3	89.05±7.2	88.54±7.5	88.61±7.5	88.54±7.6
	CRIS	26.84±16.2	88.41±8.7	88.71±8.6	88.62±8.8	88.55±8.7	88.48±8.6	88.85±8.4	88.40±9.8
synth-PT: real-FT	CLIPSeg	46.5±13.3	89.07±7.1	89.09±7.1	89.24±6.7	89.24±6.9	88.91±7.2	89.12±7.0	89.14±7.0
	CRIS	0.04±0.5	89.21±7.9	89.54±7.4	89.26±7.5	89.41±7.6	89.34±7.8	89.03±9.2	89.34±8.2

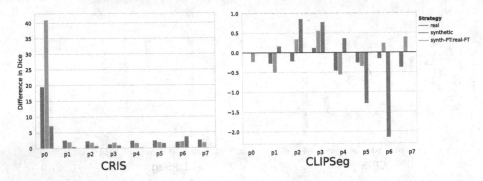

Fig. 3. Difference between mean dice scores when the encoders are frozen and when the encoders are trained for different prompts. CRIS's model performance improves when the encoders are trained along with the decoder. In contrast, CLIPSeg's performance degrades when encoders are trained.

5   Discussion

Although the VLSMs do not improve over the state-of-the-art segmentation models on the CAMUS dataset (according to the leaderboard[2], the maximum mean dice is 94.1 [14]), it is promising that they are close. Pretraining with the synthetic samples followed by finetuning in real samples improves the results compared to finetuning on real examples without synthetic pretraining. One exciting direction to explore in the future is to train real and synthetic data together while indicating in the language prompt whether the sample is real or artificial.

The VLSMs pretrained on natural image-language pairs do not seem to have captured the language-image relationships common in ultrasound images. Thus, when finetuning the encoders of VLSMs, the performance improved compared to freezing the encoders and finetuning only the decoder. CRIS's performance is always better when the encoders are finetuned for every strategy, but CLIPSeg only performs better when the synthetic dataset is introduced. Unfrozen CLIPSeg performing better when the dataset size is increased may be because, for CRIS, Wang et al. [26] finetuned the CLIP encoders and the vision-language decoder for the segmentation task, whereas, Lüddecke et al. [16] froze the encoders for CLIPSeg. Thus, CLIPSeg's encoder representation is likely not well adapted for segmentation as our finetuning of the encoder is limited to only a few thousand samples.

SDM CAMUS [23] is generated by applying random augmentations to the mask of the CAMUS dataset. As the dataset was developed by utilizing all the labeled image-mask pairs in the training set, and the images could not be generated without the corresponding mask, this questions the "synthetic" portion of the method (or dataset). This dataset does not solve the medical image segmen-

---

[2] https://www.creatis.insa-lyon.fr/Challenge/camus/results.html. Updated January 2023.

tation's limited paired-data availability problem by generating new examples. Instead, this is more akin to data augmentation, where the existing annotated set is augmented with a few thousand transformed pairs by perturbing existing masks and textures. An important direction in the future would be to find ways to generate aligned synthetic triplets of language, image, and mask at scale without annotated image-mask pairs.

6 Conclusion

Recent VLSMs trained in large image-language pairs of natural photographs perform close to the state-of-the-art on the CAMUS echocardiography dataset when finetuned on the automatically generated prompts. Augmenting training sets with synthetic images generated from SDM improves VLSMs' performance. However, using a relatively large number of synthetic data alone is still inferior to using a relatively small number of real annotated data. This suggests that more work is needed in generating better synthetic images whose distribution is closer to the real data distribution for the echocardiography dataset. Nevertheless, the synthetic data finetuned model checkpoint seems to be a good starting point for the segmentation models to finetune on the real dataset, resulting in improved metrics and faster convergence (on an average, 4.55 and 1.71 times faster for CRIS and CLIPSeg, respectively). While there is a significant potential for VLSMs for ultrasound image segmentation, there is a need to develop methods that can generate numerous consistent, realistic, but synthetic triplets of image, language, and segmentation masks if one wants to leverage the power of VLSMs.

References

1. Avola, D., Cinque, L., Fagioli, A., Foresti, G., Mecca, A.: Ultrasound medical imaging techniques: a survey. ACM Comput. Surv. (CSUR) **54**(3), 1–38 (2021)
2. Deng, K., et al.: Transbridge: a lightweight transformer for left ventricle segmentation in echocardiography. In: Noble, J.A., Aylward, S., Grimwood, A., Min, Z., Lee, S.-L., Hu, Y. (eds.) ASMUS 2021. LNCS, vol. 12967, pp. 63–72. Springer, Cham (2021). https://doi.org/10.1007/978-3-030-87583-1_7
3. Dosovitskiy, A., et al.: An image is worth 16 × 16 words: Transformers for image recognition at scale. In: International Conference on Learning Representations (2020)
4. Fürst, A., et al.: Cloob: modern hopfield networks with infoloob outperform clip. Adv. Neural Inf. Process. Syst. **35**, 20450–20468 (2022)
5. Goodfellow, I., et al.: Generative adversarial nets. Adv. Neural Inf. Process. Syst. **27**, 2672–2680 (2014)
6. Hatamizadeh, A., et al.: UNETR: transformers for 3D medical image segmentation. In: Proceedings of the IEEE/CVF Winter Conference on Applications of Computer Vision, pp. 574–584 (2022)
7. Ho, J., Jain, A., Abbeel, P.: Denoising diffusion probabilistic models. Adv. Neural Inf. Process. Syst. **33**, 6840–6851 (2020)

8. Huang, Z., Zeng, Z., Liu, B., Fu, D., Fu, J.: Pixel-BERT: aligning image pixels with text by deep multi-modal transformers. arXiv preprint arXiv:2004.00849 (2020)

9. Isensee, F., Jaeger, P.F., Kohl, S.A., Petersen, J., Maier-Hein, K.H.: nnU-Net: a self-configuring method for deep learning-based biomedical image segmentation. Nat. Methods **18**(2), 203–211 (2021)

10. Jia, C., et al.: Scaling up visual and vision-language representation learning with noisy text supervision. In: International Conference on Machine Learning, pp. 4904–4916. PMLR (2021)

11. Kazemzadeh, S., Ordonez, V., Matten, M., Berg, T.: Referitgame: referring to objects in photographs of natural scenes. In: Proceedings of the 2014 Conference on Empirical Methods in Natural Language Processing (EMNLP), pp. 787–798 (2014)

12. Leclerc, S., et al.: Deep learning for segmentation using an open large-scale dataset in 2d echocardiography. IEEE Trans. Med. Imaging **38**(9), 2198–2210 (2019)

13. Li, Y., et al.: Supervision exists everywhere: a data efficient contrastive language-image pre-training paradigm. In: International Conference on Learning Representations (2021)

14. Ling, H.J., Garcia, D., Bernard, O.: Reaching intra-observer variability in 2-d echocardiographic image segmentation with a simple u-net architecture. In: IEEE International Ultrasonics Symposium (IUS) (2022)

15. Loshchilov, I., Hutter, F.: Decoupled weight decay regularization. In: International Conference on Learning Representations (2018)

16. Lüddecke, T., Ecker, A.: Image segmentation using text and image prompts. In: Proceedings of the IEEE/CVF Conference on Computer Vision and Pattern Recognition, pp. 7086–7096 (2022)

17. Poudel, K., Dhakal, M., Bhandari, P., Adhikari, R., Thapaliya, S., Khanal, B.: Exploring transfer learning in medical image segmentation using vision-language models. arXiv preprint arXiv:2308.07706 (2023)

18. Qin, Z., Yi, H.H., Lao, Q., Li, K.: Medical image understanding with pretrained vision language models: a comprehensive study. In: The Eleventh International Conference on Learning Representations (2022)

19. Radford, A., et al.: Learning transferable visual models from natural language supervision. In: International Conference on Machine Learning, pp. 8748–8763. PMLR (2021)

20. Rao, Y., et al.: DenseCLIP: language-guided dense prediction with context-aware prompting. In: Proceedings of the IEEE/CVF Conference on Computer Vision and Pattern Recognition, pp. 18082–18091 (2022)

21. Ronneberger, O., Fischer, P., Brox, T.: U-Net: convolutional networks for biomedical image segmentation. In: Navab, N., Hornegger, J., Wells, W.M., Frangi, A.F. (eds.) MICCAI 2015. LNCS, vol. 9351, pp. 234–241. Springer, Cham (2015). https://doi.org/10.1007/978-3-319-24574-4_28

22. Singh, A., et al.: Flava: a foundational language and vision alignment model. In: Proceedings of the IEEE/CVF Conference on Computer Vision and Pattern Recognition, pp. 15638–15650 (2022)

23. Stojanovski, D., Hermida, U., Lamata, P., Beqiri, A., Gomez, A.: Echo from noise: synthetic ultrasound image generation using diffusion models for real image segmentation. arXiv preprint arXiv:2305.05424 (2023)

24. Wang, P., et al.: OFA: unifying architectures, tasks, and modalities through a simple sequence-to-sequence learning framework. In: International Conference on Machine Learning, pp. 23318–23340. PMLR (2022)

25. Wang, W., et al.: Semantic image synthesis via diffusion models. arXiv preprint arXiv:2207.00050 (2022)
26. Wang, Z., et al.: CRIS: clip-driven referring image segmentation. In: Proceedings of the IEEE/CVF Conference on Computer Vision and Pattern Recognition, pp. 11686–11695 (2022)
27. Wilcoxon, F.: Individual comparisons by ranking methods. In: Kotz, S., Johnson, N.L. (eds.) Breakthroughs in Statistics: Methodology and Distribution, pp. 196–202. Springer Series in Statistics. Springer, New York (1992). https://doi.org/10.1007/978-1-4612-4380-9_16
28. Wu, C., Lin, Z., Cohen, S., Bui, T., Maji, S.: PhraseCut: language-based image segmentation in the wild. In: Proceedings of the IEEE/CVF Conference on Computer Vision and Pattern Recognition, pp. 10216–10225 (2020)
29. Zhai, X., et al.: Lit: zero-shot transfer with locked-image text tuning. In: Proceedings of the IEEE/CVF Conference on Computer Vision and Pattern Recognition, pp. 18123–18133 (2022)

SimNorth: A Novel Contrastive Learning Approach for Clustering Prenatal Ultrasound Images

Juan Prieto[✉][iD], Chiraz Benabdelkader, Teeranan Pokaprakarn, Hina Shah,
Yuri Sebastião, Qing Dan, Nariman Almnini, Arieska Nicole Diaz,
Srihari Chari, Harmony Chi, Elizabeth Stringer, and Jeffrey Stringer

University of North Carolina at Chapel Hill, Chapel Hill, USA
jprieto@med.unc.edu

Abstract. This paper describes SimNorth, an unsupervised learning
approach for classifying non-standard fetal ultrasound images. SimNorth
utilizes a deep feature learning model with a novel contrastive loss function to project images with similar characteristics closer together in an
embedding space while pushing apart those with different image features. We then use non-linear dimensionality reduction via t-SNE and
apply standard clustering algorithms such as k-means and dbscan in 2D
embedding space to identify clusters containing similar fetal structures.
We compare SimNorth to other unsupervised learning techniques (such
as Autoencoders, MoCo, and SimCLR) and demonstrate its superior
performance based on cluster purity measures.

Keywords: Unsupervised · clustering · Ultrasound · fetal · blind
sweep

1 Introduction

Fig. 1. Images a/b are acquired by an expert to measure the fetal head and abdomen,
components of traditional gestational age (GA) estimation. Images c/d are blind sweep
frames that show non-standard views (in this case, thorax, spine, and head), yet were
deemed relevant by an AI algorithm to estimate the GA.

Supplementary Information The online version contains supplementary material
available at https://doi.org/10.1007/978-3-031-44521-7_10.

Prenatal Ultrasound (US) is a routine procedure in North America and Europe, and is considered an essential component of high-quality prenatal care. US is used to diagnose many high-risk conditions, including placenta previa, fetal growth restriction, and multiple gestation [7,12]. It is also critical to establishing gestational age (GA), a piece of clinical information that affects many aspects of patient care.

In many low- and middle-income countries (LMIC), prenatal US is less readily available due to various factors such as a shortage of qualified sonographers, lack of access to equipment, and cost barriers. As a result, many pregnant women in these countries face an increased risk of adverse pregnancy outcomes [12]. Recent breakthroughs in deep learning, and the development of portable handheld US devices is set to close the gap between expert sonographers and novices in LMICs [8].

Our previous research [1] has shown that blind sweep videos, which require minimal training and can be acquired by a nurse or a midwife, can be used to reliably estimate GA. However, as illustrated in Fig. 1, frames deemed relevant for GA estimation by this method (i.e., have high attention scores) are rarely in any one of the standard planes of fetal anatomy used by an expert sonographer [9]. This observation prompted us to devise a tool to automatically classify the images, that the underlying GA model relies upon for its estimates, into clinically meaningful categories. Such a tool could help researchers better understand the inner workings of the model, and perhaps identify novel fetal measurements associated with gestational age. The tool could also be useful for more general purposes beyond GA estimation, most notably for labeling/annotation of blind sweep videos for training other deep learning models, a task that is otherwise too costly because it requires high expertise, and cannot be reliably and efficiently outsourced.

In this paper, we present a novel method for clustering US blind sweep frames using deep feature learning, non-linear manifold embedding, and standard clustering techniques. We have opted for an unsupervised learning approach mainly because, unlike supervised learning, it potentially allows the discovery of novel fetal structures and substructures beyond those in manually annotated data. Our key contribution lies in the design of a deep feature learning model based on the contrastive learning paradigm, and a bespoke loss function that drives similar images closer in embedding space while pushing apart different images further apart. This function also contains a term based on attention scores calculated by the GA model. The rationale for using attention scores is based on the fact that they provide a direct measure of the significance of important fetal anatomy. We implement SimNorth using a dataset of US blind sweep video frames and compare it to three other unsupervised learning techniques (autoencoders, MoCo, and SimCLR), and demonstrate its superior performance based on intrinsic and extrinsic cluster evaluation measures.

Our deep feature learning model is inspired by state-of-the-art contrastive learning approaches. MoCo [5] uses the InfoNCE loss to learn a representation function by maximizing the similarity between positive pairs, and minimizing the similarity between negative pairs. SimCLR [4] simplifies the contrastive learning task by removing the queue but it requires a large batch size to learn. Both MoCo and SimCLR were successfully combined with k-means for image clustering [3, 11], which on a high level is analogous to our overall approach. Our ultrasound clustering method consists of a three-step pipeline: i) deep feature learning, ii) dimensionality reduction, iii) and clustering.

2   Method

2.1   Step 1: Deep Feature Learning

SimnNorth is primarily rooted in the well-known contrastive learning paradigm while leveraging attention scores learned from the GA prediction model. As shown in Fig. 2, the model has three main parts: i) data augmentation, ii) attention score s_i calculation, where the original image passes through the GA prediction model [1], and iii) an efficientnet [10] with a bespoke loss function that uses attention scores of all training images (top right).

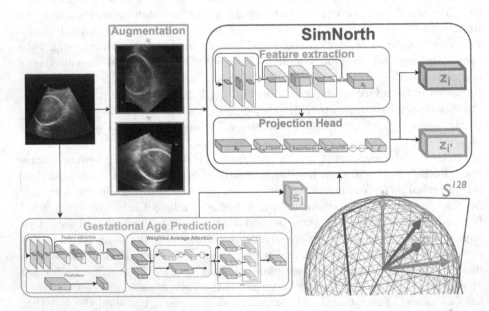

Fig. 2. SimNorth deep learning architecture. Features are extracted from pairs of augmented images and then projected to the positive quadrant of S^{128}, a 128-dimensional unit hypersphere. The model's loss function incorporates attention scores (s_i) of the training images computed by the GA prediction model and minimizes the angle between the projected pairs of images while maximizing it to other images (see text).

The loss function comprises three different components:

$$\text{Si} = \sum_i^N (1 - \text{sim}(z_i, z_{i'}))^2 \qquad \text{Co} = \sum_{i,j}^N (W * \text{S}_{\text{a}}(\text{sim}(z_{i,i'}, z_j)))^2$$

$$\text{North} = \sum_i^N 1 - s_i + \text{sim}(N_o, z_{i,i'}) \qquad L = \text{Si} + \text{Co} + \text{North}$$

where Si is similarity, Co is contrastive, $\text{sim} = \frac{z_i \cdot z_{i'}}{||A|| ||B||}$, is the cosine similarity, $W = w * (1 - x)^2, x \in [0, 1]$ are weights controlled by the hyperparameter w, $x = \frac{i}{B_s}, i \in [0, B_s]$, B_s is the batch size, S_{a} is the Sort Ascending function, and s_i is the attention score of the ith training frame. The latter is a value between 0 and 1, and is calculated using the GA prediction model - it is closer to 1 if the image is important for GA prediction, and closer to 0 otherwise. Finally, z_i and $z_{i'}$ are projections of the transformed images to the 128-dimensional unit hypersphere, denoted S^{128}, and z_j corresponds to the shuffled projections in the same batch.

The contrastive term of the loss function is computed as follows. The batch of training images is shuffled and their pairwise similarities, $\text{sim}(z_{i,i'}, z_j)$, are computed. The resulting values are sorted in ascending order with S_a, then weighted with matrix W. A graphical description of this process is provided in the Appendix. Intuitively, this term minimizes the angle between z_i and $z_{i'}$, maximizes the angle between z_i and z_j and if s_i is close to 1, it pushes the feature embedding toward the equator while pushing toward the north pole N otherwise. Also, by combining S_a and W, we encourage the model to push apart the most different frames and suppress this effect if the frames have similar features.

The importance and novelty of our weighting scheme must be emphasized. We specifically designed it to allow images with similar characteristics to be part of the same training batch. We believe this is a key factor that has enabled successful feature learning and sets our approach apart from previous contrastive learning approaches.

2.2   Step 2: Dimensionality Reduction

We reduce the dimensionality of the 128-dimensional data generated by the previous step. Clustering in a high-dimensional space is computationally challenging and prone to the curse of dimensionality, where high-dimensional points exist in sparse non-linear manifolds rather than compact regions. This makes clustering algorithms difficult to fine-tune and fragile [2]. Initially, we attempted linear dimensionality reduction using principal components analysis (PCA), however, the PCA approach did not yield any significant clusters, likely because the latent image clusters exist in non-linear manifolds that PCA's linear projection cannot preserve. Therefore, we opted for t-SNE [6], a state-of-the-art non-linear manifold embedding technique that maps input data to a space of up to 3 dimensions. We found that the 2 dimensions were equally effective for clustering.

2.3   Step 3: Clustering

The goal of a clustering problem is to find groups (or clusters) of objects that are semantically similar. In our case, objects are US images embedded in 2D t-SNE space, and the groups are expected to be fetal structures or other obstetric features. A secondary goal is to determine the smallest number of such groups so that we can easily attach meaning to each group, and use them to promote understanding. The choice of clustering method depends on the shape and sparsity of the underlying clusters. In our case, we could visually inspect the data in the 2D embedding space generated by t-SNE, simplifying the decision process. Because our model produces non-convex clusters with many dendrite-like or snake-like clusters (See Figs. 3 & 4), dbscan is well-suited for clustering our data. Finally, in order to attach meaning to the clusters calculated by the clustering method, and possibly group them into super-clusters, we extract a random sample of images from each cluster, and visually inspect them in consultation with expert sonographers. To expedite this latter process, we used a set of manually tagged images to calculate the majority label and purity of each cluster, allowing us to determine the nature of a cluster more quickly.

3   Experimental Setup

3.1   Data Set

All of our images come from blind sweep and fly-to cineloop videos collected from pregnant women enrolled in the FAMLI study during the period 2018 - 2022 at hospitals in Lusaka Zambia and Chapel Hill, North Carolina [1]. Blind sweep cineloops are obtained by following a specific data collection protocol. They are obtained in both the craniocaudal orientation and lateral orientation. The protocol is designed so novice sonographers may perform the acquisitions. Blind sweeps may or may not contain standard measurement views. The fly-to cineloops differ from blind sweeps in that they contain the 10 s prior to an expert sonographer navigating the ultrasound probe to obtain a standard view of a specific structure (in this case head, abdomen, or femur). As such, the last frame in a fly-to cineloop always contains a known measurable structure in standard view as acquired by an expert sonographer. More details about the data set can be found in the Appendix.

3.2   Experiments and Implementation Details

To demonstrate the effectiveness of *SimNorth*, we implemented and evaluated the clustering pipeline with three other state-of-the-art techniques: autoencoders, MoCo, and SimCLR. We also tested a simpler version of our model, called SimNorth−, that does not employ attention scores. Each model was trained using a sample of 3.6 million US images and over 400K were used for validation. The dimensionality reduction and clustering steps of the pipeline were performed only on a random sample of 100,000 images for the sake of computation efficiency.

The train, validation, and testing sets were split using the study ids making sure there is no overlap of videos between the sets.

We evaluated clustering performance using intrinsic (average silhouette score) and extrinsic (homogeneity or purity) cluster evaluation metrics. Cluster purity was calculated as the weighted average entropy of all clusters with respect to a set of 15,061 manually annotated images (the last frame of our fly-to cineloops; see above) - weighted by the proportion of frames in each cluster. For dimensionality reduction and clustering, we used Python's Scikit-learn library (version 1.0.2) implementations of t-SNE, dbscan and k-means. We varied t-SNE's main hyperparameter (called perplexity) in the range 10–500 and found that values around 300 yielded stable clustering results across all models.

We used the Monai 0.9.1 library to build an autoencoder with 5 downward/upward steps, Mean Squared Error loss function, and a latent dimension of 2048. For MoCo and SimCLR, we used pyTorch-lightning library implementations and trained each model with early stopping criteria, a patience value of 30 with maximum of 200 epochs, the AdamW optimizer, and a learning rate of $1e^{1-4}$. We initially used the default hyper-parameters suggested in the original papers of each model [4,5], namely using resnet50 as the backbone architecture and a temperature value of 0.07 or .05 for MoCo and SimCLR, respectively. Additional experiments were performed using batch sizes of 32, 64, 128 and temperature values of 0.1, 0.2, 0.3. for MoCo and 0.1 and 0.5 for SimCLR. Efficientnet was also tested as the base encoder for each model. For SimNorth, we varied the hyperparameter w in the range 2–16. The best hyperparameter values were determined for each model based on cluster purity with respect to our set of manually annotated images. We used PyTorch 1.12.1 and pytorch-lightning 1.8.6 All deep learning model training experiments were performed on a multi-GPU system with four NVIDIA-A100-SXM 80 GB of memory each. The average training time was 124 h. Only the best-performing models are reported in the Results section.

4   Results

Figure 3 shows results of the t-SNE embedding on the random sample of 100,000 US images for each of the five models that we implemented. SimNorth clearly outperforms the other studied contrastive learning models in bringing images of similar gestational ages images closer together. Also, the SimNorth embedding space seems to contain multiple well-separated dense regions (or clusters) while the space produced by the other models appears less well-separated.

The results of the clustering performance evaluation of all five models are shown in Table 1 and provide further evidence that SimNorth is more successful than the other models at producing meaningful clusters of ultrasound images. The silhouette score is higher for both variants of the SimNorth model, however, this result is unreliable due to the presence of non-convex clusters. The cluster purity measure indicates that SimNorth's clusters are much more homogeneous with respect to the subset of manually annotated images than all other models, meaning that they are less likely to contain images of mixed tags. The fact that SimNorth outperforms SimNorth– suggests that the GA algorithm's attention scores indeed encode information that is useful for this task.

Detailed clustering results for the SimNorth model are shown in Fig. 4 and demonstrate relative success in separating the space of ultrasound images into a small set of well-separated compact regions that each correspond to a meaningful semantic category. Specifically, applying the dbscan method produced 43 clusters (left plot), then after visually inspecting a random sample of images from each of those clusters, we were able to group these clusters into "super-clusters" that roughly correspond to known categories of fetal anatomy with some separation by gestational age. These results are quite encouraging but there remains room for improvement. In particular, the purity of the clusters could be increased and some of the super-clusters could be further separated into more granular categories (fetal sub-structures).

Table 1. Comparing clustering performance of SimNorth vs. three other unsupervised learning approaches. Purity was calculated as 1.0 - entropy (see text).

	temp/w	batch	encoder	clustering	n_clusters	Silhouette	Purity
Autoencoder	N/A	512	monai	k-means	35	.42	.55
MOCO	0.3	256	resnet	kmeans	25	.36	.39
SimCLR	0.5	256	effnet	kmeans	30	.37	.19
SimNorth–	16	256	effnet	dbscan	40	.46	**.65**
SimNorth	16	256	effnet	dbscan	43	.52	**.90**

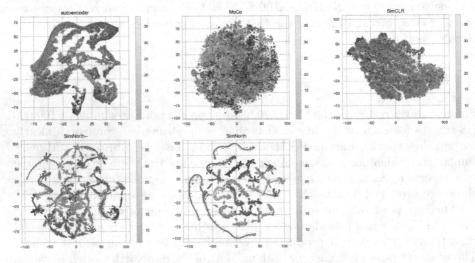

Fig. 3. t-SNE embeddings of a random sample of 100,000 US images for all five models that we implemented. Each point represents an image in the 2D space generated by t-SNE, color-coded by the corresponding gestational age (in weeks).

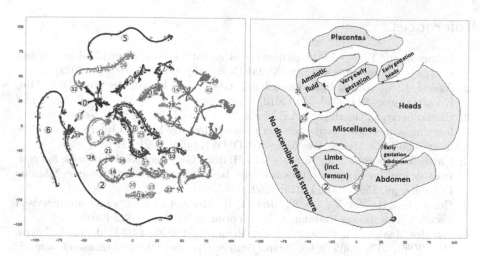

Fig. 4. Clustering results of the SimNorth model: 43 clusters were obtained by applying the dbscan clustering method on 2D embeddings of 100,000 US images (left), and true clusters were subsequently manually/visually identified by grouping neighbor dbscan clusters that are semantically similar (right).

5 Conclusions and Future Work

SimNorth is an unsupervised learning framework for US image analysis. In this paper, we compared SimNorth against other popular unsupervised learning approaches, namely autoencoders, MoCo, and SimCLR. The experiments performed demonstrate that the proposed method significantly outperforms state-of-the-art models based on a cluster purity measure calculated using 15,061 manually annotated images. SimNorth was able to automatically find head, abdomen, femur, placenta, and early gestation clusters with varying quality. A novel aspect of our approach is the use of attention scores to guide the learning task, which results have shown leads to improved cluster purity. This suggests that attention scores help the model organize important image features that better distinguish between different groups.

While SimCLR and MoCo have shown state-of-the-art performance on ImageNet, neither performed well on our US image dataset. We attribute this to the homogeneity of appearance and class imbalance in US images, in contrast to the wide range of visual characteristics and classes found in the ImageNet dataset. Our loss function was carefully designed to address this issue by enabling images with similar features to be part of the same training batch. Although the temperature hyperparameter in MoCo and SimCLR is supposed to achieve the same effect, our experiments have shown it is far less effective.

Future work will focus on improving the performance of our approach and making it generalize to other types of image data. We will use the output clusters of our model to automatically classify new blind sweep images and subsequently use those to train other deep learning models.

References

1. Pokaprakarn, T., et al.: AI estimation of gestational age from blind ultrasound sweeps in low-resource settings. NEJM Evid. **1**(5), EVIDoa2100058 (2022)
2. Assent, I.: Clustering high dimensional data. Wiley Interdiscip. Rev. Data Min. Knowl. Discov. **2**(4), 340–350 (2012)
3. Chakraborty, S., Gosthipaty, A.R., Paul, S.: G-SimCLR: self-supervised contrastive learning with guided projection via pseudo labelling. In: 2020 International Conference on Data Mining Workshops (ICDMW), pp. 912–916. IEEE (2020)
4. Chen, T., Kornblith, S., Norouzi, M., Hinton, G.: A simple framework for contrastive learning of visual representations. In: International Conference on Machine Learning, pp. 1597–1607. PMLR (2020)
5. He, K., Fan, H., Wu, Y., Xie, S., Girshick, R.: Momentum contrast for unsupervised visual representation learning. arXiv preprint arXiv:1911.05722 (2019)
6. van der Maaten, L., Hinton, G.: Visualizing data using t-SNE. J. Mach. Learn. Res. **9**(86), 2579–2605 (2008). http://jmlr.org/papers/v9/vandermaaten08a.html
7. Organization, W.H., et al.: WHO recommendations on postnatal care of the mother and newborn. World Health Organization (2014)
8. Rykkje, A., Carlsen, J.F., Nielsen, M.B.: Hand-held ultrasound devices compared with high-end ultrasound systems: a systematic review. Diagnostics **9**(2), 61 (2019)
9. Salomon, L., et al.: ISUOG practice guidelines: ultrasound assessment of fetal biometry and growth. Ultrasound Obstet. Gynecol. **53**, 715–723 (2019). https://doi.org/10.1002/uog.20272
10. Tan, M., Le, Q.: Efficientnet: rethinking model scaling for convolutional neural networks. In: International Conference on Machine Learning, pp. 6105–6114. PMLR (2019)
11. Van Gansbeke, W., Vandenhende, S., Georgoulis, S., Proesmans, M., Van Gool, L.: SCAN: learning to classify images without labels. In: Vedaldi, A., Bischof, H., Brox, T., Frahm, J.-M. (eds.) ECCV 2020. LNCS, vol. 12355, pp. 268–285. Springer, Cham (2020). https://doi.org/10.1007/978-3-030-58607-2_16
12. Whitworth, M., Bricker, L., Mullan, C.: Ultrasound for fetal assessment in early pregnancy. Cochrane Database Syst. Rev. (7) (2015)

Multimodal Imaging, Reconstruction, and Real-time Applications

HoloPOCUS: Portable Mixed-Reality 3D Ultrasound Tracking, Reconstruction and Overlay

Kian Wei Ng[1,2] , Yujia Gao[1], Mohammed Shaheryar Furqan[1], Zachery Yeo[1], Joel Lau[1], Kee Yuan Ngiam[1], and Eng Tat Khoo[2(✉)]

[1] National University Health System, Singapore 119224, Singapore
kianwei@u.nus.edu
[2] College of Design and Engineering, National University of Singapore, Singapore 117575, Singapore
etkhoo@nus.edu.sg

Abstract. Ultrasound (US) imaging provides a safe and accessible solution to procedural guidance and diagnostic imaging. The effective usage of conventional 2D US for interventional guidance requires extensive experience to project the image plane onto the patient, and the interpretation of images in diagnostics suffers from high intra- and inter-user variability. 3D US reconstruction allows for more consistent diagnosis and interpretation, but existing solutions are limited in terms of equipment and applicability in real-time navigation. To address these issues, we propose HoloPOCUS—a mixed reality US system (MR-US) that overlays rich US information onto the user's vision in a point-of-care setting. HoloPOCUS extends existing MR-US methods beyond placing a US plane in the user's vision to include a 3D reconstruction and projection that can aid in procedural guidance using conventional probes. We validated a tracking pipeline that demonstrates higher accuracy compared to existing MR-US works. Furthermore, user studies conducted via a phantom task showed significant improvements in navigation duration when using our proposed methods.

Keywords: mixed reality · 3D ultrasound · interventional guidance · tracking

1 Introduction

Modern medical imaging provides essential information for diagnostics and intervention. CT and MRI provide 3D anatomical information but exposes users to ionizing radiation and are not suitable for patients with ferrous implants respectively [1]. Ultrasound (US) imaging provides a relatively low-cost, mobile, and safe alternative [2], but in the conventional 2D form the results require more experience to interpret. This impacts diagnostic power as well as intervention efficacy. Studies have shown that using 2D US

Supplementary Information The online version contains supplementary material available at https://doi.org/10.1007/978-3-031-44521-7_11.

B. Kainz et al. (Eds.): ASMUS 2023, LNCS 14337, pp. 111–120, 2023.
https://doi.org/10.1007/978-3-031-44521-7_11

for diagnosis suffers from high inter-user variability [3], and effective intervention using 2D US is correlated with clinical experience and training [4].

Existing works have been proposed to address some of the limitations of conventional 2D US. 3D US volumes can be either captured directly via specialized probes [5], or reconstructed by stitching individual frames into a volume. Volumetric 3D US reconstruction requires an estimation of the relative pose between frames, with approaches involving electro-magnetic [6], IMU [7], and sensor-less deep learning being proposed [8]. Inter-user diagnostic variability has been shown to improve with the usage of 3D US volumes and the associated features [9].

Using medical imaging for intra-operative or interventional procedure guidance allows clinicians to navigate to or around anatomy not visible to the naked eye due to tissue occlusion [10]. The direct fusion of imaging data onto the user's vision, superimposed onto the actual anatomy, can provide a more intuitive and usable system that could improve the accuracy and speed of procedures [11]. Several works have leveraged on mixed-reality (MR) hardware, proposing to superimpose point-of-care US slices onto the user's vision, reducing the cognitive load required for clinicians to register and reproject the images onto the body [12–16].

Table 1. Summary of related works in MR-US.

	Tracking Method	Hardware	Projection/Overlay
[13]	Opto-electronic	2D Probe; HMD; tracking equipment	Image
[12]	Electro-magnetic	2D Probe; Monitor; tracking equipment	Image
[14]	Monocular + ArUco	2D Probe; HMD	Image
[15]	Depth/IR + Spheres	2D Probe; HMD	Image
[16]	Stereo + Spheres	3D Probe; HMD	Volume
Ours	Stereo + ArUco	2D Probe; HMD	Image/Volume

For the US slices to be registered and overlaid onto the body, the US probe needs to be tracked; MR-US solutions such as [13] and [12] utilized specialized tracking equipment such as opto-electronic or electromagnetic systems. While benefiting from high accuracy, the additional hardware adds to cost and reduces portability. [14] and [15] instead used cameras on head-mounted devices to directly track the probe, using fiducial markers with monocular and Infrared (IR)/Depth feeds respectively. With the acquisition, tracking and projection system integrated into one device, the need for additional equipment is removed. While portability is improved, neither have validated tracking results that are close to clinically requirements [10]. While most prior works focus on the visual overlay of 2D slices, [16] utilizes specialized probes that directly acquire and project 3D volumetric data in contrast to conventional 2D probes. We advance the domain and application of MR-US with the following contributions:

- We developed a stereo-tracking pipeline that extracts richer fiducial keypoints, which can be filtered and processed to provide higher accuracy tracking and MR-US 2D overlay compared with existing works.

- Existing solutions that utilize conventional linear probes enable the visual overlay of 2D US slices. Our proposed system allows for users to reconstruct and project 3D MR-US data, to be used in direct intervention or downstream diagnostic tasks.
- We conducted a user study to test the effectiveness of both 2D and 3D MR-US solutions against conventional US operation for a simulated biopsy task, providing insights into the potential benefits and drawbacks of implementing such systems in different (e.g. diagnostic/interventional) clinical settings.

2 Methods

2.1 System Architecture

HoloPOCUS utilizes Microsoft's HoloLens 2 for sensing and visualization [17]. HoloLens 2 provides multiple cameras – one high definition RGB, four grayscale with overlapping field-of-view (FOV), and an IR/Depth. From Table 1, [14] and [15] that use the HoloLens line of device utilized RGB and IR/Depth respectively. While the RGB feed provides high resolution images, the FOV does not cover the typical region used for tracking hand-held objects (Supp. Fig. 1) [18]. Conversely, the IR/Depth feed has a wide FOV but suffers from accuracy issues related to both random and warm-up variability [19, 20]. Given the above hardware limitations, we opted to use the stereo streams (Supp. Fig. 1) [18], with the benefit of a FOV that includes hand-object interactions, and high accuracy and reliability stemming from stereo triangulation.

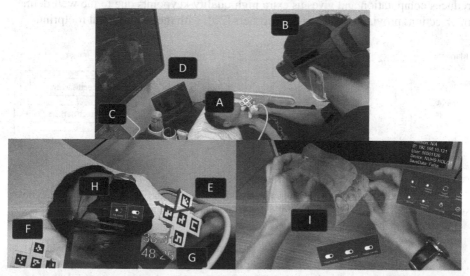

Fig. 1. (**Top**) Clinician using HoloPOCUS; (**Bottom Left**) First person view with 2D overlay (G), large virtual screen for viewing fine detail (H), operating distance/angle as user feedback; (**Bottom Right**) Tracking of US slices over time allows for 3D reconstruction of nodule and surrounding structures e.g. carotid/thyroid (I), which can be projected directly back on the acquisition location or inspected post-hoc (as shown). 150 slices were used for reconstruction.

A custom 3D-printed attachment was made to secure ArUco markers to the probe for tracking. The attachment was designed with two joints that can be rotated at 45° intervals, providing greater flexibility compared to [14] for probe positioning and orientation that can differ significantly based on anatomy and procedures.

To track and project US data onto the user's vision, US images are streamed from the US machine (Fig. 1C) to a laptop for processing (Fig. 1D). Simultaneously, the stereo feed from HoloLens (Fig. 1B) is streamed to the laptop to compute the fiducial markers' pose. Since the markers (Fig. 1A) are placed at a known offset from the probe tip, an offset transformation is applied to compute the pose of the probe tip. The pose is then paired with the US data for rendering in the user's vision. By tracking the slices across space-time (Fig. 1, **Bottom Left**), we demonstrate the ability to reconstruct the 3D anatomy for richer visualization/guidance (Fig. 1, **Bottom Right**).

2.2 Dense Fiducial Keypoints Extraction for Stereo Pose Estimation

Two stages are applied to retrieve the marker pose from a stereo pair. ArUco markers are identified in each image (*DetectMarkers*) [21]. A secondary detection pass is done on the image (*ReDetectMarkers*) to detect any previously missed markers, using the known MarkerSet mappings as reference. Given an n marker configuration, only up to $4n$ corners can be extracted. Prior works augmented ArUco for more keypoints either by adding features [22–24] or densely predicting keypoints in the binary pattern via a GPU-based deep learning approach [25]. In this stage (*ChessboardDetector*), we exploit natural chessboard corners found in ArUco patterns. This targeted approach reduces computation and gives us extra high-quality keypoints due to the well-defined intersections provided by chessboard corners [26], with the same spatial footprint.

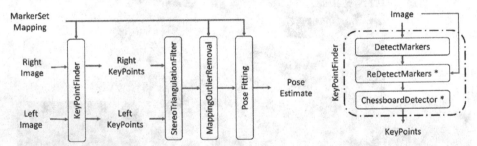

Fig. 2. Stereo pairs are processed independently with the KeyPointFinder sub-module (* denotes steps requiring MarkerSet Mapping), followed by triangulation, filtering, and pose fitting.

For each ArUco marker detected, we crop and upsample the patch to a constant size. A radon-based transform was used to extract the response map (Fig. 3, top row) [26]. Given the original 4 corners for each ArUco, we interpolated to extract candidate guesses for where chessboard corners could be located. Local maxima from the response map are matched to these guesses (Fig. 3, red points) and refined via a weighted average of the local response.

$$s_i = \frac{1}{c_1 - 1}\sum_{j\neq i}|d(i,j) - r(i,j)| \tag{1}$$

Fig. 3. Filter response for cropped ArUco patches, with local maxima filtered for points that are close to guesses interpolated from the original 4 corners.

With the enlarged keypoint sets found for both left and right images, stereo matching is done with the camera intrinsic, with stereo rays that do not intersect within a fixed tolerance (1mm) being discarded. We perform an outlier removal step on the remaining c_1 3D points. Pairwise distances $d(i, j)$ are computed exhaustively and compared against the ground truth reference $r(i, j)$ (Eq. 1). The score s_i is computed for each point, with those above a fixed threshold (0.75 mm) being discarded.

The resulting c_2 points each have a confidence value assigned from stereo intersection. We compute m candidate poses using the top $\{c_2 - 1, c_2 - 2, \ldots, c_2 - m\}$ confidence points, retaining the pose with the lowest fiducial registration error (FRE).

2.3 Projection Computation

This section describes the integration of stereo tracking output with coordinate systems across devices, for 2D slice projection or 3D reconstruction-projection tasks.

Real-time 2D Slice Reprojection. The tracking module returns the computed 4×4 transformation matrix ${}_C^P P$ that provides the pose of the probe's ArUco marker set in relation to the cameras. We retrieve the computed pose of the camera relative to a static world coordinate system ${}_W^C P$ using the ResearchMode API [17]. For the US slices to be projected at the correct location within the patient's body, we precompute another transformation ${}_P^T P$ that describes the marker's relation to the probe tip.

$$ {}_W^T P = {}_W^C P * {}_C^P P * {}_P^T P \tag{2} $$

Chaining these transformations (Eq. 2) allows us to retrieve ${}_W^T P$, the final transformation relating the position of the US slice at the probe tip relative to the application's world coordinate system. This pose is computed on a per-frame basis and sent to the headset for real-time projection and rendering of the 2D slices.

3D Reconstruction-Reprojection. US frames that are tracked in a consistent coordinate system over time can be accumulated into a 3D volume. Given the pixel-spacing (p_w, p_h) mm for the US image, a 4×4 matrix ${}_T^I P$ is pre-computed via CAD software to transform each pixel's coordinate $(x, y, 0)$ to be expressed relative to the tip in 3D.

To improve the accuracy of the 3D reconstruction process, we included an optional "anchor" marker (AM) set (Fig. 1F), identical in design to the probe tracking set (Fig. 1E). Previous works have shown that HoloLens' self-localization via its internal algorithm had an average error of 1-3cm in an indoor-mapping task [20]. While this value fluctuates depending on the environment, we mitigate this source of error by introducing the AM set. By running the tracking module in parallel to track the AM, the transformation matrix $_C^A P$ containing the pose of AM relative to the camera.

$$_A^I P = {_C^A P}^{-1} * {_C^P P} * {_P^T P} * {_T^I P} \tag{3}$$

$$_W^I P = {_W^C P} * {_C^P P} * {_P^T P} * {_T^I P} \tag{4}$$

Combining the terms through Eq. 3 gives us $_A^I P$, a new way of expressing the pixel data with respect to AM's coordinate system.

Let E_{stereo} and E_{local} represent the errors present in pose computation via the stereo tracking module and HoloLens' self-localization respectively. In terms of error contribution, accumulating the data relative to the world (Eq. 4, $_W^I P$) would result in $E_{recon|W} = E_{stereo} + E_{local}$, stemming from $_C^P P$ and $_W^C P$ respectively. On the other hand, accumulating the data relative to AM (Eq. 3, $_A^I P$) would result in $E_{recon|A} = E_{stereo} + E_{stereo}$, stemming from $_C^P P$ and $_C^A P$ being tracked independently.

Given the above, AM should be used for reconstruction if $E_{stereo} \ll E_{local}$. With an evaluation of how usage parameters affect E_{stereo}, an upper-bound for $E_{recon|A}$ can be estimated, which would not be possible in the case of $E_{recon|W}$ due to the unpredictable nature of the E_{local} component.

2.4 Implementation Details

We utilized a laptop (i9-12900H CPU) for computation together with a linear probe (Mindray DC-80A, L14-5WE) for expert-user testing and feedback. The HoloLens application was developed with Unity, gRPC and MRTK. We used the system with a wireless probe (SonoStarMed, 128E) that streamed data to an iPhone 12 mini for the user study. All processing ran in real-time for a 30 Hz HoloLens stereo feed, with full keypoint extraction and pose estimation averaging **25.6** and **5.2 ms** respectively.

3 Results

3.1 Tracking Accuracy

Of the related MR-US works described (Table 1), we excluded [16] from the tracking comparison as they utilized a unique setup (1920 × 1080 high definition RGB stereo) that is not available to HoloLens 2 and had reported FRE metrics. For MR-guided navigation, FRE has been shown to be uncorrelated with overlay accuracy [27, 28].

Instead, we focus on works utilizing HoloLens 2 for fiducial tracking [15, 29], with sensors that had a suitable FOV (Table 2). For [14], we utilized the original monocular PnP estimation on ArUco markers setup but opted to use the wide FOV grayscale 640 × 480 instead of the original low FOV RGB 1920 × 1080 feed for a fair FOV comparison.

For evaluation, past works moved markers along a known trajectory, with frame-to-frame poses compared against a gold standard. We simulated this by placing two sets of

Table 2. Tracking results comparison. * Indicates results reproduced with experimental setup changes as described. Results with inclusion of chessboard keypoints indicated in brackets.

	Tracking Method	Translation RMS	Rotation RMS
[14] *	Mono, 2x ArUco	13.8 mm	10.9°
[14] *	Mono, 5x ArUco	10.9 mm	7.91°
[15]	Depth/IR, Spheres	2.81 mm	1.70°
[29]	Stereo, Spheres	1.90 mm	1.18°
[29]	Mono, 1x ArUco	6.09 mm	6.73°
Ours	Stereo, 2x ArUco (+C)	1.08 mm (0.91 mm)	1.31° (1.24°)
Ours	Stereo, 5x ArUco (+C)	0.49 mm (0.45 mm)	0.60° (0.60°)

markers at a known offset. The viewing distance and angles were varied, with relative poses for each set computed per frame and compared against this offset.

We show that even with a 2 ArUco marker configuration (minimum of 2 markers needed for *ReDetectMarkers* module), our pose translation and rotation errors outperform existing solutions. The inclusion of chessboard corners had a stronger effect on low marker setups, with negligible improvements when 5 markers are used.

Table 3. Effect of usage distance and angle to marker on translation and rotational RMS.

		Usage Angle. (deg)		
		0–15	15–30	30–45
Usage Dist. (cm)	15–25	0.222 mm/0.417°	0.228 mm/0.407°	0.187 mm/0.459°
	25–35	0.284 mm/0.288°	0.282 mm/0.554°	0.288 mm/0.441°
	35–45	0.561 mm/0.737°	0.621 mm/0.756°	0.631 mm/0.675°
	45–55	0.859 mm/0.912°	0.854 mm/0.950°	1.015 mm/0.961°

For effective and reliable usage of HoloPOCUS, we investigated the effect of the cameras' distance and angle relative to the markers on accuracy (Table 3). Within the defined operational limits for the 5-marker configuration, translation and rotation RMS ranged from **0.19–1.02 mm** and **0.41–0.96°** respectively.

Lastly, the experimental setup allowed us to track and compute $_W^P P$ and $_A^P P$ simultaneously. We estimated E_{local}, the variation in probe tracking due to self-localization uncertainty to be around **1–2 mm**, in line with past experimental results [20].

3.2 User Study

To evaluate HoloPOCUS' effectiveness, we compared it against conventional US for a phantom biopsy task, using the time taken as a quantitative metric. Following [30], sets of three targets were submerged in agar at 10–20 mm depths (Supp. Fig. 2). Each set was contained in a 15x5 cm block, consisting of two small and one large target, with 7.5 and 15 mm diameters respectively. This design followed ATA guidelines for thyroid nodule biopsy [31]. For each trial, users were tasked to use the selected US method to locate and hit the three targets in succession with a needle. The order of methods was randomized to account for task familiarity bias.

We recruited an equal number of novices and experts, with novices defined as individuals with no medical training, and experts as specialists (from specialties that routinely use US as navigational guidance) who have had at least 5 years of post-graduate experience/training. None of the participants had a substantial background in mixed-reality usage. Novices were instructed on the principles of US operation prior to the timed task. The 3D method timing included a reconstruction sweep, which took 18 s on average to cover the 15 cm length (Table 4).

Table 4. Time taken (mean ± s.d) and statistical test results for phantom biopsy task.

	Conventional US		2D Overlay		3D Recon/Overlay	
	time (s)	–	time (s)	p-value	time (s)	p-value
Novices (n = 12)	72.2 ± 43.2	–	51.6 ± 19.7	0.1838	37.1 ± 12.5	**0.0249**
Experts (n = 12)	67.9 ± 27.2	–	58.1 ± 25.1	0.1253	35.0 ± 8.8	**0.0022**

A paired two-tailed t-test against conventional US showed a significant reduction in timings for the 3D method. The 2D method showed an insignificant reduction in timing, in line with prior results [14]. Experts performed the task faster than novices on average, except for when the 2D method was used. This is also in line with prior results [14], reflecting how the 2D method did not provide substantial improvements in mental reprojection and instead worsened timings due to technology unfamiliarity.

4 Discussion

We introduce a novel MR-US solution for 3D reconstruction-overlay of US data. This done by introducing a high accuracy stereo fiducial tracking pipeline that allows for the reliable accumulation of 2D slices across time to form a 3D volume [32].

The 3D US volume can be used directly for better interventional guidance, as anatomical structures are better perceived in 3D. A user study showed significant improvement in a simulated biopsy task when using a 3D overlay, even with the sweep duration included. We expect sweep time to be insignificant for complex real-world cases, making the benefits more significant. Apart from navigation, the volumes can be reused for diagnostics (e.g. 3D spatial features, nodule temporal progression) [33].

Future work could include using more complex phantoms to accommodate tasks where multiple structures have to be avoided and targeted. Feedback from users included difficulty in estimating phantom target depths. We hypothesize that this could be addressed with more complex phantoms/reconstructions, where the relative locations of structures, aided by mesh occlusions, could provide better 3D perception.

With a larger sample size, analysis can be done to study the effect of age and specialty on MR-US effectiveness. Finally, similar to other works, our measure of accuracy does not account for inaccuracies from the optical system used for visual overlay. A different task design can potentially shed light on this source of error.

The study was approved by the institutional ethics review board (2021/00464) and received support from the Ministry of Education, Singapore, under the Academic Research Fund Tier 1 (FY2020), and from the National University Health System (NUHSRO/2021/018/ROS+6/EIM-2nd/03).

References

1. Caraiani, C., Petresc, B., Dong, Y., Dietrich, C.F.: Contraindications and adverse effects in abdominal imaging. Med. Ultrason. **21**, 456–463 (2019)
2. Lentz, B., Fong, T., Rhyne, R., Risko, N.: A systematic review of the cost-effectiveness of ultrasound in emergency care settings. Ultrasound J. **13**, 1–9 (2021)
3. Salonen, R., Haapanen, A., Salonen, J.T.: Measurement of intima-media thickness of common carotid arteries with high-resolution B-mode ultrasonography: Inter- and intra-observer variability. Ultrasound Med. Biol. **17**, 225–230 (1991)
4. Yoon, H.K., et al.: Effects of practitioner's experience on the clinical performance of ultrasound-guided central venous catheterization: a randomized trial. Sci. Rep. **11**, 1–8 (2021)
5. Gonçalves, L.F., et al.: Applications of 2D matrix array for 3D and 4D examination of the fetus: a pictorial essay. J. Ultrasound Med. **25**, 745 (2006)
6. Daoud, M.I., Alshalalfah, A.L., Awwad, F., Al-Najar, M.: Freehand 3D ultrasound imaging system using electromagnetic tracking. In: 2015 International Conference on Open Source Software Computing, OSSCOM 2015 (2016)
7. Kim, T., et al.: Versatile low-cost volumetric 3D ultrasound imaging using gimbal-assisted distance sensors and an inertial measurement unit. Sens. (Basel). **20**, 1–15 (2020)
8. Prevost, R., et al.: 3D freehand ultrasound without external tracking using deep learning. Med Image Anal. **48**, 187–202 (2018)
9. Krönke, M., et al.: Tracked 3D ultrasound and deep neural network-based thyroid segmentation reduce interobserver variability in thyroid volumetry. PLoS ONE **17**, e0268550 (2022)
10. Fraser, J.F., Schwartz, T.H., Kaplitt, M.G.: BrainLab image guided system. In: Textbook of Stereotactic and Functional Neurosurgery, pp. 567–581 (2009)
11. Glas, H.H., Kraeima, J., van Ooijen, P.M.A., Spijkervet, F.K.L., Yu, L., Witjes, M.J.H.: Augmented reality visualization for image-guided surgery: a validation study using a three-dimensional printed phantom. J. Oral Maxillofac. Surg. **79**(1943), e1-1943.e10 (2021)
12. Ameri, G., et al.: Development and evaluation of an augmented reality ultrasound guidance system for spinal anesthesia: preliminary results. Ultrasound Med Biol. **45**, 2736–2746 (2019)
13. Rosenthal, M., et al.: Augmented reality guidance for needle biopsies: an initial randomized, controlled trial in phantoms. Med. Image Anal. **6**, 313–320 (2002)
14. Nguyen, T., Plishker, W., Matisoff, A., Sharma, K., Shekhar, R.: HoloUS: augmented reality visualization of live ultrasound images using HoloLens for ultrasound-guided procedures. Int. J. Comput. Assist. Radiol. Surg. **17**, 385–391 (2022)

15. von Haxthausen, F., Moreta-Martinez, R., Pose Díez de la Lastra, A., Pascau, J., Ernst, F.: UltrARsound: in situ visualization of live ultrasound images using HoloLens 2. Int. J. Comput. Assist. Radiol. Surg. **17**, 2081 (2022)
16. Cattari, N., Condino, S., Cutolo, F., Ghilli, M., Ferrari, M., Ferrari, V.: Wearable AR and 3D ultrasound: towards a novel way to guide surgical dissections. IEEE Access. **9**, 156746–156757 (2021)
17. Ungureanu, D., et al.: HoloLens 2 research mode as a tool for computer vision research (2020)
18. Dibene, J.C., Dunn, E.: HoloLens 2 sensor streaming (2022)
19. Tölgyessy, M., Dekan, M., Chovanec, Ľ, Hubinský, P.: Evaluation of the azure kinect and its comparison to kinect V1 and kinect V2. Sens. (Basel). **21**, 1–25 (2021)
20. Hübner, P., Clintworth, K., Liu, Q., Weinmann, M., Wursthorn, S.: Evaluation of HoloLens tracking and depth sensing for indoor mapping applications. Sensors **20**, 1021 (2020)
21. Garrido-Jurado, S., Muñoz-Salinas, R., Madrid-Cuevas, F.J., Marín-Jiménez, M.J.: Automatic generation and detection of highly reliable fiducial markers under occlusion. Pattern Recognit. **47**, 2280–2292 (2014)
22. Kedilioglu, O., Bocco, T.M., Landesberger, M., Rizzo, A., Franke, J.: ArUcoE: enhanced ArUco marker. In: International Conference on Control, Automation and Systems, vol. 2021-October, pp. 878–881 (2021)
23. Wang, Y., Zheng, Z., Su, Z., Yang, G., Wang, Z., Luo, Y.: An improved ArUco marker for monocular vision ranging. In: Proceedings of the 32nd Chinese Control and Decision Conference, CCDC 2020, pp. 2915–2919 (2020)
24. Rijlaarsdam, D.D.W., Zwick, M., Kuiper, J.M.: A novel encoding element for robust pose estimation using planar fiducials. Front. Robot. AI **9**, 227 (2022)
25. Zhang, Z., Hu, Y., Yu, G., Dai, J.: DeepTag: a general framework for fiducial marker design and detection. IEEE Trans. Pattern Anal. Mach. Intell. **45**, 2931–2944 (2021)
26. Duda, A.: Accurate detection and localization of checkerboard corners for calibration (2018)
27. West, J.B., Fitzpatrick, J.M., Toms, S.A., Maurer, C.R., Maciunas, R.J.: Fiducial point placement and the accuracy of point-based, rigid body registration. Neurosurgery **48**, 810–817 (2001)
28. Fitzpatrick, J.M.: Fiducial registration error and target registration error are uncorrelated. In: Medical Imaging 2009: Visualization, Image-Guided Procedures, and Modeling, vol. 7261, p. 726102 (2009)
29. Gsaxner, C., Pepe, A., Schmalstieg, D., Li, J., Egger, J.: Inside-out instrument tracking for surgical navigation in augmented reality. In: Proceedings of the ACM Symposium on Virtual Reality Software and Technology, VRST, p. 11 (2021)
30. Earle, M., Portu, G.D., Devos, E.: Agar ultrasound phantoms for low-cost training without refrigeration. Afr. J. Emerg. Med. **6**, 18–23 (2016)
31. Weerakkody, Y., Morgan, M.: ATA guidelines for assessment of thyroid nodules. Radiopaedia.org (2016)
32. Lindseth, F., et al.: Ultrasound-based guidance and therapy. Advancements and Breakthroughs in Ultrasound Imaging (2013)
33. Azizi, G., et al.: 3-D ultrasound and thyroid cancer diagnosis: a prospective study. Ultrasound Med. Biol. **47**, 1299–1309 (2021)

MIC-CUSP: Multimodal Image Correlations for Ultrasound-Based Prostate Cancer Detection

Indrani Bhattacharya[1]($\boxtimes$), Sulaiman Vesal[2], Hassan Jahanandish[2], Moonhyung Choi[2], Steve Zhou[2], Zachary Kornberg[2], Elijah Sommer[3], Richard Fan[2], James Brooks[2], Geoffrey Sonn[1,2], and Mirabela Rusu[1,2]

[1] Department of Radiology, Stanford University School of Medicine, Stanford, CA 94305, USA
ibhatt@stanford.edu
[2] Department of Urology, Stanford University School of Medicine, Stanford, CA 94305, USA
[3] School of Medicine, Stanford University, Stanford, CA 94305, USA

Abstract. Transrectal b-mode ultrasound images are used to guide pros-tate biopsies but are rarely used for prostate cancer detection. Cancer detection rates on b-mode ultrasound are low due to the low signal-to-noise ratio and imaging artifacts like shadowing and speckles, resulting in missing upto 52% clinically significant cancers in ultrasound-guided biopsies. Since b-mode ultrasound is widely accessible, routinely used in clinical care, inexpensive, and a fast non-invasive imaging modality, ultrasound-based prostate cancer detection has great clinical significance. Here, we present an automated ultrasound-based prostate cancer detection method, MIC-CUSP (**M**ultimodal **I**mage **C**orrelations for **C**ancer detection on **U**ltra-**S**ound leveraging **P**retraining with weak labels). First, MIC-CUSP learns richer imaging-inspired ultrasound biomarkers by leveraging registration-independent multimodal image correlations between b-mode ultrasound and two unaligned richer imaging modalities, Magnetic Resonance Imaging (MRI) and post-operative histopathology images. Second, MIC-CUSP uses the richer imaging-inspired ultrasound biomarkers as inputs to the cancer detection model to localize cancer on b-mode ultrasound images, in absence of MRI and histopathology images. MIC-CUSP addresses the lack of large accurately labeled ultrasound datasets by pretraining with a large public dataset of 1573 b-mode ultrasound scans and weak labels, and fine-tuning with 289 internal patients with strong labels. MIC-CUSP was evaluated on 41 patients, and compared with four clinician-readers with 1–12 years of experience. MIC-CUSP achieved patient-level Sensitivity and Specificity of 0.65 and 0.81 respectively, outperforming an average clinician-reader.

M. Rusu and G. Sonn—Contributed equally as senior authors.

Supplementary Information The online version contains supplementary material available at https://doi.org/10.1007/978-3-031-44521-7_12.

Keywords: ultrasound · prostate cancer · multimodal

1 Introduction

Prostate biopsies to diagnose prostate cancers are guided by transrectal b-mode ultrasound images, with or without Magnetic Resonance Imaging (MRI). MRI-Ultrasound fusion biopsies enable targeting suspicious lesions found on MRI, whereas systematic ultrasound-guided biopsies in absence of MRI "blindly" sample the prostate. These systematic ultrasound-guided biopsies miss 20–52% of clinically significant cancers, whereas MRI-ultrasound fusion biopsies only miss 12–14% clinically significant cancers [1,2]. Yet, MRI continues to be under-utilized for prostate cancer diagnosis due to limited access, high cost, and lack of interpretation expertise. As such, only about 7% of prostate biopsies in the United States are MRI-guided [3]. Since the remaining 93% biopsies are guided by b-mode ultrasound alone, there remains an unmet clinical need to enable cancer detection and localization on commonly used b-mode ultrasound images.

While b-mode ultrasound accurately identifies the prostate gland, low signal-to-noise ratio, artifacts (speckle and shadowing) and confounders that look like cancer (hypoechoic on ultrasound) prevent clinicians from reliably differentiating cancerous from non-cancerous regions, with cancer detection rates as low as 40% [4–7]. These imaging challenges coupled with lack of large labeled datasets have resulted in very few machine learning methods for b-mode ultrasound-based prostate cancer detection [8–10], with all studies using small biased populations of patients with clinically significant cancer. Other machine learning methods for ultrasound-based prostate cancer detection have used advanced investigational ultrasound (shear-wave elastography, contrast-enhanced) [5,11–14], not commonly used in routine clinical practice, limiting their clinical utility.

We present MIC-CUSP (**M**ultimodal **I**mage **C**orrelations for **C**ancer detection on **U**ltra**S**ound leveraging **P**retraining with weak labels), a b-mode ultrasound-based prostate cancer detection model that addresses existing challenges through:

1. Development and integration of a registration-independent multimodal image correlation learning framework that enables learning richer imaging-inspired ultrasound biomarkers emphasizing cancer features.
2. Development of an enhanced 3D-UNet-based cancer detection model that incorporates deep supervision on a pyramid of multi-scale predictions.
3. Integration of multi-institutional datasets with weak and strong labels.

Since spatial alignment is not required between the different imaging modalities to learn these richer imaging-inspired biomarkers, MIC-CUSP can be used in clinical settings where multimodal image registration is a challenge. Moreover, the richer imaging modalities are not required during inference, making MIC-CUSP clinically relevant for the 93% of prostate biopsies that use b-mode ultrasound alone. We evaluate MIC-CUSP on lesion- and patient-levels and also compare its performance in a multi-reader study.

2   Dataset

This study included two cohorts. **Cohort C1** is an internal cohort of 330 patients of whom 123 were cancer patients who underwent radical prostatectomy, and 207 were cancer-free patients with MRI-ultrasound fusion biopsies. Cohort C1 includes unaligned multimodal imaging data, namely b-mode ultrasound, MRI and post-operative histopathology images. All modalities have prostate gland segmentations and strong cancer labels annotated by expert human annotators. **Cohort C2** is a public cohort [15] of 1573 ultrasound scans from cancer and cancer-free men, but with weak radiologist labels derived through ultrasound-MRI registration. These radiologist outlines are 'weak labels' compared to cohort C1 due to (a) incorrect localization and extent on ultrasound arising from ultrasound-MRI registration errors, (b) absence of pathology-confirmation, and (c) absence of MRI-invisible lesions (lesions missed by radiologists).

Data Preprocessing: The ultrasound modality from both cohorts were resampled to $224 \times 224 \times 224$ pixels, with a pixel size of $0.42 \times 0.42 \times 0.42\,\mathrm{mm}^3$. All modality image-intensities were z-score normalized within the prostate mask.

3   Method

MIC-CUSP (Fig. 1) includes (1) registration-independent **M**ultimodal **I**mage **C**orrelations to learn richer imaging-inspired ultrasound biomarkers, and (2) Cancer Detection with these **U**ltr**S**ound biomarkers leveraging **P**retraining.

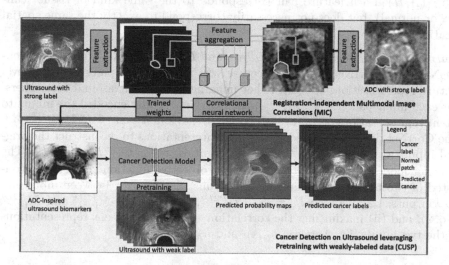

Fig. 1. Flowchart of our proposed MIC-CUSP model, with the Apparent Diffusion Coefficient (ADC)-MRI as the richer imaging modality. Same architecture is used for other richer modalities.

Registration-Independent Multimodal Image Correlations (MIC):
Apparent Diffusion Coefficient (ADC)-MRI and post-surgical prostate
histopathology images have higher information content regarding prostate cancer presence and location, than b-mode ultrasound images. ADC-inspired (AiU)
and histopathology-inspired ultrasound (HiU) biomarkers were learned by leveraging registration-independent common representation learning between ultrasound and these richer imaging modalities.

Patch-Based Feature Aggregation: Low-level texture features were extracted
from the ultrasound images (U), the ADC-MRI (A), and the whole-mount
histopathology images (H) by passing the images through the first two layers
of the pre-trained VGG-16 architecture [16], resulting in each 2D slice in each
modality having a feature map of $224 \times 224 \times 64$. The pre-trained VGG-16
architecture was chosen as the feature extractor as it has been used successfully
in prior MRI-based prostate cancer detection methods [17–19], including MRI-
pathology correlation learning frameworks [20,21]. For each patient and each
modality, multiple 2D cancer patches were extracted using the modality-specific
cancer label, and an equal number of 2D normal patches were extracted from normal regions within the prostate. Cancer patch-sizes depended on the modality-
specific cancer labels, whereas normal patch-sizes were randomly defined. An
equal number of cancer and normal patches were extracted from all three modalities. For each patch, the voxel-level features were aggregated by averaging
across the different feature channels, resulting in patch-based representations
of $U^{P2D} \in \mathbb{R}^{64}$, $A^{P2D} \in \mathbb{R}^{64}$, and $H^{P2D} \in \mathbb{R}^{64}$. Pairs of ultrasound-richer
imaging patch-level feature representations (U_i^{P2D}, M_i^{P2D}) were formed, where
$M \in (A, H)$. Each feature pair corresponds to the same kind of tissue (cancer, or normal), but does not necessarily correspond to exactly the same spatial
location.

Learning Richer Imaging-Inspired Ultrasound Biomarkers: A Correlational Neural Network (CorrNet) [22] architecture was trained with pairs of patch-level
feature representations to learn richer imaging-inspired ultrasound biomarkers.
For each input pair (U_i^{P2D}, M_i^{P2D}), the CorrNet encoder encoded the inputs to
latent representations of $h_{U_i^{P2D}} = H(WU_i^{P2D}+b)$ and $h_{M_i^{P2D}} = H(VM_i^{P2D}+b)$.
The CorrNet decoder decoded the latent representations to reconstruct the orig-
inal inputs as $U_i^{P2D\prime} = G(W'h_{U_i^{P2D}} + b')$ and $M_i^{P2D\prime} = G(V'h_{M_i^{P2D}} + b')$. The
CorrNet model was trained to optimize an objective function (Eq. 1) that con-
sisted of two terms: (i) miminizing the reconstruction error between input and
the outputs, i.e., between U_i^{P2D} and $U_i^{P2D\prime}$, and between M_i^{P2D} and $M_i^{P2D\prime}$
(Eq. 2), and (ii) maximizing the correlation between the latent representations
of the two inputs, i.e., between $h_{U_i^{P2D}}$ and $h_{M_i^{P2D}}$ (Eq. 3).

$$L_{ctotal} = L_{recon} - 2 * L_{corr} \tag{1}$$

$$L_{recon} = \sum_{i=1}^{N} \left(L(U_i^{P2D}, U_i^{P2D\prime}) + L(M_i^{P2D}, M_i^{P2D\prime}) \right) \tag{2}$$

$$L_{corr} = \frac{\sum_{i=1}^{N} \left(h_{U_i^{P2D}} - \overline{h_{U^{P2D}}} \right) \left(h_{M_i^{P2D}} - \overline{h_{M^{P2D}}} \right)}{\sqrt{\sum_{i=1}^{N} \left(h_{U_i^{P2D}} - \overline{h_{U^{P2D}}} \right)^2 \left(h_{M_i^{P2D}} - \overline{h_{M^{P2D}}} \right)^2}}. \tag{3}$$

where L in L_{recon} is the squared error between the input and the reconstructed patch-level feature representations. The L_{corr} term is weighted twice than L_{recon} term to give more weightage to the correlation error than the reconstruction error. The reconstruction error ensures that the original feature representations can be reconstructed from the latent representations, thereby ensuring that the original data is not distorted while trying to maximize the correlation.

Once trained, the latent patch-based ultrasound representations $h_{U_i^{P2D}}$ are extracted from the ultrasound images and applied on a per-voxel basis to the entire ultrasound image to form richer imaging-inspired ultrasound biomarkers. When the ultrasound biomarkers are learned through ultrasound-ADC correlations, we call them ADC-inspired ultrasound biomarker (AiU), and when they are learned through ultrasound-Histopathology correlations, we call them Histopathology-inspired ultrasound biomarkers (HiU). After training, AiU and HiU can thus be extracted in new patients without MRI or histopathology.

Cancer Detection on UltraSound (CUS) Model: Our cancer detection model is an enhanced 3D-UNet architecture [23], incorporating additional auxiliary detection heads at different resolution levels of the decoder [24], enabling integration of multi-scale information and boundary region guidance. Deep residual connections were included in both encoder and decoder blocks to allow smooth gradient propagation. Each encoder and decoder block consists of two 3D convolution layers, followed by a Rectified Linear Unit (ReLU), instance normalization layer, and a 3D convolution layer with a stride of two and a residual connection. The auxiliary detection head at each resolution level of the decoder consists of a $1 \times 1 \times 1$ convolution layer and a softmax activation function applied to the decoder output. The multi-scale predictions were upsampled to the input size, and a multi-scale deep supervision objective function (Eq. 4) consisting of a weighted sum of Dice loss and focal loss [25] was used for training:

$$\mathcal{L}_{detection}(I3D_s, y) = \frac{1}{S} \sum_{s=1}^{S} \mathcal{L}_{dice}(I3D_s, y) + \mathcal{L}_{focal}(I3D_s, y) \tag{4}$$

where $I3D_s$ denotes the 3D input at scale s, S denotes the number of multi-scale predictions, and y is the ground-truth.

Pretraining: The cancer detection model was first pre-trained with ultrasound images in Cohort C2 and weak cancer labels. The pre-trained model weights were used to initialize model training with richer imaging-inspired ultrasound biomarkers and strong labels from Cohort C1.

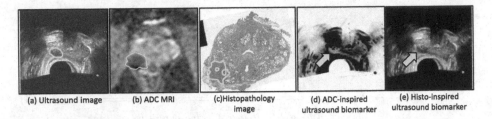

(a) Ultrasound image   (b) ADC MRI   (c)Histopathology image   (d) ADC-inspired ultrasound biomarker   (e) Histo-inspired ultrasound biomarker

Fig. 2. Ultrasound, unaligned richer modalities (ADC-MRI and histopathology), and richer imaging-inspired ultrasound biomarkers that emphasize cancer.

4   Evaluation Methods

Lesion-level, patient-level, and multi-reader comparative evaluations were performed. The evaluation metrics were averaged over lesion- and patient-level evaluations to derive a ranking score for the methods. This averaging over all metrics ensures that the evaluation strategy considers both false positives and false negatives when comparing multiple models. For both lesion-level and patient-level evaluation, $>= 1\%$ overlap between ground truth and predicted labels was considered a true positive, otherwise a false negative. Lesion-level evaluation assessed if the models detected *all* the cancerous lesions in a patient, whereas patient-level evaluation assessed if the models detected *at least* one clinically significant cancerous lesion >500 mm^3 in volume, as per the PIRADS v2 guidelines [26]. Assessment of false positives and true negatives differed for lesion- and patient-level evaluations. For lesion-level evaluation, the prostate was split into sextants, and if there were $>= 1\%$ false positive predictions in a ground truth negative sextant, it was considered a false positive. False positives in patient-level evaluations were predicted lesions with volume >500 mm^3. Four human readers M.C., S.Z., Z.K., E.S. (three medical doctors in Urology or Radiology, and one medical student) with 1–12 years of experience in interpreting prostate ultrasound images served as human readers for our multi-reader study.

5   Experimental Design

Cohort C1 was split into train-val-test splits containing 252, 37 and 41 patients respectively. The test set included 20 cancer patients and 21 cancer-free men. Entire cohort C2 was used for pretraining. The CorrNet models were trained for 500 epochs with a learning rate of 0.0005, batch size 50, and rmsprop optimizer. The cancer detection models were trained for 250 epochs with an initial learning rate of 0.0005, learning rate decay of 0.9, batch size of 2, and Adam optimizer.

Ablation Studies were performed to identify the most discriminative ADC-inspired ultrasound biomarker (AiU) and Histopathology-inspired ultrasound biomarker (HiU) from (a) two different statistical measures (mean and variance) for patch-based feature aggregation, (b) three variations of CorrNet objective function detailed in [22], and (c) variations of identity, sigmoid, and tanh CorrNet activation functions. For each ultrasound-richer imaging pair, mean absolute difference was used to rank the discriminatory power of the biomarkers and the biomarker with the highest mean absolute difference was selected. The effects of the richer imaging-inspired ultrasound biomarkers and pretraining on ultrasound-based cancer detection was then studied systematically. MIC-CUSP was also compared with (a) several top-performing medical image segmentation models, (2.5D HED [27], a 3D UNet [23], and two transformer-based approaches UNETR [28] and SwinUNETR [29]), and (b) four clinician-readers.

6   Experiments and Results

Qualitative Evaluation: AiU and HiU biomarkers help emphasize cancer features (Fig. 2). When either of these richer imaging-inspired ultrasound biomarkers are used, they improve prostate cancer detection over using b-mode ultrasound images (Fig. 3). The first two rows in Fig. 3 are from two representative cancer patients in our test cohort, while the third row shows a cancer-free man. The baseline CUS model trained with b-mode ultrasound images detected the cancer in row 1, but also had false positive predictions in all three patients. The MIC-CUSP models correctly detected both lesions in rows 1 and 2, while correctly predicting the third row patient as cancer-free. Although MIC-CUSP with HiU had small false positives in rows 2 and 3, these were <500 mm^3 in volume.

Quantitative Evaluation: When AiU and HiU are used as inputs to the CUS model instead of original ultrasound images, we see an increase in the average

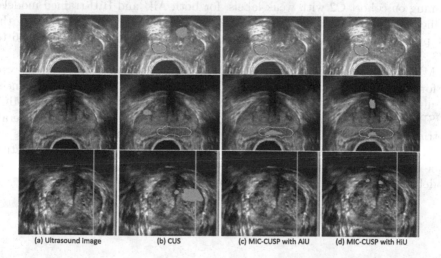

| (a) Ultrasound Image | (b) CUS | (c) MIC-CUSP with AiU | (d) MIC-CUSP with HiU |

Fig. 3. Qualitative comparison of the MIC-CUSP models with the baseline CUS model in 3 different patients (rows 1 and 2: cancer patients, row 3: cancer-free patient). Cancer labels are shown as yellow outlines, model predictions in green. (Color figure online)

Table 1. Effect of richer imaging-inspired biomarkers and pretraining on ultrasound-based cancer detection. Using richer imaging-inspired biomarkers and pre-training improves overall ultrasound-based cancer detection, as evidenced by the average metric (***bold-italic***). Se: Sensitivity; Sp: Specificity; PPV: Positive Predictive Value; NPV: Negative Predictive Value; Avg: Average

Model	Input	Lesion-level				Patient-level				Avg
		Se	Sp	PPV	NPV	Se	Sp	PPV	NPV	
Baseline ultrasound-based cancer detection model										
CUS	U	0.67	0.6	0.48	0.90	0.76	0.29	0.46	0.60	0.60
Using **richer imaging-inspired ultrasound biomarkers**										
MIC-CUS	AiU	0.41	**0.83**	0.47	0.88	0.47	**0.86**	0.73	0.67	0.66
MIC-CUS	HiU	0.52	0.78	0.52	**0.92**	0.59	**0.86**	**0.77**	0.72	0.71
Using **Pre-training** with ultrasound images and weak labels										
CUSP	U	**0.73**	0.55	0.42	0.91	**0.71**	0.33	0.46	0.58	0.59
MIC-CUSP	AiU	0.54	**0.83**	0.60	0.90	0.59	**0.86**	**0.77**	0.72	*0.73*
MIC-CUSP	HiU	0.60	0.80	**0.61**	**0.92**	0.65	0.81	0.73	**0.74**	*0.73*

performance metric from 0.60 to 0.66 and 0.71 respectively (Table 1). In particular, we notice significant improvements in patient-level specificity, positive predictive value, and negative predictive value metrics. While good at detecting cancerous patients, the CUS model with original ultrasound images also predicted significant false positives in cancer-free patients, limiting its utility. When the models are initialized with pre-trained weights obtained from pre-training on cohort C2 with weak labels, for both AiU and HiU-trained models, all metrics showed significant improvements from their respective versions without pretraining (MIC-CUSP with AiU: average metric increased from 0.66 to 0.73, MIC-CUSP with HiU: average metric increased from 0.71 from 0.73).

MIC-CUSP with either AiU or HiU also outperformed other existing top-performing medical image segmentation models when trained to detect cancer on ultrasound images (Table 2). In a multi-reader study (Table 2), our MIC-CUSP with either AiU or HiU outperformed the average human reader in overall metrics (0.73 vs. 0.70), while showing significant improvements in all metrics for patient-level evaluation, and improvement in sensitivity and negative predictive value in lesion-level evaluation. It may be noted that MIC-CUSP is the only model that outperforms an average reader (Table 2).

Table 2. Comparison of MIC-CUSP with expert clinician readers and existing top-performing medical image segmentation models. MIC-CUSP has the highest average score (***bold-italic***) among all machine learning methods, exceeding an average human reader.

		Lesion-level				Patient-level				
Human readers										
	Input	Se	Sp	PPV	NPV	Se	Sp	PPV	NPV	Avg
Reader 1	U	0.41	0.91	0.63	0.89	0.47	0.90	0.80	0.68	0.71
Reader 2	U	0.54	0.86	0.82	0.91	0.59	0.52	0.50	0.61	0.67
Reader 3	U	0.54	**0.94**	**0.96**	0.90	0.63	0.90	0.86	0.73	**0.81**
Reader 4	U	0.23	0.92	0.75	0.85	0.29	0.81	0.56	0.59	0.62
Average Reader		0.43	0.91	0.79	0.89	0.50	0.78	0.68	0.65	0.70
Top-performing medical segmentation models										
2.5D HED [27]	U	0.33	0.90	0.58	0.87	0.41	**0.95**	**0.88**	0.67	0.70
3D U-Net [23]	U	0.52	0.72	0.41	0.90	0.53	0.76	0.64	0.67	0.64
UNETR [28]	U	0.39	0.62	0.27	0.80	0.47	0.67	0.53	0.61	0.54
SwinUNETR [29]	U	**0.69**	0.62	0.40	0.91	**0.71**	0.62	0.60	0.72	0.66
Our proposed MIC-CUSP model										
MIC-CUSP	AiU	0.54	0.83	0.60	0.90	0.59	0.86	0.77	0.72	*0.73*
MIC-CUSP	HiU	0.60	0.80	0.61	**0.92**	0.65	0.81	0.73	**0.74**	*0.73*

7   Conclusion and Discussion

We presented MIC-CUSP, a b-mode ultrasound-based prostate cancer detection system that leverages registration-independent multimodal image correlations, 3D convolutional neural networks with deep supervision on a pyramid of multi-scale predictions, and pretraining to combine weakly-labeled and strongly-labeled data. Our evaluations show encouraging performance of MIC-CUSP, outperforming an average human clinician-reader. MIC-CUSP does not require richer imaging modalities during inference making it clinically relevant. Furthermore, MIC-CUSP does not require spatial alignment between multimodal imaging to learn richer imaging-inspired biomarkers, making it useful for clinical situations where multimodal image registration is challenging.

References

1. Ahmed, H.U., et al.: Diagnostic accuracy of multi-parametric MRI and TRUS biopsy in prostate cancer (PROMIS): a paired validating confirmatory study. Lancet **389**(10071), 815–822 (2017)
2. Rouvière, O., et al.: Use of prostate systematic and targeted biopsy on the basis of multiparametric MRI in biopsy-naive patients (MRI-first): a prospective, multicentre, paired diagnostic study. Lancet Oncol. **20**(1), 100–109 (2019)
3. Gaffney, C.D., et al.: Increasing utilization of MRI before prostate biopsy in black and non-black men: an analysis of the seer-medicare cohort. Am. J. Roentgenol. **217**(2), 389–394 (2021)
4. Choi, Y.H., et al.: Comparison of cancer detection rates between TRUS-guided biopsy and MRI-targeted biopsy according to PSA level in biopsy-naive patients: a propensity score matching analysis. Clin. Genitourin. Cancer **17**(1), e19–e25 (2019)
5. Azizi, S., et al.: Deep recurrent neural networks for prostate cancer detection: analysis of temporal enhanced ultrasound. IEEE Trans. Med. Imaging **37**(12), 2695–2703 (2018)
6. Schimmöller, L., et al.: MRI-guided in-bore biopsy: differences between prostate cancer detection and localization in primary and secondary biopsy settings. Am. J. Roentgenol. **206**(1), 92–99 (2016). PMID: 26700339
7. Ahmed, H.U., El-Shater Bosaily, A., et al.: Diagnostic accuracy of multi-parametric MRI and TRUS biopsy in prostate cancer (PROMIS): a paired validating confirmatory study. Lancet **389**(10071), 815–822 (2017)
8. Hassan, M.R., et al.: Prostate cancer classification from ultrasound and MRI images using deep learning based explainable artificial intelligence. Futur. Gener. Comput. Syst. **127**, 462–472 (2022)
9. Han, S.M., Lee, H.J., Choi, J.Y.: Computer-aided prostate cancer detection using texture features and clinical features in ultrasound image. J. Digit. Imaging **21**(1), 121–133 (2008)
10. Wildeboer, R.R., Mannaerts, C.K., van Sloun, R.J.G., et al.: Automated multiparametric localization of prostate cancer based on b-mode, shear-wave elastography, and contrast-enhanced ultrasound radiomics. Eur. Radiol. **30**(2), 806–815 (2020)
11. Azizi, S., et al.: Learning from noisy label statistics: detecting high grade prostate cancer in ultrasound guided biopsy. In: Frangi, A.F., Schnabel, J.A., Davatzikos, C., Alberola-López, C., Fichtinger, G. (eds.) MICCAI 2018. LNCS, vol. 11073, pp. 21–29. Springer, Cham (2018). https://doi.org/10.1007/978-3-030-00937-3_3
12. Moradi, M., Abolmaesumi, P., Siemens, et al.: P6C-7 ultrasound RF time series for detection of prostate cancer: feature selection and frame rate analysis. In: 2007 IEEE Ultrasonics Symposium Proceedings, pp. 2493–2496 (2007)
13. Imani, F., Abolmaesumi, P., Gibson, M., et al.: Computer-aided prostate cancer detection using ultrasound RF time series: in vivo feasibility study. IEEE Trans. Med. Imaging **34**(11), 2248–2257 (2015)
14. Sedghi, A., Pesteie, M., Javadi, G., et al.: Deep neural maps for unsupervised visualization of high-grade cancer in prostate biopsies. IJCARS **14**(6), 1009–1016 (2019)
15. Natarajan, S., Priester, A., Margolis, D., Huang, J., Marks, L.: Prostate MRI and ultrasound with pathology and coordinates of tracked biopsy (prostate-MRI-US-biopsy) (2020)

16. Simonyan, K., Zisserman, A.: Very deep convolutional networks for large-scale image recognition. In: Bengio, Y., LeCun, Y. (eds.) 3rd International Conference on Learning Representations, ICLR 2015, San Diego, CA, USA, 7–9 May 2015, Conference Track Proceedings (2015)

17. Abraham, B., Nair, M.S.: Automated grading of prostate cancer using convolutional neural network and ordinal class classifier. Inform. Med. Unlock. **17**, 100256 (2019)

18. Salama, W.M., Aly, M.H.: Prostate cancer detection based on deep convolutional neural networks and support vector machines: a novel concern level analysis. Multimed. Tools Appl. **80**, 1–13 (2021)

19. Alkadi, R., Taher, F., El-Baz, A., Werghi, N.: A deep learning-based approach for the detection and localization of prostate cancer in t2 magnetic resonance images. J. Digit. Imaging **32**(5), 793–807 (2019)

20. Bhattacharya, I., et al.: CorrSigNet: learning CORRelated prostate cancer SIGnatures from radiology and pathology images for improved computer aided diagnosis. In: Martel, A.L., et al. (eds.) MICCAI 2020. LNCS, vol. 12262, pp. 315–325. Springer, Cham (2020). https://doi.org/10.1007/978-3-030-59713-9_31

21. Bhattacharya, I., Seetharaman, A., Kunder, C., et al.: Selective identification and localization of indolent and aggressive prostate cancers via corrsignia: an MRI-pathology correlation and deep learning framework. Med. Image Anal. **75**, 102288 (2022)

22. Chandar, S., Khapra, M.M., Larochelle, H., Ravindran, B.: Correlational neural networks. Neural Comput. **28**(2), 257–285 (2016)

23. Çiçek, Ö., Abdulkadir, A., Lienkamp, S.S., Brox, T., Ronneberger, O.: 3D U-net: learning dense volumetric segmentation from sparse annotation. In: Ourselin, S., Joskowicz, L., Sabuncu, M.R., Unal, G., Wells, W. (eds.) MICCAI 2016. LNCS, vol. 9901, pp. 424–432. Springer, Cham (2016). https://doi.org/10.1007/978-3-319-46723-8_49

24. Lin, T.Y., Dollar, P., Girshick, R., He, K., Hariharan, B., Belongie, S.: Feature pyramid networks for object detection. In: Proceedings of the IEEE Conference on Computer Vision and Pattern Recognition (CVPR) (2017)

25. Yeung, M., Sala, E., Schönlieb, C.B., Rundo, L.: Unified focal loss: generalising dice and cross entropy-based losses to handle class imbalanced medical image segmentation. Comput. Med. Imaging Graph. **95**, 102026 (2022)

26. Turkbey, B., et al.: Prostate imaging reporting and data system version 2.1: 2019 update of prostate imaging reporting and data system version 2. Eur. Urol. **76**(3) (2019) 340–351

27. Xie, S., Tu, Z.: Holistically-nested edge detection. In: Proceedings of the IEEE International Conference on Computer Vision, pp. 1395–1403 (2015)

28. Hatamizadeh, A., Tang, Y., Nath, et al.: UNETR: transformers for 3D medical image segmentation. In: 2022 WACV, pp. 1748–1758 (2022)

29. Hatamizadeh, A., Nath, V., Tang, Y., Yang, D., Roth, H.R., Xu, D.: Swin UNETR: swin transformers for semantic segmentation of brain tumors in MRI images. In: Crimi, A., Bakas, S. (eds.) BrainLes 2021. LNCS, vol. 12962, pp. 272–284. Springer, Cham (2022). https://doi.org/10.1007/978-3-031-08999-2_22

GAJA - Guided self-Acquisition of Joint ultrAsound images

Marco Colussi[1]([✉]), Sergio Mascetti[1], Dragan Ahmetovic[1],
Gabriele Civitarese[1], Marco Cacciatori[1], Flora Peyvandi[2,3],
Roberta Gualtierotti[2,3], Sara Arcudi[2,3], and Claudio Bettini[1]

[1] Department of Computer Science, Universitá Degli Studi di Milano,
Via Celoria, 18, 20133 Milan, Italy
marco.colussi@unimi.it
[2] Department of Pathophysiology and Transplantation, Universitá Degli Studi di
Milano, Via Pace, 9, 20122 Milan, Italy
[3] Fondazione IRCCS Ca' Granda Ospedale Maggiore Policlinico, Angelo Bianchi
Bonomi Hemophilia and Thrombosis Center, Via Pace, 9, 20122 Milan, Italy

Abstract. People with hemophilia require frequent diagnoses of joint
bleeding. This is currently achieved with visits to specialized centers.
One possibility is to have a point-of-care acquisition of the ultrasound
joint image by the patients themselves, followed by a remote evaluation
by the practitioner. However, the acquisition of US images is operator-
dependent, so it is unclear to what extent patients can acquire images
that are suitable for remote diagnosis. In this paper, we present GAJA
(Guided Acquisition of Joint ultrAsound), an application designed to
guide the patient in collecting US images of their own joints, which are
then transmitted to a medical practitioner. GAJA uses a collaborative
interaction approach, in which an expert practitioner collects a reference
US image of a specific scan during an in-person clinical visit. Anatomical
markers for the target joint are automatically extracted and then used
as a reference to guide the patient in properly positioning the US probe.

Keywords: Ultrasound · Guidance · Portable probe · Hemophilia

1 Introduction

People with hemophilia can experience joint bleeding that, if not promptly
treated, can result in synovial hyperplasia, osteochondral damage, and hemophilic
arthropathy [12]. To promptly recognize joint bleeding, hemophilic patients

This work was partially supported by the project MUSA - Multilayered Urban Sustain-
ability Action - project, funded by the European Union - NextGenerationEU, under the
National Recovery and Resilience Plan (NRRP) Mission 4 Component 2 Investment
Line 1.5: Strenghtening of research structures and creation of R&D "innovation ecosys-
tems", set up of "territorial leaders in R&D", and by the Italian Ministry of Health
- Bando Ricerca Corrente. The Fondazione IRCCS Ca' Granda Ospedale Maggiore
Policlinico is member of the European Reference Network (ERN) EuroBloodNet.

B. Kainz et al. (Eds.): ASMUS 2023, LNCS 14337, pp. 132–141, 2023.
https://doi.org/10.1007/978-3-031-44521-7_13

should be regularly visited in specialized centers, particularly in the presence of joint aches. The diagnosis of joint bleeding performed in specialized centers is based on a series of medical history questions and an instrumental examination using magnetic resonance (MRI) or ultrasound (US) images [11,18]. Although MRI is considered the gold standard for this diagnosis, it is not always a practical solution due to its high costs, limited availability, and long examination times [17]. Instead, US is known to be highly operator dependent and therefore requires a highly specialized practitioner [2].

One limitation of the current approach is that it is not always possible for the patient to attend frequent visits (e.g., due to the distance from the specialized center). Similarly, frequent and urgent visits can be hard to manage by the specialized center for a number of reasons, including the limited availability of medical personnel and the costs. In order to address these issues, the University of Milan and the Policlinico of Milan are designing a telemedicine system for at-home joint bleeding diagnosis. The idea of the system is that each hemophilic patient is provided with a portable ultrasound probe connected to a portable computer. When necessary, as a routine check or in case of pain, the patient uses the probe to acquire ultrasound images of the joints[1] and sends them through the computer to the specialized center where a medical practitioner remotely assesses the presence of joint bleeding, supported by a CAD tool using techniques already proposed in the literature for this problem [6,10].

One of the main challenges of the system is that the acquisition of ultrasound images is operator dependent, so it is unclear to what extent the patients can acquire images that are suitable for remote diagnosis. This problem has been addressed in the literature with two different approaches: to teach the patients how to acquire the image so that they can repeat the process without additional support [9] or to guide the acquisition in real-time with remote support by a medical practitioner [3]. The limit of the former approach is that patients tend to forget how to acquire the images [1], while the latter approach is time-consuming for the medical practitioners.

To overcome the limitations of existing approaches, this paper presents GAJA (Guided self-Acquisition of Joint ultrAsound images), an application that provides an automated guiding system to support the patient in the acquisition of joint ultrasound images. GAJA is designed to combine the benefits of existing solutions: on one side, it guides the patient in real-time during the acquisition process, on the other side it does not require the practitioner to remotely supervise the acquisition process. Currently, GAJA is a working prototype that supports the acquisition of knee joint ultrasound images.

2   State of the Art

The use of portable US imaging systems has been extensively investigated in the literature [7,13,15]. Such devices were initially conceived to allow clinicians

---

[1] We use the term "patient" to denote the person in charge of acquiring the ultrasound images but actually it can be the patient or a caregiver.

to make diagnoses at point-of-care (*e.g.*, scene of an accident, patient's home). Three approaches have been proposed in the literature.

The first approach is to train the patients so that they can independently acquire US images [5,9,19].A different approach is to rely on teleguidance, meaning that a medical practitioner supports in real-time the patient during US image acquisition. Teleguidance can be provided by the medical practitioner that observes the US feed (as in [3,16]), possibly combined with the video from other cameras [16]. In [4], the authors suggest that 5G technologies will play a major role to make teleguidance practical in real-world scenarios, and indeed several research groups are exploring it in the general medical domain [3,16]. One limitation of teleguidance is that it requires the availability of human experts to remotely support the patients in performing US scans.

A recent and closely related study compares these two approaches considering the problem of hemophilic patients that use portable probes for self-collection of US images of their joints, with the objective of reducing hospital visits [1]. One of the results of this work is that, even if patients follow a dedicated training session (lasting 4–5 h), the quality of the self-collected images (without any type of real-time assistance) significantly degrades over time. This suggests that simply training the patients is not sufficient for high-quality self-imaging. Interestingly, this work also shows that high-quality images can be self-collected when patients were assisted with teleguidance (*i.e.*, with human operators remotely assisting the patients). However, the problem analysis conducted in our study uncovered that this solution is impractical in our scenario because it is considered too time-consuming for medical practitioners.

The third approach is based on automated guidance, meaning that the patient is guided to correctly position the probe by an AI system. Existing works adopt a camera mounted on the probe to locate and guide the probe positioning [8,20]. The proposed system, GAJA, also adopts an automated guidance approach, but it does not require an external camera, and instead, it only uses the feed from the probe.

3 Interaction Design

GAJA was designed by a multi-disciplinary research team involving computer scientists and medical practitioners. The *Automate-Guide-Remind* design principle was defined in the process and a collaborative interaction approach was adopted.

3.1 "Automate-Guide-Remind" Design Principle

Previous papers show that learning to self-acquire US images is difficult and that patients tend to forget how to use and position the probe after some time. We conjecture that this is partially due to the large number of actions that the patient is required to complete and that affect the successful acquisition of US images: the probe positioning on the body, its inclination, the joint flexion, putting the gel on the probe, and setting the probe parameters. To mitigate this problem we introduce the *Automate-Guide-Remind* design principle. According to this principle, as many actions as possible should be **automated** so that the patient is not in charge of them. The actions that cannot be automated, and that require extensive practice and deep domain knowledge, which usually only medical practitioners acquire during their training, should be **guided**, meaning that the system should provide automatic instructions in real-time on how to use the system. For the remaining actions, which cannot be automated or guided, clear **reminders** should be automatically provided by the system. These actions should only include those that are easy to explain to the patient and that the patient can easily complete.

To implement the *Automate-Guide-Remind* design principle we identified the set of all actions required to successfully acquire a US image, and divided them into three classes:

- **Automated actions**. This class contains actions that can be totally automated and hence are not in charge of the patient. For example, in GAJA the probe parameters (scan depth and gain) are tuned by the practitioner in a setup phase and saved as presets for each scan. During self-acquisition, these parameters are automatically loaded without intervention by the patient.
- **Guided actions**. These are the actions that the patient does while guided in real-time by the system. In GAJA they include the fine positioning of the probe on the body as well as the exact joint flexion.
- **Reminded actions**. These actions are performed independently by the patient, possibly after initial training and with reminders provided during use. In GAJA these actions include general probe usage (*e.g.*, apply the gel on the probe) as well as scan-specific coarse positioning. For example, in the sub-quadricipital recess (SQR) longitudinal scan the probe should be centered on the leg and parallel to the femur. The patient learns to use the probe and to position it during an initial physical visit with the medical practitioner (the setup step, see Sect. 3.2). When patients need to use GAJA independently, they can access quick reminders as well as a detailed video explanation (by clicking the 'HELP' button) (*e.g.*, see Fig. 1).

Based on this design criterion, in the specific case of the SQR longitudinal scan, we identified two **Guided actions** shown in Fig. 2 where the solid orange boxes represent the current patella position, while the dashed boxes represent the target area where the patella should be positioned. Similarly, the purple boxes represent the femur. The two **Guided actions** are: positioning the probe with the correct distance from the knee (see Fig. 2a) and flexing the knee to the right angle (see Fig. 2b). These actions are particularly important because even small errors can make the acquired US image unsuitable for the diagnosis. In particular, as the probe gets closer to the knee (see Fig. 2a left), the patella (rigid orange box in Fig. 2a right) moves right in the scan. Similarly, increasing the knee flexion angle (see Fig. 2b left) moves the femur down in the scan. We empirically selected these two actions based on the experience of the medical practitioners in our research team.

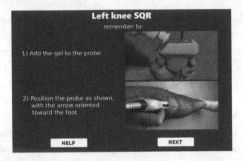

Fig. 1. Instructions provided before the self-acquisition

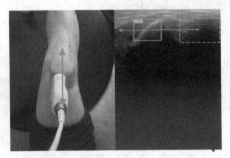
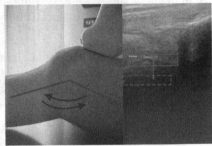

(a) Probe distance from the knee   (b) Knee flexion

Fig. 2. Effect of moving the probe or the knee angle

3.2   Collaborative Interaction Approach

GAJA adopts a collaborative interaction approach between the medical practitioner and the patient. The approach consists of a *setup* step in which the medical practitioner and the patient collaborate in person and a *self-acquisition* step in which the patient independently acquires the image.

Setup Step. The setup step is conducted during an in-person clinical visit by an expert medical practitioner who trains the patient (preliminary results show that a training session of about 10 min is sufficient) and collects a **reference image** for each target joint scan[2]. The collection of reference images is particularly relevant because the correct probe positioning may vary between patients having different physical characteristics and health conditions, hence it is important to personalize the probe position for each patient.

During the training, the practitioner shows how to use the system and provides basic instructions on how to coarsely position the probe and how to follow the guidance instructions. During the reference image collection, scan-specific

---

[2] A scan is a specific view of a body part obtained by positioning the probe in a consistent way.

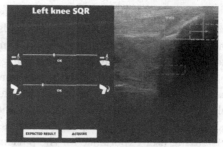

(a) Setup step by the practitioner   (b) Self-acquisition by the patient

Fig. 3. GAJA two-step image acquisition procedure

anatomical markers are automatically extracted from the US image using object detection techniques. For example, Fig. 3a shows the detected positions of the patella and of the femur in the SQR scan of the knee. The practitioner positions the probe, confirming that the markers are positioned correctly, and acquires a single US image for each scan. While performing this procedure, the practitioner also specifies the scan depth and gain parameters that are stored by GAJA. Note that these parameters should be tuned for each scan and patient.

Self-acquisition Step. Self-acquisition requires the patient to complete a set of tasks. First, the target joint to scan is selected from a list, thus loading the probe parameters (**Automated action**). The patient then files a clinical history questionnaire (*e.g.*, does the joint hurt?). Then, a screen containing text indications and images (see Fig. 1) reminds the patient to perform **Reminded actions** which include adding the gel on the probe and its coarse positioning.

Next, the patient fine-tunes the probe position through a **Guided action**. The guidance is provided with two simultaneous modalities. On the right side of the interface (see Fig. 3b), visual feed from the probe is overlaid with the bounding boxes of the detected anatomical markers present in the feed (continuous border). The patient has to align the anatomical markers with the target areas (with dashed border) of the same color, which are extracted from the reference image collected by the practitioner. For example, in Fig. 3b the solid boxes represent the current position of the patella (orange) and femur (purple), while the dashed rectangles represent their position in the reference image.

The left frame provides symbolic indicators of the quality of the current positioning, rendered as sliders, each corresponding to a positioning parameter. Icons at the beginning and at the end of the slider indicate the range of the movements that govern the corresponding parameter. The sliding indicator is centered on the line when the positioning is correct, and it is displaced laterally if the patient needs to perform alignment corrections with respect to that parameter. In the above example, the upper sliding indicator is displaced slightly to the left, indicating that the probe should be approached to the knee.

Once the probe is correctly positioned (see Sect. 4.2) a message informs the user to hold the probe still for 3 seconds. This was required because we empirically observed that the first acquired images are motion-blurred and requiring the patient to hold the device still mitigates this problem.

We also observe that, although the probe is correctly positioned, it is possible that the acquired image is unsuitable, for example, due to blurriness or lack of gel. However, sending an unsuitable image to the practitioner would result in a delay in the diagnosis process, a loss of time for the practitioner, and in a frustrating user experience for the patient. To mitigate this problem, we adopted two solutions. First, GAJA acquires a set of images (instead of a single one), as this increases the chances that at least one of them is suitable. Second, we use a ML model to check if at least one of the collected images is suitable. Thanks to this model, the user can be immediately informed if no image is suitable and can re-acquire the images. Once a set of images is acquired, they are sent to the server where they are stored for the medical practitioner to use in order to formulate a diagnosis. Note that the larger the set of images sent to the medical practitioners, the longer it could take them for finding a suitable one. In order to speed up the diagnosis process, images are ordered according to the suitability as computed by the ML model, so that the images with the highest likelihood of being suitable can be processed first.

4   Implementation

4.1   Architecture

GAJA was implemented as a Windows application and current prototype runs on *Surface GO3*[3], a touchscreen-based portable device. The device is connected to the portable probe *MicrUS Pro-L40S* manufactured by *Telemed, Lithuania*[4] through a USB-C cable. The application requires bi-directional communication with the ultrasound probe in order to acquire images in real-time and to change the settings (*e.g.*, depth and gain). This was achieved through an SDK made available by the probe manufacturer. Thanks to this solution, the GAJA app can access the ultrasound stream of images in real-time, hence making it possible to locally process the images and show the result in real-time.

The data produced by GAJA (questionnaire answers, images, and other metadata, including the detected bounding boxes, and acquisition time) are transmitted to a remote server, hosted at the hospital, which stores them. The server also hosts a web app that the practitioner can use to visualize the data acquired by various patients through GAJA and to provide the diagnoses.

4.2   Implementation of Machine Learning Models

GAJA uses two machine learning models: one to detect the anatomical markers, and the other for classifying images suitability.

---

[3] https://tinyurl.com/go-3-surface.
[4] https://www.telemedultrasound.com/micrus-pro.

In order to implement the former model we trained a YOLO V5 [14] architecture that provides a nano version specifically designed to require low memory and provide fast computation also on low-performance devices. Our preliminary results show a mean Average Precision at 0.5 IoU (mAP@0.5) of 0.986 and 0.922 for the patella and femur, respectively. The model was then exported in the *onnx* format to be used in GAJA. The model processing time on the portable device is about 150 milliseconds. Considering the other computations that are required for each frame (e.g., drawing the bounding boxes, acquiring the frame) GAJA is able to process approximately 4 images per second.

The detection model returns, for each processed frame, the bounding boxes of the detected anatomical markers. Since the model can recognize each anatomical marker more than once in each frame, we only consider the prediction for each class with the highest confidence.

The bounding boxes are then displayed as an overlay over the US frame stream. In order to smooth the movements of the bounding boxes as they appear to the user, we adopted a moving average that considers the current and the two previous frames.

Preliminary results suggest that the features that most impact image suitability are the horizontal position of the center of the patella bounding box and the vertical position of the center of the femur bounding box. Hence, for each processed frame, the procedure computes the horizontal distance between the centers of the patella bounding boxes of the current frame and of the reference image. If the distance is smaller than a given threshold, the patella is considered in the correct position. Similarly, GAJA detects if the femur is in the correct position by considering the vertical distance. If both the patella and the femur are in the correct position, then the probe is correctly positioned.

The latter model (classification of image suitability) was implemented as a convolutional neural network based on **InceptionV3** [21]. Our preliminary results show an average F1-score of 0.85. In this particular task, the processing time is slower as a result of the model complexity. Hence this model does not run in real-time. The model is currently running on the device but we plan to run it on the server in the future.

5   Conclusions and Future Work

Portable ultrasound (US) devices have the potential to play a significant role in the context of e-health due to their affordability and non-invasive nature. This is particularly relevant for people with chronic diseases (like hemophilia) that could use self-acquisition to ease the diagnosis process. One of the main factors that are currently limiting the diffusion of this solution is the lack of a practical solution that allows the patient to independently self-acquire suitable images. GAJA addresses this problem, in the specific case of joint US images for hemophilic patients, with a solution that is practical in terms of hardware and software requirements and that appears to be effective in the preliminary experiments we conducted.

The main limitation of this contribution is the lack of formal system validation, in particular from the point of view of its usability by the patient. We are indeed in the process of conducting a user study, aimed at assessing the ability of the system to guide patients in collecting reliable US scans. The two main metrics which we will consider in the evaluation are the time required by the patient to fine-tune the probe position and the percentage of auto-acquisition sessions that contain at least one suitable image (as assessed by a medical practitioner). A longitudinal study will also measure to what extent GAJA can be used by the patients over a long period, as previous works [1] uncovered that it can be challenging for patients to remember how to use the system. We conjecture that, since GAJA adopts the *Automate-Guide-Remind* design principle, it will substantially mitigate this problem.

References

1. Aguero, P., Barnes, R.F., Flores, A., von Drygalski, A.: Teleguidance for patient self-imaging of hemophilic joints using mobile ultrasound devices: A pilot study. J. Ultrasound Med. **42**(3), 701–712 (2023)
2. American College of Radiology (ACR), Society for Pediatric Radiology (SPR), Society of Radiologists in Ultrasound (SRU): AIUM practice guideline for the performance of a musculoskeletal ultrasound examination. J. Ultrasound Med. Official J. Am. Inst. Ultrasound Med. **31**(9), 1473–1488 (2012)
3. Baribeau, Y., et al.: Handheld point-of-care ultrasound probes: the new generation of pocus. J. Cardiothorac. Vasc. Anesth. **34**(11), 3139–3145 (2020)
4. Berlet, M., et al.: Emergency telemedicine mobile ultrasounds using a 5g-enabled application: development and usability study. JMIR Formative Res. **6**(5), e36824 (2022)
5. Chiem, A.T., Lim, G.W., Tabibnia, A.P., Takemoto, A.S., Weingrow, D.M., Shibata, J.E.: Feasibility of patient-performed lung ultrasound self-exams (patient-plus) as a potential approach to telemedicine in heart failure. ESC Heart Failure **8**(5), 3997–4006 (2021)
6. Colussi, M., et al.: Ultrasound detection of subquadricipital recess distension. Intelligent Systems with Applications p. 200183 (2023)
7. Corte, G., et al.: Performance of a handheld ultrasound device to assess articular and periarticular pathologies in patients with inflammatory arthritis. Diagnostics **11**(7), 1139 (2021)
8. Culbertson, H., Walker, J.M., Raitor, M., Okamura, A.M., Stolka, P.J.: Plane Assist: The Influence of Haptics on Ultrasound-Based Needle Guidance. In: Ourselin, S., Joskowicz, L., Sabuncu, M.R., Unal, G., Wells, W. (eds.) MICCAI 2016. LNCS, vol. 9900, pp. 370–377. Springer, Cham (2016). https://doi.org/10.1007/978-3-319-46720-7_43
9. Duggan, N.M., et al.: Novice-performed point-of-care ultrasound for home-based imaging. Sci. Rep. **12**(1), 20461 (2022)
10. Gualtierotti, R., et al.: A computer-aided diagnosis tool for the detection of hemarthrosis by remote joint ultrasound in patients with hemophilia. Blood **140**(Supplement 1), 464–465 (2022)
11. Gualtierotti, R., Solimeno, L.P., Peyvandi, F.: Hemophilic arthropathy: current knowledge and future perspectives. Journal of Thrombosis and Haemostasis **19**(9), 2112–2121 (2021)

12. Hilgartner, M.W.: Current treatment of hemophilic arthropathy. Current Opin. Podiatr. **14**(1), 46–49 (2002)

13. Huang, Q., Zheng, Y., Lu, M., Chi, Z.: Development of a portable 3d ultrasound imaging system for musculoskeletal tissues. Ultrasonics **43**(3), 153–163 (2005)

14. Jocher, G.: YOLOv5 by Ultralytics (2020). https://doi.org/10.5281/zenodo. 3908559, https://github.com/ultralytics/yolov5

15. Kim, G.D.: A single FPGA-based portable ultrasound imaging system for point-of-care applications. IEEE Trans. Ultrasonics Ferroelectr. Freq. Control **59**(7), 1386–1394 (2012)

16. McBeth, P.B., et al.: Simple, almost anywhere, with almost anyone: remote low-cost telementored resuscitative lung ultrasound. J. Trauma Acute Care Surg. **71**(6), 1528–1535 (2011)

17. Plut, D., et al.: Diagnostic accuracy of haemophilia early arthropathy detection with ultrasound (head-us): a comparative magnetic resonance imaging (mri) study. Radiol. Oncol. **53**(2), 178–186 (2019)

18. Roosendaal, G., Lafeber, F.P.: Blood-induced joint damage in hemophilia. In: Seminars in thrombosis and hemostasis. vol. 29, pp. 037–042. Copyright 2003 by Thieme Medical Publishers Inc, 333 Seventh Avenue, New... (2003)

19. Schneider, E., et al.: Can dialysis patients identify and diagnose pulmonary congestion using self-lung ultrasound? J. Clin. Med. **12**(11), 3829 (2023)

20. Sun, S.Y., Gilbertson, M., Anthony, B.W.: Computer-guided ultrasound probe realignment by optical tracking. In: 2013 IEEE 10th International Symposium on Biomedical Imaging. pp. 21–24. IEEE (2013)

21. Szegedy, C., Vanhoucke, V., Ioffe, S., Shlens, J., Wojna, Z.: Rethinking the inception architecture for computer vision. In: Proceedings of the IEEE Conference on Computer Vision and Pattern Recognition, pp. 2818–2826 (2016)

Privileged Anatomical and Protocol Discrimination in Trackerless 3D Ultrasound Reconstruction

Qi Li[1]([✉]), Ziyi Shen[1], Qian Li[1,2], Dean C. Barratt[1], Thomas Dowrick[1], Matthew J. Clarkson[1], Tom Vercauteren[3], and Yipeng Hu[1]

[1] Centre for Medical Image Computing, Wellcome/EPSRC Centre for Interventional and Surgical Sciences, Department of Medical Physics and Biomedical Engineering, University College London, London, UK
qi.li.21@ucl.ac.uk
[2] State Key Laboratory of Robotics and System, Harbin Institute of Technology, Harbin, China
[3] School of Biomedical Engineering & Imaging Sciences, King's College London, London, UK

Abstract. Three-dimensional (3D) freehand ultrasound (US) reconstruction without using any additional external tracking device has seen recent advances with deep neural networks (DNNs). In this paper, we first investigated two identified contributing factors of the learned interframe correlation that enable the DNN-based reconstruction: anatomy and protocol. We propose to incorporate the ability to represent these two factors - readily available during training - as the privileged information to improve existing DNN-based methods. This is implemented in a new multi-task method, where the *anatomical* and *protocol* discrimination are used as auxiliary tasks. We further develop a differentiable network architecture to optimise the branching location of these auxiliary tasks, which controls the ratio between shared and task-specific network parameters, for maximising the benefits from the two auxiliary tasks. Experimental results, on a dataset with 38 forearms of 19 volunteers acquired with 6 different scanning protocols, show that 1) both anatomical and protocol variances are enabling factors for DNN-based US reconstruction; 2) learning how to discriminate different subjects (anatomical variance) and predefined types of scanning paths (protocol variance) both significantly improve frame prediction accuracy, volume reconstruction overlap, accumulated tracking error and final drift, using the proposed algorithm.

Keywords: Freehand ultrasound · Privileged information · Multi-task learning

1 Introduction

3D ultrasound (US) reconstruction is a promising technique both for diagnostics and image guidance, such as image fusion with other image modalities [5],

B. Kainz et al. (Eds.): ASMUS 2023, LNCS 14337, pp. 142–151, 2023.
https://doi.org/10.1007/978-3-031-44521-7_14

registration with preoperative data during surgery [3], volume visualisation and measurement [2]. Currently, most clinically applied 3D reconstruction of 2D freehand US imaging use spatial tracking devices, such as optical, electromagnetic or mechanical positioning [12]. Research for reducing dependency on external devices in such 3D US reconstruction has been motivated for its portability, accessibility and low-cost. Previous non-learning-based methods utilised the speckle correlation between US frames [1,3]. In recent learning-based approaches, convolutional neural networks and their variants have been proposed to use two adjacent frames as network input [10,15,16], for predicting spatial transformation between them. More generally, sequential modelling methods, e.g. using recurrent neural network [4,7,8,11] and transformer [14], have also been tested with the same goal of localising relative positions between two or more US frames.

With the promising results from deep learning, one might question what was learned in these data-driven approaches for predicting inter-frame transformations. Specifically, in addition to speckle patterns (which holds within a limited spatial scale), what are other factors that generated correlation between US frames, such that their relative locations can be inferred?

We first hypothesized that two factors, common anatomical characteristics between subjects and predefined scanning protocols, are responsible for such predictability in this application. A variance-reduction study is presented in Sect. 3.2 to demonstrate that sufficient anatomical and protocol variance in training data is indeed required for the reconstruction.

In this work, we propose to encode the anatomical and protocol patterns using two classification tasks, discriminating between subjects and between types of scanning paths, respectively. We then investigate methods to train these tasks together with the main reconstruction task to improve the performance of the main task.

In addition to US images as network input, previous studies have also integrated additional information or signals, such as optical flow [21] between US frames and acceleration, orientation, angular rates from inertial measurement units (IMU) [8,9]. Optical flow was derived from image sequence itself, while the IMU-measured signals are required at both training and inference. Different to these applications, the proposed discrimination task labels, subject and protocol indices, are in general available during training, but not required at inference, thus known as privileged information [19], further discussed in Sect. 2.1.

In summary, our contributions include 1) a multi-task learning approach to formulate two factors in freehand US as privileged information, for improving reconstruction accuracy; 2) a mixture model formulation for optimisable branching locations for auxiliary tasks, implemented with a differentiable network and a gradient-based bi-level optimisation; 3) extensive experimental results to quantify the improved performance due to the privileged tasks; and 4) open-source code and data[1] for public access and reproducibility.

---

[1] https://github.com/ucl-candi/freehand.

2 Method

2.1 Preliminaries: Privileged Auxiliary Tasks and Shared Parameters

Assume a main task $f_\theta(y|x)$ that predicts y with input data x (here, using a θ-parameterised neural network), which is optimised alongside $\mathcal{J}$ auxiliary tasks $f_{\theta_j^s, \theta_j^a}(y_j^a|x)$, $j = 1, ..., \mathcal{J}$, where θ_j^s are shared parameters (with the main task), and θ_j^a are task-specific parameters, both for predicting y_j^a. Therefore, $\theta_j^s \subseteq \theta$ and $\theta_j^a \cap \theta = \emptyset$. When the goal is to predict y from x, the supervision and prediction of auxiliary task are only required during training. The main task benefits from this privileged information, which is not required at inference.

Such multi-task learning incorporates the privileged information but may suffer from absolute negative transfer [20] - here, when the additional auxiliary tasks negatively impact the main task performance, and/or relative negative transfer - one auxiliary task reduces the main-task-improving potentials from the other auxiliary task(s). One approach for reducing negative transfer, or optimising the transferability, is adjusting the ratio between the shared θ_j^s and task-specific θ_j^a parameters [13]. As no parameters are shared (i.e. $\theta_j^s = \emptyset$), no negative transfer is possible (although any benefit from this auxiliary task also diminishes).

Assume a binary task descriptor z_j (extended to a one-hot vector in Sect. 2.3) indicating the use of the jth auxiliary task. The main task is thus conditioned on the use of the auxiliary task $f_{\theta, \theta_j^a}(y|x, z_j)$. Importantly, where to place the task descriptor z_j determines which and how many network parameters θ_j^s are shared. As in Fig. 1 (a), the closer the task descriptor is to the input, i.e. early branching, the less shared parameters.

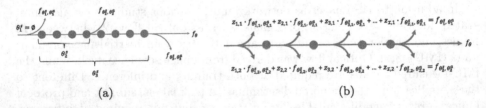

(a)   (b)

Fig. 1. Example of network architectures with (a) various possible branching locations with different shared parameters and (b) two auxiliary tasks, each modelled as a mixture of $\mathcal{I}$ candidate tasks.

2.2 Example Auxiliary Tasks: Anatomical and Protocol Discrimination

Each auxiliary task is trained with a cross-entropy loss, between predicted class probability vectors y_j^a and ground-truth targets t_j^a in one-hot vectors.

$$\mathcal{L}_j^{CE} = -\sum_{N_j}(t_j^a \cdot log[f_{\theta_j^s, \theta_j^a}(y_j^a|x)]) \tag{1}$$

The two tasks, minimising $\mathcal{L}_{j=1}^{CE}$ and $\mathcal{L}_{j=2}^{CE}$, classify different training subjects and types of scanning protocols, with $N_{j=1}$ and $N_{j=2}$ number of classes, respectively. An underlying assumption is that the anatomical and protocol variance can impact the 3D US reconstruction performance. This assumption is tested by quantifying the reconstruction accuracy changes, as number of subjects and/or protocol types are reduced. Results are reported in Sect. 3.2.

2.3 Parameterised Task Descriptor Locations

Assume $\mathcal{I}$ locations in the main task network, at which a task descriptor $z_{i,j}$ can be conditioned, where $i = 1, ..., \mathcal{I}$ for j^{th} auxiliary task. For a single main task in this case, each auxiliary task can branch out from these $\mathcal{I}$ locations, as illustrated in Fig. 1 (b). The task descriptor thus represents the probability of branching location, with additional constraints $z_{i,j} \in [0, 1]$ and $\sum_i z_{i,j} = 1$.

With the task descriptor $z_{i,j}$, the jth auxiliary task is parameterised by a mixture model of $\mathcal{I}$ candidate tasks $f_{\theta_{i,j}^s, \theta_{i,j}^a}(y_{i,j}^a|x)$, each performed by one branch, where the additional subscript i is the candidate task index.

$$f_{\theta, \theta_{1,j}^a, ..., \theta_{\mathcal{I},j}^a}(y_j^a|x, z_j) = \sum_{i=1}^{\mathcal{I}}[z_{i,j} \cdot f_{\theta_{i,j}^s, \theta_{i,j}^a}(y_{i,j}^a|x)] \tag{2}$$

where $z_j = [z_{i,j}]_{i=1,...,\mathcal{I}}^{\top}$ is the task descriptors for all the auxiliary tasks, with shared parameters $\theta_j^s = [\theta_{i,j}^s]_{i=1,...,\mathcal{I}}^{\top}$ and task-specific parameters $\theta_j^a = [\theta_{i,j}^a]_{i=1,...,\mathcal{I}}^{\top}$. For j^{th} auxiliary task, the final prediction is therefore the matrix product of all candidate (branch) predictions $y_j^a = [y_{i,j}^a]_{i=1,...,\mathcal{I}}^{\top}$ (a $N_j \times \mathcal{I}$ matrix) and the location weights z_j (a $\mathcal{I} \times 1$ vector, generated by a softmax function). Multiplicative task conditioning is also known as gating. The loss defined in Eq. 1 remains.

This formulation allows all candidate branches trained together without a predefined architecture decision. We show in Sect. 2.5 that the task descriptor may be considered as a hyperparameter and optimised using a gradient-based bi-level optimisation algorithm, for efficient inference using a single branch.

2.4 The Main Task and Evaluation

We adopt the approach in our previous work [4] for the main task, reconstructing a 3D US scan by sequentially predicting inter-frame transformations with inputs of frame sequences. The same reconstruction loss is used, but is now conditioned on the two auxiliary tasks, denoted as $\mathcal{L}^{Rec}(t, f_{\theta, \theta_1^a, \theta_2^a}(y|x, z_1, z_2))$ where the network output is the six parameters for rigid spatial transformation. It is important to clarify that this proposed loss function also utilises a multi-task learning for predicting transformations between nearby frames, but different to and independent of that used in this work. Unless specified otherwise, the methodology and the implementation of the main task network, based on EfficientNet (b1) [18], remain the same, with further details in the original publication [4].

To test the generalisation and reconstruction performance of the proposed method, four evaluation metrics are used. For each frame, *frame prediction accuracy* (ϵ_{frame}) is used to evaluate the generalisation of the method, denoting the Euclidean distance between the ground-truth and prediction- transformed four corner points of each frame. The scan reconstruction performance is quantified by an *accumulated tracking error* ($\epsilon_{acc.}$), indicating the averaged point distance on all frame pixels, a *volume reconstruction overlap* (ϵ_{dice}), denoting the overlap of all pixels between the ground-truth and prediction volume, and a *final drift* (ϵ_{drift}), denoting the *frame prediction accuracy* of the last frame in a scan.

2.5 Bi-level Optimisation of Task Descriptor

Given a loss for the main task $\mathcal{L}^{Rec}(t, f_{\theta, \theta_1^a, \theta_2^a}(y|x, z_1, z_2))$ and those for the two auxiliary tasks defined in Eq. 1, the overall loss function thus is:

$$\mathcal{L}(\theta, \theta_1^a, \theta_2^a, z_1, z_2|D) = \mathcal{L}^{Rec}(\theta|x, t) + \sum_{j=1}^{2} \mathcal{L}_j^{CE}(\theta, \theta_j^a, z_j|x, t_1^a, t_2^a) \qquad (3)$$

where the loss is rearranged as a function of relevant network parameters $\{\theta, \theta_1^a, \theta_2^a\}$ and task descriptors $\{z_1, z_2\}$, with observed data $D = \{x, t, t_1^a, t_2^a\}$. Given a training data set $\mathcal{D}_{train}$ and a validation data set $\mathcal{D}_{val}$, the empirical losses are $\mathcal{L}_{train}(\cdot) = \mathbf{E}_{D \in \mathcal{D}_{train}}[\mathcal{L}(\cdot|D)]$ and $\mathcal{L}_{val}(\cdot) = \mathbf{E}_{D \in \mathcal{D}_{val}}[\mathcal{L}(\cdot|D)]$, respectively. Optimising the task descriptors subject to optimised network parameters leads to the following meta-learning task with a bi-level optimisation problem:

$$\hat{z}_1, \hat{z}_2 = \arg\min_{z_1, z_2} \mathcal{L}_{val}(\hat{\theta}, \hat{\theta}_1^a, \hat{\theta}_2^a; z_1, z_2)$$

$$\text{s.t.}\ \ \hat{\theta}, \hat{\theta}_1^a, \hat{\theta}_2^a = \arg\min_{\theta, \theta_1^a, \theta_2^a} \mathcal{L}_{train}(\theta, \theta_1^a, \theta_2^a; z_1, z_2) \qquad (4)$$

Since the $\frac{\partial \mathcal{L}_{val}}{\partial z_j}$ can be estimated, the task descriptors can be optimised by gradient-based updates alternating between minimising the two empirical loss functions [17]. The numerical algorithm is summarised in Algorithm 1. The three tasks are weighed equally in Eq. 3 as the task descriptor hyperparameters make explicit optimising or predefining these weights redundant.

3 Experiments and Results

3.1 Dataset and Network Settings

The US data used in this study was from our previously published data set in [4], acquired at 20 frame per second (fps) by an Ultrasonix machine (BK, Europe) with a curvilinear probe (4DC7-3/40, 6 MHz, 9 cm depth and a median level of speckle reduction) and an NDI Polaris Vicra (Northern Digital Inc., Canada) tracker. All US images with a size of 480×640 pixels, after spatial and temporal calibration, acquired from 38 forearms of 19 volunteers were used

---

Algorithm 1: The bi-level optimisation algorithm.

---

1. Initialise task descriptors $\{z_1, z_2\}$ for two auxiliary tasks.
2. Optimise the task descriptors using meta-learning algorithm in a differentiable network:
   while *not converged* **do**
       (1) Update network parameters $\{\theta, \theta_1^a, \theta_2^a\}$ for the main task and all auxiliary tasks
       by descending $\nabla_{\theta, \theta_1^a, \theta_2^a} \mathcal{L}_{train}(\theta, \theta_1^a, \theta_2^a; z_1, z_2)$
       (2) Update task descriptors $\{z_1, z_2\}$
       by descending $\nabla_{z_1, z_2} \mathcal{L}_{val}((\theta, \theta_1^a, \theta_2^a) - \xi \nabla_{\theta, \theta_1^a, \theta_2^a} \mathcal{L}_{train}(\theta, \theta_1^a, \theta_2^a; z_1, z_2); z_1, z_2)$.
3. Finalise the network architecture using the optimised task descriptors $\{z_1, z_2\}$.

In this work, the first-order approximation was used when optimising task descriptors with $\xi = 0$, i.e., $\nabla_{z_1, z_2} \mathcal{L}_{val}(\theta, \theta_1^a, \theta_2^a; z_1, z_2)$ [6].

in this study, more than 40,000 US frames in total. For each forearm, three predefined scanning protocols (straight line shape, 'C' shape and 'S' shape, as in Fig. 2 (a)), in a distal-to-proximal direction, with the US probe perpendicular of and parallel to the forearm, were acquired, resulting in 6 different protocols and 228 scans in total. The US scans have a various number of frames, from 36 to 430 frames, equivalent to a probe travel distance of between 100 and 200 mm. The data was split into train, validation and test sets by a ratio of 3:1:1 on a scan level.

With the EfficientNet (b1) for the main reconstruction task [4], nine locations were used for candidate branches, with each being a single fully-connected classification layer, denoted as Branches 1–9 and Branch 1 being closest to network input. The nine candidate predictions are weighted by the softmax-generated task predictor, as described in Sect. 2.3, to form each final auxiliary task prediction. The two auxiliary tasks resulted in total of 18 branches.

A minibatch of 32, an Adam optimizer were used for model training, with a learning rate of 10^{-4} (tested among $\{10^{-3}, 10^{-4}, 10^{-5}\}$) and the input sequence length being $M = \{100, 140\}$ (tested among $M = \{49, 75, 100, 140\}$), selected based on the validation set performance. Each model was trained for at least 15,000 epochs until convergence, for up to 4 days, on Ubuntu 18.04.6 LTS with a single NVIDIA Quadro P5000 GPU card. The model with the best validation set performance was selected to evaluate test set performance. Other hyperparameters were found relatively insensitive to model performance and configured empirically based on validation performance.

3.2 The Effect of Anatomical and Protocol Variances

The impact on performance of the main task was tested by training models with various anatomical and protocol variance in the training data: 1) all training data (All); 2) straight only (Straight); 3) C-shape and S-shape (C-S); 4) 25% subjects in training data (Sub 25%); 5) 50% training subjects (Sub 50%); 6) 75% training subjects (Sub 75%); 7) 50% of frames in a scan (Frm 50%) and 8) 75%

of frames (Frm 75%), and tested on the same test set. Figure 2 (b) plotted $\epsilon_{acc.}$ with $M = 20$ as an example of the reconstruction performance using different training sets. The other models and metrics yielded a consistent trend, which saw $\epsilon_{acc.}$ increased with both reduced anatomical and protocol variances. It indicates both are factors impacting the main reconstruction task performance.

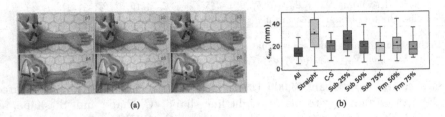

(a)   (b)

Fig. 2. Illustration of different US acquisition protocols and their imapct to reconstruction accuracy. (a) Protocols of straight line shape (p1, p4), 'C' shape (p2, p5) and 'S' shape (p3, p6) with US probe perpendicular of and parallel to the forearm, (b) $\epsilon_{acc.}$ changes due to reduced anatomical and protocol variance.

3.3 Ablation Studies and Comparison

In our experiments, two types protocol discrimination tasks are considered, six-class classification (as in Fig. 2) and three-class classification (combining the perpendicular and parallel scans for the same scan shapes). Each is combined with the 38-class classification task (38 training subjects) as the anatomical discrimination task. Results from different $M = 100, 140$ are also included, together with those from the main task network without any branches (no-branch).

The optimised $z_{i,j}$ values versus the training epochs are plotted in Fig. 3 (a) and (b), where the optimum branch was selected by the maximum $z_{i,j}$ value, at the epoch. Table 1 summarised the reconstruction performance of the proposed method, using the optimised branches (their indices are denoted with asterisks) for the two auxiliary tasks. Comparing with the no-branch models, the improved performances from the proposed methods can be seen, for both $M = 100$ and $M = 140$, regardless of the three- or six-class were used as protocol discrimination tasks. For example, at $M = 100$, ϵ_{drift} was lowered from 14.52 to 6.56 mm, using the proposed methods with optimised Branches 4 and 4, for protocol and anatomical discrimination tasks, with p-value = 0.013 (unpaired t-test, at a significance level $\alpha = 0.05$). Statistical significance was found in performance improvement using all four evaluation metrics.

Although no previous work utilise these discrimination tasks as privileged information for assisting this application, two baseline models were implemented as alternatives to the main task network. We have re-implemented the proposed method using one of the first proposed approaches for this application [16] as the main task network, with two adjacent frames as input and outputting the transformation between them. In addition, the same network architecture using more (10) input frames were also tested, denoted as '[16]-10'. These results are also summarised in Table 1, with and without optimised branches. However, we would like to emphasize that the reported inferior results from these compared baselines need to be interpreted with caution, as they were neither designed for nor tuned with incorporating these auxiliary tasks used in this study. They are included for completeness and reference values.

Table 1. Mean and standard deviation of four metrics of the proposed method and no-branch method.

M	Num. of protocols	Branch index (protocol/anatomy)	ϵ_{frame}	$\epsilon_{acc.}$	ϵ_{dice}	ϵ_{drift}
100	n/a	No-branch	0.18 ± 0.05	7.03 ± 3.97	0.84 ± 0.08	14.52 ± 10.51
100	3	Branches 5*/4*	0.19 ± 0.06	3.92 ± 3.50	0.73 ± 0.21	7.06 ± 7.30
100	6	Branches 4*/4*	0.17 ± 0.08	3.80 ± 3.97	0.76 ± 0.24	6.56 ± 7.53
140	n/a	No-branch	0.14 ± 0.05	3.68 ± 3.10	0.62 ± 0.28	7.30 ± 7.40
140	3	Branches 9*/4*	0.15 ± 0.08	3.36 ± 3.26	$\mathbf{0.94 \pm 0.00}$	$\mathbf{6.20 \pm 6.31}$
140	6	Branches 5*/7*	$\mathbf{0.13 \pm 0.05}$	$\mathbf{2.90 \pm 2.10}$	0.89 ± 0.00	6.53 ± 5.98
[16]	n/a	No-branch	0.59 ± 0.28	29.03 ± 9.15	0.43 ± 0.32	35.67 ± 11.20
[16]	3	Branches 1*/9*	0.70 ± 0.50	32.71 ± 18.10	0.60 ± 0.22	59.53 ± 36.87
[16]	6	Branches 4*/9*	0.68 ± 0.46	30.29 ± 17.44	0.67 ± 0.16	55.05 ± 32.69
[16]-10	n/a	No-branch	0.38 ± 0.21	17.60 ± 9.77	0.67 ± 0.22	22.64 ± 12.47
[16]-10	3	Branches 4*/4*	0.42 ± 0.30	19.37 ± 10.63	0.50 ± 0.30	26.32 ± 13.33
[16]-10	6	Branches 9*/4*	0.43 ± 0.38	21.72 ± 12.74	0.50 ± 0.25	29.64 ± 16.29

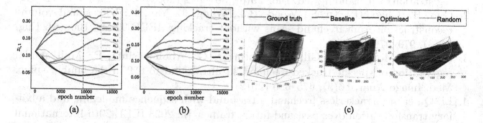

(a)   (b)   (c)

Fig. 3. The trend of task descriptor for anatomy (a) and protocol (b), $M = 100$, and the reconstruction performance (c). The epoch indicating best performance of the model on validation set is denoted by a gray dotted line. Scans with various scanning path are reconstructed using no-branch, optimised branches, and random branches strategies, $M = 100$. (Color figure online)

4 Conclusion and Discussion

This work demonstrated the impact of anatomical and protocol variance towards the 3D reconstruction of trackerless freehand US and formulated two respective discrimination tasks for taking advantage these privileged information during training. Using the proposed algorithm, substantially improved reconstruction performance was achieved, which may indicate a promising new direction for improving the potentials of this application for clinical adoption. Future work includes testing clinical applications with specific challenges, such as those without predefined protocol classes (where a clustering task may be used instead), and comparison with approaches such as gradient surgery [22], which may need adaptation for a single main task.

Declarations. This work was supported by the EPSRC [EP/T029404/1], a Royal Academy of Engineering / Medtronic Research Chair [RCSRF1819\7\734] (TV), Wellcome/EPSRC Centre for Interventional and Surgical Sciences [203145Z/16/Z], and the International Alliance for Cancer Early Detection, an alliance between Cancer Research UK [C28070/A30912; C73666/A31378], Canary Center at Stanford University, the University of Cambridge, OHSU Knight Cancer Institute, University College London and the University of Manchester. TV is co-founder and shareholder of Hypervision Surgical. Qi Li was supported by the University College London Overseas and Graduate Research Scholarships. For the purpose of open access, the authors have applied a CC BY public copyright licence to any Author Accepted Manuscript version arising from this submission. This study was performed in accordance with the ethical standards in the 1964 Declaration of Helsinki and its later amendments or comparable ethical standards. Approval was granted by the Ethics Committee of local institution (UCL Department of Medical Physics and Biomedical Engineering) on 20th Jan. 2023 [24055/001].

References

1. Chang, R.F., et al.: 3-D us frame positioning using speckle decorrelation and image registration. Ultrasound Med. Bio. **29**(6), 801–812 (2003)
2. Guo, H., Chao, H., Xu, S., Wood, B.J., Wang, J., Yan, P.: Ultrasound volume reconstruction from freehand scans without tracking. IEEE Trans. Biomed. Eng. **70**(3), 970–979 (2022)
3. Lang, A., Mousavi, P., Gill, S., Fichtinger, G., Abolmaesumi, P.: Multi-modal registration of speckle-tracked freehand 3d ultrasound to CT in the lumbar spine. Med. Image Anal. **16**(3), 675–686 (2012)
4. Li, Q., et al.: Trackerless freehand ultrasound with sequence modelling and auxiliary transformation over past and future frames. In: 2023 IEEE 20th International Symposium on Biomedical Imaging (ISBI), pp. 1–5. IEEE (2023)
5. Lindseth, F., et al.: Multimodal image fusion in ultrasound-based neuronavigation: improving overview and interpretation by integrating preoperative mri with intraoperative 3d ultrasound. Comput. Aided Surg. **8**(2), 49–69 (2003)
6. Liu, H., Simonyan, K., Yang, Y.: Darts: Differentiable architecture search. arXiv preprint arXiv:1806.09055 (2018)
7. Luo, M., et al.: Self context and shape prior for sensorless freehand 3D ultrasound reconstruction. In: de Bruijne, M., et al. (eds.) MICCAI 2021. LNCS, vol. 12906, pp. 201–210. Springer, Cham (2021). https://doi.org/10.1007/978-3-030-87231-1_20
8. Luo, M., Yang, X., Wang, H., Du, L., Ni, D.: Deep motion network for freehand 3d ultrasound reconstruction. In: Medical Image Computing and Computer Assisted Intervention-MICCAI 2022: 25th International Conference, Singapore, September 18–22, 2022, Proceedings, Part IV. pp. 290–299. Springer (2022). https://doi.org/10.1007/978-3-031-16440-8_28
9. Mikaeili, M., Bilge, H.Ş: Trajectory estimation of ultrasound images based on convolutional neural network. Biomed. Signal Process. Control **78**, 103965 (2022)
10. Miura, K., Ito, K., Aoki, T., Ohmiya, J., Kondo, S.: Localizing 2D ultrasound probe from ultrasound image sequences using deep learning for volume reconstruction. In: Hu, Y., et al. (eds.) ASMUS/PIPPI -2020. LNCS, vol. 12437, pp. 97–105. Springer, Cham (2020). https://doi.org/10.1007/978-3-030-60334-2_10

11. Miura, K., Ito, K., Aoki, T., Ohmiya, J., Kondo, S.: Pose estimation of 2D ultrasound probe from ultrasound image sequences using CNN and RNN. In: Noble, J.A., et al. (eds.) ASMUS 2021. LNCS, vol. 12967, pp. 96–105. Springer, Cham (2021). https://doi.org/10.1007/978-3-030-87583-1_10
12. Mozaffari, M.H., Lee, W.S.: Freehand 3-D ultrasound imaging: a systematic review. Ultrasound Med. Bio. **43**(10), 2099–2124 (2017)
13. Newell, A., Jiang, L., Wang, C., Li, L.J., Deng, J.: Feature partitioning for efficient multi-task architectures. arXiv preprint arXiv:1908.04339 (2019)
14. Ning, G., Liang, H., Zhou, L., Zhang, X., Liao, H.: Spatial position estimation method for 3d ultrasound reconstruction based on hybrid transfomers. In: 2022 IEEE 19th International Symposium on Biomedical Imaging (ISBI), pp. 1–5. IEEE (2022)
15. Prevost, R., et al.: 3D freehand ultrasound without external tracking using deep learning. Med. Image Anal. **48**, 187–202 (2018)
16. Prevost, R., Salehi, M., Sprung, J., Ladikos, A., Bauer, R., Wein, W.: Deep learning for sensorless 3D freehand ultrasound imaging. In: Descoteaux, M., Maier-Hein, L., Franz, A., Jannin, P., Collins, D.L., Duchesne, S. (eds.) MICCAI 2017. LNCS, vol. 10434, pp. 628–636. Springer, Cham (2017). https://doi.org/10.1007/978-3-319-66185-8_71
17. Rajeswaran, A., Finn, C., Kakade, S.M., Levine, S.: Meta-learning with implicit gradients. Adv. Neural Inf. Process. Syst. **32** (2019)
18. Tan, M., Le, Q.: Efficientnet: Rethinking model scaling for convolutional neural networks. In: International conference on machine learning. pp. 6105–6114. PMLR (2019)
19. Vapnik, V., Vashist, A.: A new learning paradigm: learning using privileged information. Neural Netw. **22**(5–6), 544–557 (2009)
20. Wu, S., Zhang, H.R., Ré, C.: Understanding and improving information transfer in multi-task learning. arXiv preprint arXiv:2005.00944 (2020)
21. Xie, Y., Liao, H., Zhang, D., Zhou, L., Chen, F.: Image-based 3D ultrasound reconstruction with optical flow via pyramid warping network. In: 2021 43rd Annual International Conference of the IEEE Engineering in Medicine & Biology Society (EMBC). pp. 3539–3542. IEEE (2021)
22. Yu, T., Kumar, S., Gupta, A., Levine, S., Hausman, K., Finn, C.: Gradient surgery for multi-task learning. Adv. Neural Inf. Process. Syst. **33**, 5824–5836 (2020)

Diagnostic Enhancements and Novel Ultrasound Innovations

The Open Kidney Ultrasound Data Set

Rohit Singla[1,2]([envelope]), Cailin Ringstrom[3], Grace Hu[3], Victoria Lessoway[3], Janice Reid[3], Christopher Nguan[4], and Robert Rohling[3,4,5]

[1] School of Biomedical Engineering, University of British Columbia, Vancouver, BC, Canada
[2] MD/PhD Program, University of British Columbia, Vancouver, BC, Canada
rsingla@ece.ubc.ca
[3] Electrical and Computer Engineering, University of British Columbia, Vancouver, BC, Canada
[4] Urological Sciences, University of British Columbia, Vancouver, BC, Canada
[5] Mechanical Engineering, University of British Columbia, Vancouver, BC, Canada

Abstract. Ultrasound is widely used and affordable diagnostic tool for medical imaging. With the increasing popularity of machine learning, ultrasound research has also expanded, but limited access to open data sets hinders progress. Despite being a frequently examined organ, the kidney lacks a publicly available ultrasonography data set. To address this issue, the proposed Open Kidney Ultrasound Data Set is the first publicly available, high-quality data set of kidney B-mode ultrasound data, collected over five years from over 500 adult patients with common primary diseases. The data set includes annotations for multi-class semantic segmentation, with fine-grained manual annotations from two expert sonographers. It contains images from a patient population with a mean ($\pm$ stdev) age of 53.2 ± 14.7 years, with 63% males and 37% females. The primary diagnoses included include diabetes mellitus (32%), immunoglobulin A nephropathy (11%), hypertension (10%), and other diseases ($\leq$ 10% each). Of the images, 91.2% were rated as fair or good quality, while 8.8% were deemed poor or unsatisfactory. Intra-rater and inter-rater variability were assessed, and initial benchmarking demonstrated a state-of-the-art algorithm achieving a Dice Sorenson Coefficient of 0.85 for kidney capsule segmentation. Furthermore, the data set includes both native and transplanted kidneys, providing a comprehensive data set for future researchers to develop novel image analysis techniques for tissue characterization, disease detection, and prognostication.

Keywords: ultrasound · segmentation · data · kidney · transplantation

1 Introduction

1.1 Background and Motivation

Ultrasound is an essential tool in abdominal radiology due to its low cost, non-invasiveness, real-time capability, and lack of ionizing radiation [18]. The Amer-

B. Kainz et al. (Eds.): ASMUS 2023, LNCS 14337, pp. 155–164, 2023.
https://doi.org/10.1007/978-3-031-44521-7_15

ican College of Radiologists recommends it as the first-line imaging modality for suspected kidney dysfunction in both native and transplanted kidneys [16,19]. Kidney ultrasound plays a potential role in the clinical management of patients with chronic kidney disease; a condition that affects 1 in 10 adults globally [10]. Changes in morphological characteristics as measured by ultrasound imaging, such as kidney length, total kidney volume, and cortical thickness, are correlated with kidney disease severity [8,9,17]. However, these variables are often extracted manually by experts, resulting in intra- and inter-rater heterogeneity as well as significant time and labour needed [17]. Automatic analysis for segmentation and measurement is needed to reduce these discrepancies. Automated kidney ultrasound image analysis can be split into two segmentation tasks: the binary segmentation of the renal capsule border from the background ultrasound image and the semantic segmentation of specific areas of the kidney, such as the cortex and medulla, using a multi-class approach. These regions are difficult for novices to interpret visually, and changes in their size and echogenicity also have clinical importance.

Machine learning is a promising solution for automatic segmentation of ultrasound images, but accessing high-quality medical imaging data remains a challenge. An extensive authorization process, including institutional and research ethics board approvals, anonymization of images, and privacy considerations, must be implemented before data can be made broadly accessible. The Medical Segmentation Decathlon provides publicly available medical data for ten distinct organ data sets, but it does not include kidney ultrasound imaging [1].

The literature on kidney ultrasound segmentation has frequently reported limited sample sizes, inconsistent evaluation methods, and proprietary data sets [7,12,13,20,21]. This exacerbates the reproducibility dilemma in machine learning for medical imaging [11]. Moreover, transplanted kidneys have been omitted in many studies, although monitoring these organs for early detection of disease is critical to improve clinical outcomes and reduce the likelihood of rejection. Therefore, there is an urgent need for a high-quality, reproducible data set of kidney ultrasound images, with detailed expert annotations and thorough characterization, that includes transplanted kidneys to advance the field of machine learning in medical imaging. The inclusion of transplanted kidneys in such a data set would allow researchers to better investigate novel image analysis techniques for tissue characterization, disease detection, and prognostication, and improve the generalizability of machine learning models for clinical applications.

As our main contribution, the Open Kidney Ultrasound Data Set is introduced: 514 two-dimensional kidney ultrasound images with manual annotations from two expert sonographers. The annotations follow a systematic protocol and include labels for view type and kidney type. The data set also includes benchmark findings using a state-of-the-art segmentation neural network, which may contribute to ultrasound machine learning research. Its goal is to set a benchmark for ultrasound segmentation and simplify interpretation in the future.

2   Methods

2.1   Image Acquisition and Pre-processing

The retrospective collection of the anonymized B-mode ultrasound images was approved by our institution's Research Ethics Board (H21-02375). The ultrasound images were originally acquired between January 2015 and September 2019. One image was randomly selected from each video to obtain various kidney cross-sections, and non-kidney images were removed manually. The files were annotated using VIA software [3]. Any additional graphics or illustrations were automatically removed after annotation, and the images are provided in their original dimensions. The ultrasound images were taken from patients with clinical indications for kidney ultrasound rather than controlled conditions. The images include adults with chronic kidney disease, prospective donors, and transplanted kidneys, and were taken using different manufacturers and machine models. This includes the ACUSON Sequoia with 6C2 and 4V1 transducers, the General Electric LOGIQ E10 with C1-6 and C2-9 transducers, the Philips Affiniti 70G with C5-1 and C9-2 transducers, the Philips Epiq 5G with C5-1 and C9-2 transducers, the Philips Epiq 7G with C5-1 and C9-2 transducers, the Philips iU22 with the C5-1 transducer, the Siemens S2000 with 4V1 and 6C1 transducers, and the Toshiba TUS-A500 with a PVT-375BT transducer. Transducer information for each image is made available along with the data set. Clinical data such as age and primary diagnosis were obtained from a provincial institution that oversees care for all patients with kidney disease.

2.2   Annotations and Quality Assurance

Experienced sonographers (V.L. and J.R.), each with over 30 years of ultrasound imaging experience, performed manual annotations on 514 kidney ultrasound images. Annotation goals, definitions, and guidelines were established before labeling for image quality, view, and four segmentation classes: kidney capsule, cortex, medulla, and central echogenic complex (CEC). A practice set of 20 random images was used to determine categories for quality assessment (unacceptable, poor, fair, and good) and view labels (transverse, longitudinal, and other for non-standard views). These images are not part of the data set. Annotations for each class were hand-drawn closed polygons, and no guidelines were provided for vertices or minimum size. Annotations were reviewed collectively, and guidelines were established online. The released data includes individual annotations of each sonographer. The annotations are not aggregated or fused.

With regards to the segmentation classes, the functional anatomy of the kidney is comprised of the renal parenchyma and the renal pelvis [14]. The parenchyma consists of the cortex (the outermost portion of the kidney) and the medulla [14]. The renal pelvis however is more complex, consisting of minor and major calyces, blood vessels, and fat [14]. As these components are not able to be individually delineated in these images by the sonographers, the CEC term was introduced to represent the renal pelvis and other components.

Two biomedical engineers (R.S. and C.R.) reviewed all images with annotations. Any errors such as a missing capsule boundary or repeated class label were returned for correction. At the time of release, a date-stamped list of errata is maintained and is available online should further errors be identified.

2.3 Imaging Data and Trained Models

The Open Kidney Ultrasound Data Set (https://rsingla92.github.io/kidneyUS/) includes 514 PNG files corresponding to distinct patients, along with 20 copied images used for validation. The data itself is shared via our institution's instance of Microsoft OneDrive (Microsoft, Redmond, WA). Each sonographer's annotations are provided in a comma-separated value (CSV) file following the structure provided by VIA, and example images are shown in Fig. 1. A data sheet for the data set is available online in the format from Gebru et al. [4].

The patient-level demographic details are not publicly available due to privacy considerations; however, aggregated summary statistics of the patient population are provided. The population had a mean ($\pm$ stdev) age of 53.2 $\pm$ 14.7 years, with 63% males and 37% females. The mean ($\pm$ stdev) BMI was 27.0 $\pm$ 5.4 kg/m^2. At the time of imaging, the mean ($\pm$ stdev) estimated glomerular filtration rate (eGFR) was 28.7 $\pm$ 21.3 mL/min/1.73m^2. The primary diagnoses causing end-stage kidney disease were type 1 or type 2 diabetes mellitus (32%), immunoglobulin A (IgA) nephropathy (11%), hypertension (10%), and other diseases ($\leq$ 10% each). The diagnoses were obtained from electronic medical records for each patient, and were determined through their clinical care. This indicates the data is sampled from a diverse and representative patient population. Technical details on image quality, class frequency, and sonographer annotations are described in subsequent sections.

To facilitate initial benchmarks in segmentation tasks, we provide pre-trained models. We use nnU-net by [6] to represent the current state-of-the-art in medical image segmentation. This network is a fully automatic and self-configuring solution using a data-adaptive variant of U-net. This approach has demonstrated leading results in several image segmentation challenges through a combination of fixed parameterization, heuristics, and empirical measures. We use nnU-net to obtain results for binary segmentation of the kidney capsule and multi-class segmentation of the kidney compartments. The networks were trained using an 80:20 training-test split, with five folds of the training data used for training an ensemble model. Each network was trained for 500 epochs with a batch size of 4, using a learning rate of 0.01 annealed throughout training and a combined loss of DSC and cross-entropy loss. The University of British Columbia's Advanced Research Computing (ARC) platform was used with one 32GB Nvidia Tesla V100 GPU. Three versions of nnU-net were trained including sonographer-specific models and a model with annotations randomly sampled from both sonographers. The data and code that are made available are under the Creative Commons Attribution Non-commercial Share Alike (CC BY-NC-SA) license. Data may not be used for commercial purposes. Due to accessibility and privacy terms, registration is required for manual verification prior to the release

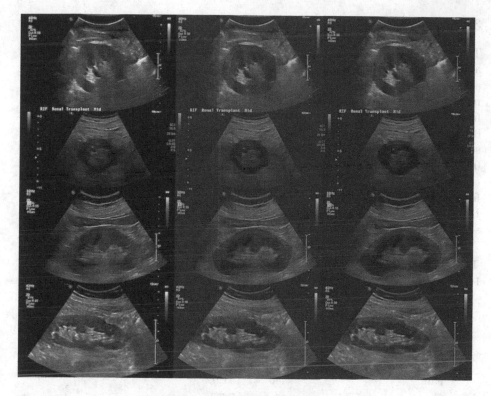

Fig. 1. Example images. (L to R columns): original image, the sonographer's annotation, and the predicted segmentations. Capsule in blue, cortex in yellow, medulla in red and CE in green. Transplant kidneys are in even rows, native ones in odd rows. (Color figure online)

of data. Relevant code for masking, cropping data, reading, and processing summary statistics of labels, pre-trained models and weights, and additional code is available at the following repository: https://github.com/rsingla92/kidneyUS

2.4   Technical Validation

We analyzed sonographers' annotations, comparing quality, view, and kidney types, class frequency, and average pixels per class. We evaluated intra- and inter-rater variability by randomly selecting 10 images and having the annotators perform annotations three times in a blinded manner, reporting DSC values. Segmentation accuracy for each class in all three models was measured by DSC and Hausdorff distance. A sensitivity analysis is performed by eroding and dilating polygons by 1 and 10 pixels with mean absolute percent change in DSC value for each class provided.

3   Results

Table 1 summarizes image quality, view frequency, kidney types, class frequency, and average annotation size per class. Table 2 reports the number of vertices, absolute pixel coverage per class, and relative pixel coverage of kidney compartments to the capsule in sonographers' annotations. Intra-rater variability for the first sonographer was 0.95 ± 0.02 for the capsule, 0.62 ± 0.26 for the cortex, 0.75 ± 0.21 for the medulla, and 0.85 ± 0.07 for the CEC. Similarly, for the second sonographer was 0.96 ± 0.01 for the capsule, 0.72 ± 0.20 for the cortex, 0.80 ± 0.18 for the medulla, and 0.89 ± 0.06 for the CEC. The inter-rater variability was 0.93 ± 0.10 for the capsule, 0.48 ± 0.37 for the cortex, 0.54 ± 0.38 for the medulla, and 0.82 ± 0.17 for the CEC. Table 3 summarizes the DSC and HD values per class for each of the three models. Finally, Table 4 highlights the sensitivity of the annotations and models with erosion and dilation changes.

Table 1. Summary of quality, view, kidney type, class frequency, and average pixels per class in terms of number of frames and pixels.

Category	Frames	Frequency (percentage)	Pixels per 1000 pixels
Quality			
Good	1	0.2%	-
Fair	486	91.0%	-
Poor	41	7.7%	-
Unsatisfactory	6	1.1%	-
View			
Transverse	145	27.2%	-
Longitudinal	371	69.5%	-
Other	18	3.4%	-
Kidney Type			
Native	386	72.2%	-
Transplanted	148	27.8%	-
Class			
Capsule	452	-	237 ± 7.7
Cortex	452	-	65.1 ± 1.3
Medulla	316	-	35.2 ± 0.2
Central Echogenic Complex	315	-	21.2 ± 0.6

4   Discussion

The Open Kidney Ultrasound Data Set is a data set of high quality, available to the public and thoroughly characterized in terms of image and annotation quality, as well as initial benchmark segmentation results. Over 90% of the images were suitable for annotation, and the data set includes both native and transplanted kidneys. However, it is worth noting that the cortex and medulla each make up less than 5% of the overall image and less than 15% of the kidney, which highlights the challenge of segmenting these small regions of interest. Given that the cortex is the functional part of the kidney, where glomeruli filter blood, it is a class of significant interest. Measurements of the cortex, such as cortical thickness, has demonstrated prognostic value.

Table 2. Summary of fidelity of annotations in terms of number of vertices, as well as the pixel coverage in absolute and relative terms. Absolute coverage is the size of the class compared to the size of the overall image. Relative coverage is the size of the class compared to the size of the capsule in that frame. Px: pixel, S1: sonographer 1, S2: sonographer 2.

	Sonographer 1	Sonographer 2
No. vertices (mean ± standard deviation)		
Capsule	18.9 ± 8.0	20.2 ± 8.0
Cortex	16.7 ± 15.2	15.3 ± 14.4
Medulla	16.5 ± 15.5	21.5 ± 20.7
Central Echogenic Complex	21.7 ± 13.5	31.3 ± 17.2
Absolute Px Coverage (median %, [min, max])		
Capsule	26.6 [0, 87.7]	29.2 [0,93.0]
Cortex	1.8 [0, 19.6]	1.7 [0, 19.6]
Medulla	3.1 [0, 28.8]	2.9 [0, 26.0]
Central Echogenic Complex	6.8 [0, 30.6]	7.3 [0, 32.2]
Relative Px Coverage (median %, [min, max])		
Cortex	7.3 [0, 44.5]	6.7 [0,65.3]
Medulla	13.9 [0, 48.4]	12.6 [0, 77.6]
Central Echogenic Complex	26.3 [0, 64.0]	25.3 [0, 54.4]

Moreover, the pixel-to-millimeter scale factors for abdominal imaging are typically around 0.1 mm, meaning that a 1 mm error (10 pixels) in prediction can significantly impact the DSC score. Therefore, using the DSC as an accuracy metric for these small regions is challenging due to its sensitivity to size and shape unawareness [15]. Nonetheless, with the data, code, and models available, the Open Kidney Ultrasound Data Set can serve as a benchmark for future efforts.

This study has several limitations that need to be addressed. First, although the data set contains a wide range of adult patients with varying sex, age, and primary diseases, it was obtained from a single urban tertiary hospital, which may limit its generalizability due to geographic disparities. Second, while the terms cortex and medulla are well-established, their anatomical delineation is unclear, and there is no prior definition of the central echogenic complex. The definition used in this study includes different minor parts of the kidney's anatomy, and

Table 3. Segmentation validation using nnU-net and sensitivity analysis of both the sonographer's annotations and the model's predictions given an erosion or dilation in each class's annotation. Network accuracies using annotations from models trained on individual sonographers and a random even sampling from both is reported. Hausdorff distance is reported in millimeters. CEC: central echogenic complex. DSC: Dice Sorenson Coefficient. HD: Hausdorff Distance. S1: Sonographer 1. S2: Sonographer 2.

Method	Capsule	Cortex	Medulla	CEC	Mean
Segmentation validation					
DSC (S1 Model)	0.87	0.43	0.48	0.76	0.63
DSC (S2 Model)	0.85	0.51	0.57	0.66	0.67
DSC (Both)	0.85	0.52	0.59	0.78	0.69
HD (S1 Model)	11.0	16.4	11.8	10.7	12.5
HD (S2 Model)	15.5	13.7	9.3	15.9	13.6
HD (Both)	12.2	12.9	9.8	10.8	11.4
Sensitivity analysis	Cortex	Medulla	CEC		
1px erosion (S1)	3.9	2.0	2.5		
1px erosion (S2)	5.2	2.8	2.4		
1px erosion (Model 1)	7.2	5.8	0.8		
1px erosion (Model 2)	7.0	3.3	1.4		
10px erosion (S1)	46.8	26.1	28.4		
10px erosion (S2)	62.3	36.2	27.2		
10px erosion (Model 1)	37.7	29.9	16.4		
10px erosion (Model 2)	44.1	27.0	15.9		
1px dilation (S1)	3.4	1.9	2.4		
1px dilation (S2)	4.5	2.7	2.3		
1px dilation (Model 1)	6.7	6.2	0.8		
1px dilation (Model 2)	6.5	3.1	1.4		
10px dilation (S1)	22.5	14.8	19.2		
10px dilation (S2)	29.7	20.5	18,8		
10px dilation (Model 1)	42.5	55.1	9.0		
10px dilation (Model 2)	44.9	18.9	14.3		

there may still be discrepancies between expert sonographers' annotations. To improve consistency in defining this region, the labeling instructions have been provided. Third, the importance of each class is task-dependent, and no distinction is made between the importance of each class. For example, the capsule measures size and shape, the cortex assesses cortical thinning, and both medulla and cortex detect the loss of corticomedullary differentiation. Weighting different classes could lead to task-specific or class-specific improvements. Finally, several potential exogenous factors, including acquisition shift within medical imaging, may affect the performance of machine learning techniques [2,5]. Thus, it's unclear how well methods trained on the Open Kidney Data Set will adapt to unrepresented ultrasound transducers, and alternative training data may yield different results.

5   Conclusion

In conclusion, the Open Kidney Ultrasound Data Set is designed to cover native and transplant kidneys, as well as a variety of diagnoses and ultrasound systems, with significant effort to provide useful and high-quality annotations from two experienced sonographers. The data set provides an excellent opportunity for researchers to develop and test segmentation algorithms and ultimately enhance the accuracy of kidney disease diagnosis and treatment.

Acknowledgments. R.S. acknowledges funding from the Vanier Graduate Scholarship, the Kidney Foundation of Canada, and the American Society of Transplant Surgeons. C.R. acknowledges funding from Natural Sciences and Engineering Council of Canada.

References

1. Antonelli, M., et al.: The medical segmentation decathlon. Nat. Commun. **13**(1), 4128 (2022)
2. Castro, D.C., Walker, I., Glocker, B.: Causality matters in medical imaging. Nat. Commun. **11**(1), 3673 (2020)
3. Dutta, A., Zisserman, A.: The VIA annotation software for images, audio and video. In: Proceedings of the 27th ACM International Conference on Multimedia, pp. 2276–2279 (2019)
4. Gebru, T., et al.: Datasheets for datasets. Commun. ACM **64**(12), 86–92 (2021)
5. Glocker, B., Robinson, R., Castro, D.C., Dou, Q., Konukoglu, E.: Machine learning with multi-site imaging data: an empirical study on the impact of scanner effects. arXiv preprint arXiv:1910.04597 (2019)
6. Isensee, F., Jaeger, P.F., Kohl, S.A., Petersen, J., Maier-Hein, K.H.: nnU-Net: a self-configuring method for deep learning-based biomedical image segmentation. Nat. Methods **18**(2), 203–211 (2021)
7. Jokar, E., Pourghassem, H.: Kidney segmentation in ultrasound images using curvelet transform and shape prior. In: 2013 International Conference on Communication Systems and Network Technologies, pp. 180–185 (2013)
8. Kim, H.C., Yang, D.M., Lee, S.H., Cho, Y.D.: Usefulness of renal volume measurements obtained by a 3-dimensional sonographic transducer with matrix electronic arrays. J. Ultrasound Med. **27**(12), 1673–1681 (2008)
9. Korkmaz, M., Aras, B., Güneyli, S., Yılmaz, M.: Clinical significance of renal cortical thickness in patients with chronic kidney disease. Ultrasonography **37**(1), 50–54 (2018)
10. Kovesdy, C.P.: Epidemiology of chronic kidney disease: an update 2022. Kidney Int. Suppl. **12**(1), 7–11 (2022)
11. Maier-Hein, L., et al.: BIAS: transparent reporting of biomedical image analysis challenges. Med. Image Anal. **66**, 101796 (2020)

12. Marsousi, M., Plataniotis, K.N., Stergiopoulos, S.: An automated approach for kidney segmentation in three-dimensional ultrasound images. IEEE J. Biomed. Health Inform. **21**(4), 1079–1094 (2016)
13. Mendoza, C.S., Kang, X., Safdar, N., Myers, E., Peters, C.A., Linguraru, M.G.: Kidney segmentation in ultrasound via genetic initialization and active shape models with rotation correction. In: 2013 IEEE 10th International Symposium on Biomedical Imaging, pp. 69–72 (2013)
14. Netter, F.H.: Atlas of Human Anatomy: Latin Terminology. Elsevier Health Sciences (2018)
15. Reinke, A., et al.: Common limitations of image processing metrics: a picture story (2022)
16. Remer, E.M., et al.: ACR appropriateness criteria on renal failure. Am. J. Med. **127**(11), 1041–1048 (2014)
17. Singla, R.K., Kadatz, M., Rohling, R., Nguan, C.: Kidney ultrasound for nephrologists: a review. Kidney Med. **4**(6), 100464 (2022)
18. Szabo, T.L.: Diagnostic Ultrasound Imaging: Inside Out. Academic Press (2004)
19. Taffel, M.T., et al.: ACR appropriateness criteria renal transplant dysfunction. J. Am. Coll. Radiol. **14**(5), S272–S281 (2017)
20. Xie, J., Jiang, Y., Tsui, H.-T.: Segmentation of kidney from ultrasound images based on texture and shape priors. IEEE Trans. Med. Imaging **24**(1), 45–57 (2005)
21. Yin, S., et al.: Automatic kidney segmentation in ultrasound images using subsequent boundary distance regression and pixelwise classification networks. Med. Image Anal. **60**, 101602 (2020)

Anatomical Landmark Detection for Initializing US and MR Image Registration

Zhijie Fang[✉], Hervé Delingette, and Nicholas Ayache

Centre Inria d'Université Côte d'Azur,
2004 Rte des Lucioles, 06902 Valbonne, France
zhijie.fang@inria.fr

Abstract. Targeted MR/ultrasound (US) fusion biopsy is a technology made possible by overlaying ultrasound images of the prostate with MRI sequences for the visualization and the targeting of lesions. However, US and MR image registration requires a good initial alignment based on manual anatomical landmark detection or prostate segmentation, which are time-consuming and often challenging during an intervention. We propose to explicitly and automatically detect anatomical landmarks of prostate in both modalities to achieve initial registration. Firstly, we train a deep neural network to detect three anatomical landmarks for both MR and US images. Instead of relying on heatmap regression or coordinate regression using a fully connected layer, we regress coordinates of landmarks directly by introducing a differentiable layer in U-Net. After being trained and validated on 900 and 152 cases, the proposed method predicts landmarks within a Mean Radial Error (MRE) of 5.55 ± 2.63 mm and 5.77 ± 2.67 mm in 263 test cases for US and MR images, separately. Secondly, least-squares fitting is applied to calculate a rough rigid transformation based on detected anatomical landmarks. Surface registration error (SRE) of 6.62 ± 3.97 mm and Dice score of 0.77 ± 0.11 are achieved, which are both comparable metrics in clinical setting when comparing with previous method.

Keywords: Landmark detection · Image-guided intervention · Convolutional neural network and Prostate cancer

1 Introduction

Prostate cancer is the 2nd most commonly occurring cancer in men and the 4th most common cancer overall, with around 1.4 million new cases and 370 000 deaths worldwide in 2020 [1]. There are several tests that indicative of a potential prostate cancer, but biopsy analysis is the gold standard. The introduction of multiparametric magnetic resonance imaging (mp-MRI) now allows for imaging-based detection of prostate cancer, which may improve diagnostic accuracy for higher-risk tumors. Targeted MR/ultrasound (US) fusion biopsy is a technology made possible by overlaying ultrasound images of the prostate with MRI sequences for visualization and targeting lesions [2]. However, image fusion is a challenging and time consuming task especially for multi-modal images. For mono-modal medical image registration, it can be solved as an optimization problem [3] by maximizing image similarity, which indicates how well image

B. Kainz et al. (Eds.): ASMUS 2023, LNCS 14337, pp. 165–174, 2023.
https://doi.org/10.1007/978-3-031-44521-7_16

intensities correspond. However, it is difficult to engineer a similarity metric for multi-modal image registration. Last but not least, even if many researchers [4–6] worked on the US-MR image registration task, the proposed methods demand an approximate initial alignment for US and MR images, which are usually based on manual anatomical landmark detection or prostate segmentation. However, manually detecting landmarks from both modalities is time-consuming and often challenging during an intervention [7]. Therefore, computer assistance is necessary for anatomical landmarks detection in both modalities in order to achieve a good initialization for US and MR images registration.

Landmark-Based Image Registration. Natarajan *et al.* [8] proposed an elastic warping of MR volume to match the US volume acquired for targeted prostate biopsy. The fusion method involves rigid alignment of the two volumes using manually selected anatomical landmarks. Heinrich *et al.* [9] proposed a landmark detection method specifically designed for lung computed tomography (CT) registration, which is not generalizable to other tasks. Grewal *et al.* [10] presented DCNN-Match, that learns to predict landmark correspondences in lower abdominal CT scans and in a self-supervised manner, which significantly improves the performance in deformable image registration. Song *et al.* [11] proposed an affine registration method for US and MR images based on four anatomical landmarks, which requires not only landmark detection network, but also segmentation network.

Landmark Detection. Detecting landmarks in images is a well-studied topic, and this problem has been explored with traditional machine learning techniques [12,13]. Recently, deep learning methods have been proposed with fully-convolutional architecture such as U-Net [14] to compute a heatmap image as an output that highlights the location of the landmark(s). Thus, landmark localization is turned into an image-to-heatmap regression problem [11,15,16], where the ground truth coordinates are used to generate Gaussian blobs (of often arbitrary size) to create training data. Another coordinate regression approach is to add a fully connected layer which produces numerical coordinates [17]. An attractive property of this approach is that it is possible to backpropagate all the way from the predicted numerical coordinates to the input image. However, the weights of the fully-connected layer are highly dependent on the spatial distribution of the inputs during training, hampering the generalization ability of the overall network. Nibali *et al.* [18] proposed differentiable spatial to numerical transform (DSNT) layer for 2D human pose estimation, which is fully differentiable, and exhibits good spatial generalization.

Proposed Method. As shown in Fig. 1, we propose a pipeline to achieve initialization for US and MR image registration automatically. We use three anatomical landmarks, including the apex, the bladder neck, and the posterior median, which are displayed in Fig. 1a. A neural network is adopted to detect three anatomical landmarks in each US and MR image, separately. Least-squares fitting [19] is applied to calculate a rough rigid transformation based on the detected landmarks from both modalities.

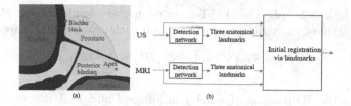

Fig. 1. Overview of the proposed pipeline for initializing US and MR image registration. (a) Three prostate anatomical landmarks: the apex, the bladder neck, the posterior median. (b) Workflow for detecting anatomical landmarks in both modalities and for computing a rough rigid transformation using least-squares fitting.

Contribution. In summary, our work to the state of the art in the following aspects:

1. The proposed pipeline can detect three prostate anatomical landmarks of both US and MR images automatically, and least-squares fitting is applied to calculate a rough rigid transformation based on detected anatomical landmarks, thus achieving initialization for US and MR image registration.
2. Instead of heatmap regression or coordinate regression using fully connected layer, we adopt the differentiable spatial to numerical transform (DSNT) layer [18,20] and combine it with a 3D U-Net in order to regress coordinates of landmarks.
3. We introduce a novel heatmap regularization term, which penalizes large heatmap values far away from the ground truth location.

2   Methodology

Given a 3D US and MR image pair, F, M, respectively, with corresponding landmarks $G_i{}^f \in \mathbb{R}^3$ and $G_i^m \in \mathbb{R}^3$, where i is the landmark index, $i = [1, 2 \ldots L]$, and L is the number of landmarks. Our goal is to train a neural network that predicts the coordinates of L landmarks, then calculate a rigid transformation based on the detected landmark coordinates from both modalities.

2.1   End-to-end Landmark Detection Network

Inspired by landmark detection in human pose estimation [18], we formulate landmark detection problem as a direct coordinate regression task. The proposed neural network consists in a 3D U-Net and a differentiable spatial to numerical transform (DSNT) layer, which transforms spatial heatmaps from the output of U-Net into numerical coordinates, shown in Fig. 2. We consider an input image I, which is either F or M, of size N, and the network outputs a matrix P of size $L \times 3$. To generate this matrix, each raw heatmap $\tilde{H}^i$ of size N is first normalized with a softmax activation function into H^i such that $\sum_{j \in I} H_j^i = 1$,

$H_j^i \in]0,1[$ for $i = 1 \ldots L$. The DNST layer computes each landmark $\boldsymbol{P}_i \in \mathbb{R}^3$ as the expectation of the voxel position based on each probabilistic maps:

$$\boldsymbol{P}_i = \mathbb{E}_{H^i}(\boldsymbol{V}) = \mathrm{DSNT}(H^i) = \sum_{j \in I} H_j^i \boldsymbol{v}_j \tag{1}$$

where $\boldsymbol{v}_j$ is the 3D position of voxel j in image I and $\boldsymbol{P}_i$ is the estimated i_{th} landmark position.

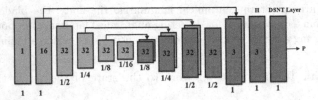

Fig. 2. Overview of the proposed end-to-end landmark detection network with $L = 3$, consisting of 3D U-Net and DSNT layer. The proposed network is trained separately for each modality. It's inspired by Balakrishnan *et al.* [21].

2.2   Regression Loss Function

Since DSNT layer transforms spatial heatmaps into numerical coordinates directly, it's possible to calculate the L1 and L2 norms between the ground truth and prediction coordinate vector (Eq. 2), and it is named as vanilla DSNT.

$$\mathcal{L}(\boldsymbol{G}, \boldsymbol{P}) = \|\boldsymbol{P} - \boldsymbol{G}\|_1 + \lambda_1 \|\boldsymbol{P} - \boldsymbol{G}\|_2 \tag{2}$$

where G is the matrix of ground truth landmark position.

The spread of the heatmap has no effect on the output such that heatmaps with small or large variance can produce the same landmark position. Based on [18], we propose to regularize the probabilistic map H variance to achieve better performance than vanilla DSNT. The overall loss function is a combination between coordinate regression loss and heatmap regularization loss.

$$\mathcal{L}(\boldsymbol{G}, \boldsymbol{P}) = \|\boldsymbol{P} - \boldsymbol{G}\|_1 + \lambda_1 \|\boldsymbol{P} - \boldsymbol{G}\|_2 + \lambda_2 \mathcal{L}_{re.g.}(\boldsymbol{H}) \tag{3}$$

Variance Regularization. As a first option, the variance of each probabilistic map is used to regularize the regression. In [18], the authors proposed a regularization term based on a specific target variance. We instead propose to minimize the overall variance (equivalent to specifying a zero target variance) thus avoiding to pick an additional hyperparameter which may be data dependent. Besides, this choice forces the network to make a bias-variance trade-off in a data driven way. The computation of the variance as the second order moment of the probabilistic maps which extends the approach proposed in [18]:

$$\mathcal{L}_{\mathrm{Var}} = \mathbb{E}_{H^i}(\|\boldsymbol{P}_i - \mathbb{E}_{H^i}(\boldsymbol{V})\|^2) = \sum_{j \in I} H_j^i \|\boldsymbol{v}_j - \boldsymbol{P}_i\|^2 \tag{4}$$

Distance Map Regularization. As a second option, we propose a new regularization term $\mathcal{L}_{\text{Dist}}$, which penalizes high probability values that are far way from the ground truth landmark position G_i:

$$\mathcal{L}_{\text{Dist}} = \sum_{i=1}^{L} \sum_{j \in I} H_j^i \|v_j - G_i\| \tag{5}$$

2.3   Multimodal Landmark-Based Rigid Registration

Once anatomical landmark coordinates have been predicted in both modalities, the calculation of rigid matrix can be formulated as the least-square optimization problem. P_i^m and P_i^f are the coordinate vectors of the ith landmark in the MR and US images, R is a 3×3 rotation matrix, and t is a 3×1 translation vector. To solve this problem, we use the noniterative SVD-based algorithm proposed in [19], and the equation is $\min_{R,t} \sum_{i=1}^{3} \left\| P_i^f - (RP_i^m + t) \right\|^2$.

3   Experiments

3.1   Data and Training

The database contains 1315 patients, each of them consisting of a MRI-US volume pair, prostate segmentations, and landmarks. All cases were scheduled for prostate biopsy. Each MRI volume has $256 \times 256 \times 128$ voxels with a voxel size of $0.5 \times 0.5 \times 1.0$ mm^3, and each US volume has $256 \times 256 \times 256$ voxels with 0.4 mm resolution in all directions. US images are coming from various ultrasound systems, with various probes, both end-fire and side-fire probes. For both MR and US images, three anatomical landmarks (the apex, the bladder neck, the posterior median) are detected by medical experts. We used 900 cases of MRI-US volume pair for training, 152 cases for validation, and 263 cases for testing. For each modality, we train a landmark detection network. As shown in Fig. 2, we used 3D U-Net structure to map a whole 3D image to 3 probability maps ($L = 3$), one for each landmark. We apply 3D convolutions in both the encoder and decoder stages using a kernel size of 3, and a stride of 2. Each convolution is followed by a LeakyReLU layer with parameter 0.2. In the encoder, we use strided convolutions to reduce the spatial dimensions in half at each layer. The softmax activation function is applied to normalize each heatmap. Finally, the DSNT layer transforms spatial heatmaps into numerical coordinates. The loss hyperparameter was empirically chosen as $\lambda_1 = 1$ and $\lambda_2 = 5 \times 10^{-4}$ on MR images (resp. $\lambda_2 = 2 \times 10^{-3}$ on US images) for the variance regularization and $\lambda_2 = 5 \times 10^{-3}$ on MR images (resp. $\lambda_2 = 10^{-2}$ on US images) for the distance map regularization. An Adam optimizer is used with a learning rate initialized to lr $= 1 \times 10^{-4}$. The neural network was implemented with PyTorch framework and trained on one NVIDIA RTX 8000 GPU with batch size of 4.

3.2   Experimental Results

Landmark Detection Results and Ablation Study. Various landmark detection methods were evaluated qualitatively and quantitatively in Table 1. Following previous works [22], we use Mean Radial Error (MRE) as a metric, which is the average Euclidean distance between the predicted landmarks and the ground-truth landmarks measured in mm. As baseline method, we consider the proposed end-to-end method with DSNT layer without any heatmap regularization. From Table 1, we can see that regularizing heatmap improves significantly the model's performance. The proposed method (with and without regularization) outperforms the heatmap matching or direct regression coordinates methods [15,17] based on MRE. In Fig. 3, a successful example of posterior median landmark detection is shown for both modalities.

Table 1. Landmark detection results on MR and US images using different methods. We report statistically significant differences based on the Wilcoxon test from the baseline model with a * sign, and from the variance regularization model with a † sign.

Method	US MRE (mm)	MRI MRE (mm)
Direct regression coordinate [17]	11.43 ± 3.82	13.83 ± 7.25
Heatmap matching [15]	6.91 ± 5.12	6.93 ± 7.57
Baseline (no regularization)	5.90 ± 2.91	6.24 ± 2.79
Variance regularization	$5.53 \pm 2.85^*$	$6.05 \pm 2.97^*$
Distance map regularization	$5.55 \pm 2.63^*$	$5.77 \pm 2.67^{*\dagger}$

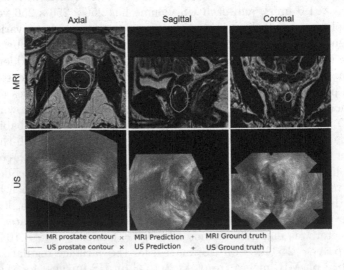

Fig. 3. Visualization results of the posterior median landmark for both modalities. The contour of US and MR prostate segmentation is highlighted in green and blue, separately. (Color figure online)

Registration Error Based on Detected Landmarks. Following [6], we also evaluate the proposed method based on surface registration error (SRE). In the remainder, we consider that the ground truth rigid transformation is best estimated by performing an Iterative Closest Point (ICP) algorithm between the prostate meshes extracted from binary segmentation masks in the US and MR images. We write T_{gt} as the mesh-based rigid transformation from MR to US images, T_{man} as the rigid transform estimated from manual landmarks and T_{pred} as the rigid transform predicted by applying the automatic landmark detection on both MR and US images. The SRE metric measures the displacement error due to a rigid misalignment on the prostate surface. If we write $S_i \in \mathbb{R}^3, i = 1 \ldots n$, a surface point of a segmented prostate mesh from the MR T2w image, the SRE for the automatic landmark detection computes as:

$$\text{SRE}(T_{gt}, T_{pred}) = \frac{1}{n} \sum_{i=1}^{n} \|T_{\text{gt}}(S_i) - T_{\text{pred}}(S_i)\|_2 \tag{6}$$

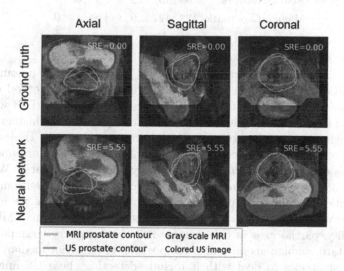

Fig. 4. Visualization of registration result. The top (resp. bottom) row show the rigid registration based on ICP algorithm (resp. neural network landmark detection) aligning MR and US images.

The registration results on all 263 MR-US image pairs in the test set are shown in Table 2, including the surface registration error (SRE) and the Dice score between the transformed MR prostate mask and US prostate mask. Visual comparison between the ground truth transformation T_{gt} and the automatic network prediction is shown in Fig. 4.

It shows that our fully automatic approach does not match the manual landmark accuracy but is comparable to initial SRE and Dice score in clinical setting from Song *et al.* [23] (resp. 7.98 ± 5.01 mm and 0.77 ± 0.14 Dice).

Table 2. Image registration performance of different methods.

Metric	Neural Network	Manual Landmark
SRE (mm)	6.62 ± 3.97	5.80 ± 3.08
Dice score	0.77 ± 0.11	0.82 ± 0.06

We can see the histogram of SRE values for our fully automatic approach and the manual landmark approach in Table 3. For fully automatic approach, most cases are smaller than 15 mm with few outliers, similarly to the SRE based on manual landmark cases.

Table 3. Frequency distribution (histogram) of SRE on the test set.

Threshold (mm)	5	10	15	20	25	30	45
Neural Network	93	137	28	1	3	0	1
Manual Landmark	122	127	9	4	0	1	0

The residual rotation matrix $R_{res} = R_{gt} R_{pred}^{-1}$ captures the amount of rotation that needs to be compensated by any rigid registration method estimated after the rigid initialization stage based on predicted landmarks. If we convert this residual matrix into a rotation vector, then we produce the histogram of the rotation angle given by the norm of rotation vector, as seen in Table 4. For the fully automatic landmark selection approach, 213 (81%) cases are under 20°C, whereas this occurs 229 (87%) for the manually selected landmarks. While both histograms are similar, this suggests that the robustness of the automated landmark detection should be improved. After looking at the data, we found that large registration errors are associated with the following reasons : MR and US image quality, partial view of the prostate in US image, very large deformation of the prostate, ambiguous ground truth position of posterior median landmark (#3). The strategies to deal with it include detecting these US images using intensity, detecting discrepancies between the predictions of two different models (with and without regularization), and visual inspection.

Table 4. Frequency distribution (histogram) of the norm of the residual rotation vector on the test set.

Threshold (degree)	5	10	20	30	40	60	70
Neural Network	18	71	124	37	8	5	0
Manual Landmark	29	88	112	24	3	6	1

4 Conclusion

We have proposed a pipeline to detect prostate anatomical landmarks of both US and MR images automatically, then least-squares fitting is applied to calculate a rough rigid transformation based on detected anatomical landmarks, thus achieving initialization for US and MR image registration. Intense experimental results have demonstrated that our method can detect anatomical landmarks for US and MR images in terms of MRE. A rough rigid transformation is calculated based on detected anatomical landmarks, which achieves comparable results in terms of SRE and Dice score in clinical setting when comparing with previous method.

Acknowledgments. This work has been supported by the French government, through the 3IA Côte d'Azur Investments in the Future project managed by the National Research Agency (ANR) with the reference number ANR-19-P3IA-0002.

References

1. Sung, H., et al.: Global cancer statistics 2020: GLOBOCAN estimates of incidence and mortality worldwide for 36 cancers in 185 countries. CA Cancer J. Clin. **71**(3), 209–249 (2021)
2. Siddiqui, M.M., et al.: Comparison of MR/ultrasound fusion-guided biopsy with ultrasound-guided biopsy for the diagnosis of prostate cancer. JAMA **313**(4), 390–397 (2015)
3. Mok, T.C.W., Chung, A.C.S.: Large deformation diffeomorphic image registration with Laplacian pyramid networks. In: Martel, A.L. (ed.) MICCAI 2020. LNCS, vol. 12263, pp. 211–221. Springer, Cham (2020). https://doi.org/10.1007/978-3-030-59716-0_21
4. Sun, Y., Jing Yuan, W., Qiu, M.R., Romagnoli, C., Fenster, A.: Three-dimensional nonrigid MR-TRUS registration using dual optimization. IEEE Trans. Med. Imaging **34**(5), 1085–1095 (2014)
5. Hu, Y., et al.: Weakly-supervised convolutional neural networks for multi image registration. Med. Image Anal. **49**, 1–13 (2018)
6. Song, X., et al.: Cross-Modal attention for MRI and ultrasound volume re In: de Bruijne, M. (ed.) MICCAI 2021. LNCS, vol. 12904, pp. 66–7 Cham (2021). https://doi.org/10.1007/978-3-030-87202-1_7
7. Li, H., Lee, C.H., Chia, D., Lin, Z., Huang, W., Tan, C.H.: Mac prostate MRI for prostate cancer: current status and future op nostics **12**(2), 289 (2022)
8. Natarajan, S., et al.: Clinical application of a 3D ultrasound-g system. Urologic Oncol.: Seminars Original Invest. **29** 334
9. Heinrich, M.P., Hansen, L.: Voxelmorph++ Going beyo keypoint supervision and multi-channel instance op Image Registration: 10th International Workshop, W July 10–12, 2022, Proceedings, pp. 85–95. Spring 1007/978-3-031-11203-4
10. Grewal, M., Wiersma, J., Westerveld, H., Bosm matic landmark correspondence detection in to deformable image registration. J. Med. I

Song, X., et al.: Distance map supervised landmark localization for MR-TRUS registration. In: Medical Imaging 2023: Image Processing, vol. 12464, pp. 708–713. SPIE (2023)

12. Criminisi, A., et al.: Regression forests for efficient anatomy detection and localization in computed tomography scans. Med. Image Anal. **17**(8), 1293–1303 (2013)

13. Alansary, A., et al.: Evaluating reinforcement learning agents for anatomical landmark detection. Med. Image Anal. **53**, 156–164 (2019)

14. Ronneberger, O., Fischer, P., Brox, T.: U-Net: convolutional networks for biomedical image segmentation. In: Navab, N., Hornegger, J., Wells, W.M., Frangi, A.F. (eds.) MICCAI 2015. LNCS, vol. 9351, pp. 234–241. Springer, Cham (2015). https://doi.org/10.1007/978-3-319-24574-4_28

15. Payer, C., Štern, D., Bischof, H., Urschler, M.: Regressing heatmaps for multiple landmark localization using CNNs. In: Ourselin, S., Joskowicz, L., Sabuncu, M.R., Unal, G., Wells, W. (eds.) MICCAI 2016. LNCS, vol. 9901, pp. 230–238. Springer, Cham (2016). https://doi.org/10.1007/978-3-319-46723-8_27

16. Wang, X., Yang, X., Dou, H., Li, S., Heng, P-A., Ni, D.: Joint segmentation and landmark localization of fetal femur in ultrasound volumes. In: 2019 IEEE EMBS International Conference on Biomedical Health Informatics (BHI), pp. 1–5. IEEE, (2019)

17. Qian, J., Ming Cheng, M., Tao, Y., Lin, J., Lin, H.: CephaNet: an improved faster R-CNN for cephalometric landmark detection. In: 2019 IEEE 16th international symposium on biomedical imaging (ISBI 2019), pp 868–871. IEEE, (2019)

18. Nibali, A., He, Z., Morgan, S., Prendergast, L.: Numerical coordinate regression with convolutional neural networks. arXiv preprint arXiv:1801.07372 (2018)

19. Arun, K.S., Huang, T.S., Blostein, S.D.: Least-squares fitting of two 3-D point sets. IEEE Trans. Pattern Anal. Mach. Intell. **9**(5), 698–700 (1987)

20. Gajowczyk, M., et al.: Coronary ostia localization using residual U-Net with heatmap matching and 3D DSNT. In: Rygiel, P., Grodek, P., Korbecki, A., Sobanski, M., Podgorski, P., Tomasz Konopczynski, T. (eds.) International Workshop on Machine Learning in Medical Imaging, vol. 13583, pp 318–327. Springer, Cham (2022). https://doi.org/10.1007/978-3-031-21014-3_33

21. Balakrishnan, G., Amy Zhao, A., Sabuncu, M.R., Guttag, J., Dalca, A.V.: VoxelMorph: a learning framework for deformable medical image registration. IEEE Trans. Med. Imaging **38**(8), 1788–1800 (2019)

22. McCouat, J., Voiculescu, I.: Contour-hugging heatmaps for landmark detection. In: Proceedings of the IEEE/CVF Conference on Computer Vision and Pattern Recognition, pp. 20597–20605 (2022)

23. Xinrui Song, X., et al.: Cross-modal attention for multi-modal image registration. Med. Image Anal. **82**, 102612 (2022)

Can Ultrasound Confidence Maps Predict Sonographers' Labeling Variability?

Vanessa Gonzalez Duque[1,2]([✉]), Leonhard Zirus[1], Yordanka Velikova[1],
Nassir Navab[1,3], and Diana Mateus[2]

[1] Computer Aided Medical Procedures, Technical University of Munich,
Munich, Germany
vanessag.duque@tum.de
[2] LS2N laboratory at Ecole Centrale Nantes, UMR CNRS, 6004 Nantes, France
[3] Computer Aided Medical Procedures, John Hopkins University, Baltimore, USA

Abstract. Measuring cross-sectional areas in ultrasound images is a
standard tool to evaluate disease progress or treatment response. Often
addressed today with supervised deep-learning segmentation approaches,
existing solutions highly depend upon the quality of experts' annotations. However, the annotation quality in ultrasound is anisotropic and
position-variant due to the inherent physical imaging principles, including attenuation, shadows, and missing boundaries, commonly exacerbated with depth. This work proposes a novel approach that guides
ultrasound segmentation networks to account for sonographers' uncertainties and generate predictions with variability similar to the experts.
We claim that realistic variability can reduce overconfident predictions
and improve physicians' acceptance of deep-learning cross-sectional segmentation solutions. Toward that end, we rely on a simple and efficient
method to estimate Confidence Maps (CM)s from ultrasound images.
The method provides certainty for each pixel for minimal computational
overhead as it can be precalculated directly from the image. We show
that there is a correlation between low values in the confidence maps and
expert's label uncertainty. Therefore, we propose to give the confidence
maps as additional information to the networks. We study the effect
of the proposed use of ultrasound CMs in combination with four state-
of-the-art neural networks and in two configurations: as a second input
channel and as part of the loss. We evaluate our method on 3D ultrasound
datasets of the thyroid and lower limb muscles. Our results show ultrasound CMs increase the Dice score, improve the Hausdorff and Average
Surface Distances, and decrease the number of isolated pixel predictions.
Furthermore, our findings suggest that ultrasound CMs improve the

V.G. Duque and L. Zirus—Both authors share first authorship.

This work has been supported in part by the European Regional Development. Fund,
the Pays de la Loire region on the Connect Talent scheme (MILCOM Project) and
Nantes Metropole (Convention 2017-10470),

Supplementary Information The online version contains supplementary material
available at https://doi.org/10.1007/978-3-031-44521-7_17.

penalization of uncertain areas in the ground truth data, thereby improving problematic interpolations. Our code and example data will be made
public at https://github.com/IFL-CAMP/Confidence-segmentation.

Keywords: Confidence maps · 3D ultrasound · 3D segmentation ·
fully convolutional neural networks

1   Introduction

Volumetry information of muscles and organs is used to evaluate the treatment
response for diseases such as hyperthyroidism [17] or Duchenne dystrophy [19].
One way of measuring the volume or the evolution is by performing segmentation
of the affected organs on 3D ultrasound images. This process is time-consuming
and operator dependent if done manually. Moreover, expert segmentations are
anisotropic and position-variant due to the inherent physical principles governing
ultrasound images: sound interacts with surface layers generating areas of attenuation, shadows, missing boundaries, etc. This paper investigates how to make deep
learning segmentation models aware of the specific uncertainties the ultrasound
modality introduces, which also affect experts' annotations. To this end, we rely on
the concept of Confidence Maps (CMs) introduced by Kalamaris et al. [12]. Based
on an image-based simplified approximation of the wave propagation through the
imaged mediums, CMs proposed to estimate an uncertainty value for each pixel
in the image. The problem is formulated as a label propagation on a graph solved
with a random walker algorithm. The resultant confidence maps (CMs) have been
used until now for improving reconstruction [3], registration [24], and non-deep-
learning bone segmentation [2] in ultrasound. To the best of our knowledge, we are
the first to study ultrasound confidence maps in the context of Neural Networks
for semantic segmentation and analyze its influence on border variability.

  To address the differences in interpretation among observers in medical image
segmentation, supervised learning methods often rely on ground truth data generated by popular fusion techniques such as majority voting [8] or Staple [23].
Nevertheless, these techniques do not capture the variations when making predictions with the model. Different approaches integrate segmentation uncertainty
directly as part of the model's ability to make probabilistic predictions. Baumgartner et al. [1], for example, propose a hierarchical probabilistic model, while
Jungo et al. [11] analyse the uncertainty and calibration of brain tumor segmentation using U-Net-like architectures [21]. Both methods are trained with
annotations from single or multiple annotators. In a similar manner, training is
done for stochastic segmentation networks [15] and Post hoc network calibration methods [22]. Such approaches require modifications in the architectures and
extra labeling that are time-consuming and demand a hyper-parameter search.
Instead, our first proposal consists in providing a pre-calculated Confidence Map
as a second channel to a segmentation network, which does not require multiple
annotations, and does not change the loss but slightly increases the number of
parameters (of the input layer).

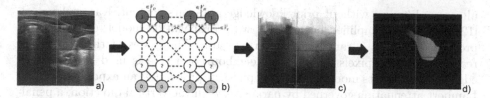

Fig. 1. From confidence maps to confidence masks: a) US image and overlaid segmentations, b) image graph representation, c) Confidence map [12], d) Confidence mask

There exist other approaches to learn label variability without modifying the network, such as label smoothing [9,14,16], temperature scaling [6], annotator error Disentangling [10], and non-parametric calibration [25]. Most of them are applied on MRI or CT. We align ourselves with these ideas, applying our method to ultrasound, a modality characterized by blurred edges, low signal-to-noise ratio, speckle noise, and other challenges. Our second proposition to cope with these challenges is to define a cross-entropy loss based on a probabilistic ground truth called "confidence mask", computed from the CMs and the ground truth labels. This new label is probabilistic not only in the borders, like other methods, but in the whole structure. Thereby, we propose to predict the "Confidence Masks" in order to make predictions both a good segmentation but also calibrate the output probability to the confidence content. Following our experiments, we discover that confidence masks teach the network to penalize areas with high confidence and interpolate areas with low confidence.

2   Methodology

Guiding Segmentation Networks with Confidence Maps. The core of our method is to guide the training with pre-calculated CMs. Let $\mathbf{X} \in \mathbb{R}^{W \times H \times D}$ be the input volume and $\mathbf{Y}, \hat{\mathbf{Y}} \in \mathbb{R}^{W \times H \times D \times C}$ respectively the one-hot encoding labels and the network prediction for C classes. We first compute the CM from the image: $\mathbf{CM} : \mathbf{X} \mapsto (0,1)^{W \times H \times D}$ (c.f. the next subsection). Our first proposition is to use the CMs as an additional channel so that the input to the network becomes $[\mathbf{X}|\mathbf{CM}]$, with $\cdot|\cdot$ a concatenation. In our second proposition, we combine the CMs with the labels to create a "Confidence Mask" $(Y \cdot CM)$, where "$\cdot$" represents the element-wise multiplication, and define the Cross entropy confidence loss over the m voxels of the image as:

$$\text{CE}_{conf}(\mathbf{Y}, \hat{\mathbf{Y}}) = -\frac{1}{m} \sum_{i=1}^{m} (Y_i \cdot CM_i) \cdot \log\left(\hat{Y}_i\right) \qquad (1)$$

Pre-calculated Confidence Maps: In ultrasound imaging, pressure waves are transmitted and reflected primarily to the transducers, but traversed tissues absorb, diverge, refract, and disperse the sound as well. Therefore, as the wave progresses, the recorded intensities become less reliable. The goal of the confidence map algorithm is to assign uncertainty values to each pixel in any ultrasound image, without prior knowledge about its content. Karamalis et al. [12] proposed a simplified but efficient wave propagation model to address this problem based on a random walk on a graph. The nodes of the graph represent the image pixels while an 8 neighbourhood rule is used to define the edges. Edge weights model ultrasound physical properties: an exponential Beer-Lambert attenuation governed by parameter α in the vertical direction; a penalization for horizontal and diagonal propagations associated with the beam shape; and a penalization between neighbour pixels with different intensities, controlled by parameter β, modeling the negative correlations between reflection and transmission across tissue boundaries. At each step of the random walk, the probability of moving from one pixel to another is based on the defined edge weights. By definition, source and sink nodes are placed at the top and bottom of the image, respectively. The problem is then formulated as computing the probability of the random walk starting from a transducer/source pixel to reach a sink node (c.f. Fig. 1-c). The sought probabilities are obtained by solving a linear system of equations, we refer the reader to [12] for more details. In practice, and following the above model, the random walk goes from the top to the bottom approximately perpendicular to the beam/scanline direction. Deviations in the horizontal/diagonal directions are possible to a small degree, according to the image content, and controlled by the α and β hyper-parameters.

Datasets: Two different 3D ultrasound datasets were used for the experiments and are presented in Fig. 2. They consist of 2D B-mode ultrasound sweeps that can generate compounded 3D volumes. The first dataset is open-source and available from [13]. It contains scans of the *thyroid* of 16 volunteers, with 3 labels: thyroid, aorta, and jugular vein. Each volume contains around 200 images of size $W \times H = 400 \times 270$, for a total of more than 1600 images. The second in-house dataset [5] contains 4 to 6 scans per volume of the left *low-limb legs* of 16 participants with 3 labels: Soleus, Gastrocnemius lateralis, and Gastrocnemius Medialis muscles. Each volume of size $W \times H = 500 \times 420$ contains around 1500 images, for a total of more than 24000 images.

For both datasets, confidence maps were calculated over 2D ultrasound images using the implementation of the random walker algorithm [12] available in the ImFusion[1] [24] software, version 2.36.3, with α and β parameters set to 0.5, 100 respectively. The data was split patient-wise into 11 train volumes, 2 for validation and 3 for testing, in each case.

Evaluation Metrics: For multi-label segmentation, we compute 8 different metrics: Dice Similarity Coefficient (DSC), mean Intersection over Union (mIoU), precision, recall, Average Surface Distance (ASD), Hausdorff distance(HD), miss rate, and fall out. Following [20], we evaluate the metrics for each class and average them over the organs and participants.

---

[1] ImFusion GmbH, Munich, Germany.

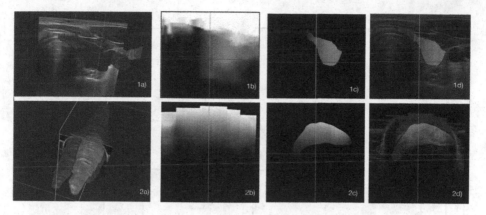

Fig. 2. Examples of the thyroid (top row) and the low-limb muscles (bottom row), respectively. (a) corresponds to the 3D view of the labels at the top, the red, blue, and yellow correspond to the Thyroid, the carotid artery, and the Jugular vein, while at the bottom, they correspond to the Soleus, the Gastrocnemius lateralis, and the Gastrocnemius Medialis. (b) the CM cross-sectional view, (c) the confidence Mask used for the loss, (d) the CM overlapped over the image with red signalizing the areas with low confidence. (Color figure online)

3 Experiments and Results

Contribution of the Confidence Maps: We denote the models relying on the CMs as a second channel with names including the term (*-2ch-*) and those with CMs in the loss with the pattern (*-*-*conf). Based on a U-Net architecture we evaluate a total of 10 configurations:

- **Baselines:** unet-1ch-dice, unet-1ch-crossentropy(CE), unet-1ch- Dice cross entropy (diceCE)
- **CMs as 2nd channel:** unet-2ch-dice, unet-2ch-CE, unet-2ch-diceCE,
- **CMs within the loss :** unet-1ch-CEconfidence, unet-1ch-diceCEconfidence
- **CMS both as 2nd channel and within the loss:** unet-2ch-diceCE confidence and unet-2ch-CEconfidence

The results are reported in Fig. 3, where we keep the best configuration for each group. We computed a 3-fold-cross validation to verify the independence of the results to the participants split. We found that CMs decrease the standard deviation of the DSC in general. While the HD of CM configurations is similar or increased for the thyroid dataset, the positive effect of CMs in the muscles dataset is clear. We attribute this behavior to the more complex muscle shapes. More boxplots metrics can be found in our github. Based on the balance between DSC and HD scores, the best two configurations are: unet-2ch-dice and unet-1ch-CEconfidence. Figure 4 showcases segmentation improvements using CMs. For the thyroid dataset, CMs reduced isolated regions, enhancing accuracy. For the leg dataset, CMs improved interpolation and smoothness of segmented structures.

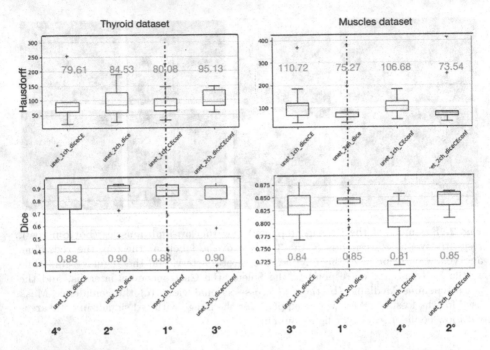

Fig. 3. First and second columns report the results for the thyroid and the muscles metrics, respectively. The best four performing methods are ranked 1°, 2°, 3°, 4°.

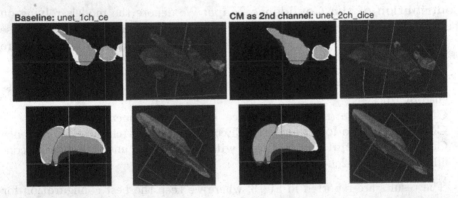

Fig. 4. Prediction for one participant of the thyroid dataset in the top and the leg in the bottom. At left the baseline method:**unet-1ch-ce**, at the right our proposal:**unet-2ch-dice**

Expert Uncertainty and Prediction Variability: To evaluate the areas where the network is less certain, we ask the same expert to perform the labeling of the same image 100 times at different times. We compare the variability with the entropy of 100 Monte Carlo Dropout predictions for the unet-1ch-dice and unet-2ch-dice. We observe in Fig. 5, how CMs bring the predictions variability closer to the expert's uncertainty, with an anisotropic behaviour that reflects difficult areas (the intersection of the three muscles) and increases with depth.

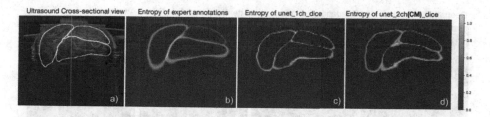

Fig. 5. Labelling variability: Ultrasound image with labeling of the muscles, b) Expert variability, c) Monte Carlo dropout for the baseline method. d) Monte Carlo dropout of our method with CMs as the second channel.

CMs with State of the Art Architectures: For both datasets, we tested four different 3D networks available in MONAI [4]. We trained the models for 120 epochs, with a learning rate of 0.001 and the ADAM optimizer, on a Nvidia 390 GPU. Qualitative images are presented in Fig. 6. The evaluation metrics for the Muscles dataset, computed in a 3-fold cross-validation manner, are presented in Table 1.

Unet transformer (UNETR) presents a very low accuracy probably as they need more data. Instead, Attention Unet obtains a very high accuracy using confidence maps, we attribute this behavior to the way the attention layers learn from the new meaningful additional information in the CMs.

Table 1. Metrics on the muscle dataset for the baselines and the modified versions of 4 different networks: UNet3D [21], attention Unet (AttUNet) [18], DeepAtlas [26] and UNet Transformer(UNETR) [7].

Network	DSC ↑	precision ↑	miss rate ↓	ASD ↓
UNet 1ch dice CE	0.84 ± 0.02	0.84 ± 0.06	0.16 ± 0.04	8.37 ± 2.19
UNet 2ch dice*	**0.85 ± 0.01**	0.85 ± 0.01	**0.16 ± 0.02**	**8.20 ± 1.81**
UNet 1ch diceCEconf*	0.81 ± 0.01	**0.86 ± 0.05**	0.18 ± 0.04	8.36 ± 0.78
AttUNet 1ch CE	0.57 ± 0.49	0.58 ± 0.50	0.44 ± 0.49	40.00 ± 15.01
AttUNet 2ch dice *	**0.86 ± 0.00**	**0.85 ± 0.04**	**0.12 ± 0.04**	**7.03 ± 1.08**
AttUNet 1ch diceCEconf	0.57 ± 0.50	0.59 ± 0.51	0.44 ± 0.48	40.00 ± 14.09
DeepAtlas Dice	0.82 ± 0.02	0.84 + 0.05	0.18 ± 0.06	**11.22 ± 1.54**
DeepAtlas 2ch dice *	0.84 ± 0.01	0.84 ± 0.06	0.15 ± 0.07	11.89 ± 6.00
DeepAtlas 1ch diceCEconf *	**0.85 ± 0.01**	0.84 ± 0.02	**0.13 ± 0.02**	11.74 ± 5.50
UNETR 1ch CE	**0.66 ± 0.06**	0.72 ± 0.12	**0.37 ± 0.02**	23.52 ± 8.97
UNETR 2ch dice*	0.48 ± 0.12	0.77 ± 0.11	0.62 ± 0.12	23.74 ± 8.72
UNETR 1ch diceCEconf*	0.56 ± 0.07	**0.82 ± 0.13**	0.55 ± 0.09	**19.54 ± 9.65**

We performed the Friedman statistical significance test for the Null hypothesis: "all methods perform equally". A pair-wise post-hoc cross-validation between

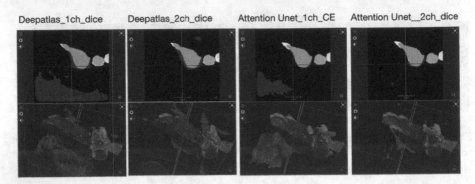

Fig. 6. (**top row**) 2D cross-sectional view of the predictions overlaid over the expert's labels. (**bottom row**) 3D predictions in color and labels in gray for the 2 best configurations and their corresponding baselines: 1. Deep-atlas 1ch dice, 2. Deep-atlas 2ch dice, 3. Attention Unet 1ch CE, 4.Attention Unet-2ch-Dice. (Color figure online)

the baseline networks and the modified networks (2ch and dice-CEconf) was performed. The methods that reject the null hypothesis, $p < 0.05$, for the Hausdorff distance, are marked with $*$. The results in the table show that CMs improve segmentation metrics by a small factor. However, looking at the qualitative results, we see CM-models favor better interpolation of the bottom areas where uncertainty is higher, improve the segmentation of small structures, and decrease the number of islands, as it can be seen in Fig. 6.

4   Discussion and Conclusions

In conclusion, this study presents an original approach to improve the awareness of ultrasound deep learning segmentation methods to label variability. Our method, based on ultrasound Confidence Maps, takes into account the basic ultrasound wave propagation principles, which affect sonographers' uncertainty when annotating. Introduced as an additional input channel or within the loss, CMs guide the network to predict segmentations that effectively reproduce expert-like borders variability and whose drop-out uncertainty grows with the depth, as expected for ultrasound images. Thereby, our method can be used to generate multiple solutions for the physicians to judge, with fixed borders for certain and variable mask predictions for uncertain regions. Two advantages of the approach with the CM loss is that it does not increase the number of parameters, which indicates that it is architecture agnostic. In this sense, the approach could be applied as a fine-tuning strategy after transfer learning.

Our experimental results show that the training of CM models does not affect the convergence for either of the proposed approaches. Moreover, the CMs precomputation is very fast as it consists of the resolution of a linear system with a sparse matrix. In sum, this novel, simple and effective approach to introduce ultrasound and expert knowledge can be easily implemented in combination with various ultrasound segmentation architectures without incurring additional computational costs. We evaluated our method on two datasets, one private and another public, to ensure repeatability. Future work aims at distilling the confidence map automatically. Although we used the dice loss and cross-entropy loss, other losses or combinations could also be considered.

References

1. Baumgartner, C.F., et al.: PHiSeg: capturing uncertainty in medical image segmentation. In: Shen, D., et al. (eds.) MICCAI 2019. LNCS, vol. 11765, pp. 119–127. Springer, Cham (2019). https://doi.org/10.1007/978-3-030-32245-8_14

2. Beitzel, J., Ahmadi, S.A., Karamalis, A., Wein, W., Navab, N.: Ultrasound bone detection using patient-specific CT prior. In: 2012 Annual International Conference of the IEEE Engineering in Medicine and Biology Society, pp. 2664–2667. IEEE (2012)

3. Berge, C.S., Kapoor, A., Navab, N.: Orientation-driven ultrasound compounding using uncertainty information. In: Stoyanov, D., Collins, D.L., Sakuma, I., Abolmaesumi, P., Jannin, P. (eds.) IPCAI 2014. LNCS, vol. 8498, pp. 236–245. Springer, Cham (2014). https://doi.org/10.1007/978-3-319-07521-1_25

4. Cardoso, M.J., et al.: Monai: An open-source framework for deep learning in healthcare. arXiv preprint arXiv:2211.02701 (2022)

5. Crouzier, M., Lacourpaille, L., Nordez, A., Tucker, K., Hug, F.: Neuromechanical coupling within the human triceps Surae and its consequence on individual force-sharing strategies. J. Exp. Biol. **221**(21), jeb.187260 (2018)

6. Guo, C., Pleiss, G., Sun, Y., Weinberger, K.Q.: On calibration of modern neural networks. In: International Conference on Machine Learning, pp. 1321–1330. PMLR (2017)

7. Hatamizadeh, A., et al.: Unetr: transformers for 3d medical image segmentation. In: Proceedings of the IEEE/CVF Winter Conference on Applications of Computer Vision, pp. 574–584 (2022)

8. Iglesias, J.E., Sabuncu, M.R.: Multi-atlas segmentation of biomedical images: a survey. Med. Image Anal. **24**(1), 205–219 (2015)

9. Islam, M., Glocker, B.: Spatially varying label smoothing: capturing uncertainty from expert annotations. In: Feragen, A., Sommer, S., Schnabel, J., Nielsen, M. (eds.) IPMI 2021. LNCS, vol. 12729, pp. 677–688. Springer, Cham (2021). https://doi.org/10.1007/978-3-030-78191-0_52

10. Jacob, J., Ciccarelli, O., Barkhof, F., Alexander, D.C.: Disentangling human error from the ground truth in segmentation of medical images. In: ACL (2021)

11. Jungo, A., et al.: On the effect of inter-observer variability for a reliable estimation of uncertainty of medical image segmentation. In: Frangi, A.F., Schnabel, J.A., Davatzikos, C., Alberola-López, C., Fichtinger, G. (eds.) MICCAI 2018. LNCS, vol. 11070, pp. 682–690. Springer, Cham (2018). https://doi.org/10.1007/978-3-030-00928-1_77

12. Karamalis, A., Wein, W., Klein, T., Navab, N.: Ultrasound confidence maps using random walks. Med. Image Anal. **16**(6), 1101–1112 (2012)

13. Krönke, M., et al.: Tracked 3d ultrasound and deep neural network-based thyroid segmentation reduce interobserver variability in thyroid volumetry. PLoS ONE **17**(7), e0268550 (2022)

14. Lourenço-Silva, J., Oliveira, A.L.: Using soft labels to model uncertainty in medical image segmentation. In: Crimi, A., Bakas, S. (eds.) Brainlesion: Glioma, Multiple Sclerosis, Stroke and Traumatic Brain Injuries. BrainLes 2021. LNCS, vol. 12963. Springer, Cham (2021). https://doi.org/10.1007/978-3-031-09002-8_52
15. Monteiro, M., et al.: Stochastic segmentation networks: modelling spatially correlated aleatoric uncertainty. Adv. Neural Inf. Process. Syst. **33**, 12756–12767 (2020)
16. Müller, R., Kornblith, S., Hinton, G.E.: When does label smoothing help? In: Advances in Neural Information Processing Systems, vol. 32 (2019)
17. Nguyen, D.T., Choi, J., Park, K.R.: Thyroid nodule segmentation in ultrasound image based on information fusion of suggestion and enhancement networks. Mathematics **10**(19), 3484 (2022)
18. Oktay, O., et al.: Attention u-net: learning where to look for the pancreas. In: IMIDL Conference (2018) (2018)
19. Pichiecchio, A., et al.: Muscle ultrasound elastography and MRI in preschool children with Duchenne muscular dystrophy. Neuromuscul. Disord. **28**(6), 476–483 (2018)
20. Reinke, A., et al.: Common limitations of image processing metrics: a picture story. arXiv preprint arXiv:2104.05642 (2021)
21. Ronneberger, O., Fischer, P., Brox, T.: U-Net: convolutional networks for biomedical image segmentation. In: Navab, N., Hornegger, J., Wells, W.M., Frangi, A.F. (eds.) MICCAI 2015. LNCS, vol. 9351, pp. 234–241. Springer, Cham (2015). https://doi.org/10.1007/978-3-319-24574-4_28
22. Rousseau, A.J., Becker, T., Bertels, J., Blaschko, M.B., Valkenborg, D.: Post training uncertainty calibration of deep networks for medical image segmentation. In: 2021 IEEE 18th International Symposium on Biomedical Imaging (ISBI), pp. 1052–1056. IEEE (2021)
23. Warfield, S.K., Zou, K.H., Wells, W.M.: Simultaneous truth and performance level estimation (staple): an algorithm for the validation of image segmentation. IEEE Trans. Med. Imaging **23**(7), 903–921 (2004)
24. Wein, W., Karamalis, A., Baumgartner, A., Navab, N.: Automatic bone detection and soft tissue aware ultrasound-CT registration for computer-aided orthopedic surgery. Int. J. Comput. Assist. Radiol. Surg. **10**, 971–979 (2015)
25. Wenger, J., Kjellström, H., Triebel, R.: Non-parametric calibration for classification. In: International Conference on Artificial Intelligence and Statistics, pp. 178–190. PMLR (2020)
26. Xu, Z., Niethammer, M.: DeepAtlas: joint semi-supervised learning of image registration and segmentation. In: Shen, D., et al. (eds.) MICCAI 2019. LNCS, vol. 11765, pp. 420–429. Springer, Cham (2019). https://doi.org/10.1007/978-3-030-32245-8_47

Multi-task Learning for Hierarchically-Structured Images: Study on Echocardiogram View Classification

Jerome Charton[1]([envelope]), Hui Ren[1], Sekeun Kim[1], Carola Maraboto Gonzalez[1], Jay Khambhati[1], Justin Cheng[2], Jeena DeFrancesco[2], Anam Waheed[2], Sylwia Marciniak[2], Filipe Moura[2], Rhanderson Cardoso[2], Bruno Lima[2], Michael Picard[1], Xiang Li[1], and Quanzheng Li[1]

[1] Massachusetts General Hospital, Harvard Medical School, Boston, USA
jcharton@mgh.harvard.edu
[2] Brigham and Women's Hospital, Boston, USA

Abstract. Echocardiography is a crucial and widely adopted imaging modality for diagnosing and monitoring cardiovascular diseases. Deep learning has been proven effective in analyzing medical images but is limited in echocardiograms due to the complexity of image acquisition and interpretation. One crucial initial step to address this is automatically identifying the correct echocardiogram video views. Several studies have used deep learning and traditional image-processing techniques for this task. The authors propose an ablation study on a multi-task learning scheme with a hierarchically structured model output that arranges views in a tree structure. The proposed model, named "Multi-task Residual Neural Network (MTRNN) with masked loss", uses a conditional probabilistic training method and demonstrates superior performance for echocardiogram view classification. While the model has only been validated for the echocardiogram video classification task, it can be easily generalized to any medical image classification scenario with a hierarchical structure among the data labels.

Keywords: Echocardiagram · Multi-task learning · View classification

1 Introduction

Echocardiography is a critical and widely adopted imaging modality for the screening, diagnosing, differential diagnosing, and follow-up of various cardiovascular diseases [13]. Deep learning has emerged as a powerful tool for analyzing medical images and has shown its potential to reduce the burden on cardiologists and radiologists [17]. However, applying deep learning methods for echocardiogram analysis is more challenging than other modalities due to the complexity of image interpretation and identification of the desired imaging view(s) and the focus in that view [8]. To address this issue, the first step toward comprehensive computer-assisted echocardiographic image analysis is to automatically

B. Kainz et al. (Eds.): ASMUS 2023, LNCS 14337, pp. 185–194, 2023.
https://doi.org/10.1007/978-3-031-44521-7_18

identify the correct views for echocardiogram videos [16]. Recently, there have been multiple studies targeting this task, both using deep learning-based techniques [3,9,10,12,19] and traditional image processing-based techniques [1,20] and many others.

On the other hand, from the perspectives of the sonographers, obtaining an echocardiogram generally involves several standard steps, such as localization, rotation, and tilting of the probe or transducer. These steps will naturally result in a hierarchical structure among echocardiogram views. We observe that these views could be arranged in a tree structure depending on the location (Apical, Parasternal, Others), the orientation of the probe (e.g., short axis views vs long axis views, orientation notch towards the right side or the up side of the body) and the focus in the view (e.g., short axis view at the level of the aortic valve vs apical long axis view with three chambers). Motivated by the imaging procedure and observations, we proposed a multi-task learning scheme with hierarchically-structured model outputs in this study. The proposed scheme simultaneously predicts the corresponding labels at each tree layer via different branches implemented as model heads. In addition, motivated by the multi-task learning schemes proposed by [4,14], which utilizes model training with conditional probability and a masked loss function, we integrate the conditional probabilistic training into the branch-based model design. The final model, named "Multi-task Residual Neural Network (MTRNN) with masked loss", fully leverages the intrinsic tree structure of the relationship among video labels (views) and has demonstrated superior performance for the echocardiogram view classification task using an in-house dataset. Formulating the view classification task in a hierarchical multi-task learning framework can: 1) improve model generalizability by learning the related data labels simultaneously with shared representations learned across tasks, which can help capture standard features [15]; 2) reduce overfitting towards a single task by defining the loss function across multiple related tasks [22]; 3) improve model explainability as not only the leaf-level label (e.g., whether the given video belongs to A4C view) is predicted, but also along with the labels of each layer (e.g., whether the video belongs to apical view or parasternal views).

2   Methodology

2.1   Model Architecture

Hierarchically-structured image classification has been discussed through several research works but is still a largely overlooked topic. We can distinguish two approaches for leveraging the hierarchical structure among labels: revisiting the loss function or designing the hierarchical classification network. These two approaches were considered in [23] (also in [7]) and [4] (also in [2]). While [23] relay on a network architecture adapted to the hierarchical classification (BCNN: branch convolutional neural network for hierarchical classification) with a specific loss function designed for its network (Weighted Loss), [4] focuses on the definition of a loss function adapted to a hierarchical classification (Masked loss). This paper will compare these two loss functions upon several networks similar to the BCNN.

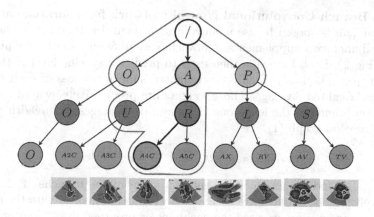

Fig. 1. Tree structure of the classification labels of this task. Echocardiography videos are classified into nine regular views, including Apical 2, 3, 4, 5 chambers (A2c, A3c, A4c, A5c, respectively), Parasternal long axis (AX), Parasternal long axis with right ventricle focus (RV), Parasternal short axis at the level of aortic valve (AV), Parasternal short axis at the level of tricuspid valve (TV), and Others (O), shown as leaf nodes on the hierarchical tree. Those views are associated at the first level by the orientation of the probe during image acquisition, including the Upper (U), Right (R), Long axis (L), Short axis (S), and Others (O). These five classes are then regrouped into three classes depending on the location of the probe Apical (A), Parasternal (P), and Others (O). Outlined nodes are A4c and its ancestors. The red contour draws the mask defined Eq. (2). Illustrations of the images for each view are visualized at the bottom, which were originally presented in [11]. (Color figure online)

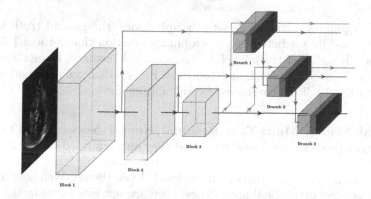

Fig. 2. Multi-task network architectures tested in this work on a VGG16 backbone. Black arrows: connections of the backbone network. BCNN (Branch Neural Network) [23] added two classifier heads (branches 1 and 2) with the green arrow connections, where the branches 1, 2, and 3 predict the green, purple, and red levels of the tree Fig. 1, respectively. We also tested the following combinations: black+green+red connections (R-BCNN: Residual Branch Neural Network); black+grey connections (MTNN: multi-task neural network); black+grey+red connections (MTRNN: multi-task residual neural network) (Color figure online)

BCNN: Branch Convolutional Neural Network for Hierarchical Classification [23] proposed to use a convolutional neural network as a backbone and to adjunct two supplementary branches at different depths defining the BCNN (Fig. 2). Each branch is then used to predict a specific level of the classification tree. The loss is finally the weighted sum of the loss of each branch, called the Weighted Average. Those weights are progressively swayed from the higher level branch to the lower one. This approach suggests a breadth path of the classification graph (1).

$$L_{WeightedAvg} = \alpha \cdot L_1 + \beta \cdot L_2 + \gamma \cdot L_3, \tag{1}$$

where L_1, L_2, and L_3 are the cross-entropy losses of the branches 1, 2, and 3, respectively, and α, β, and γ are normalized weight that evolves with the epochs. In our experimentation, we used the backbone as proposed in [23] and preserved the original coefficients, but we increased the periodicity of their changes to match our convergence curves.

Masking for Evaluating the Loss. In opposition to [23], which proposed a network for progressively learning the hierarchical graph level by level for the root to the leaves, [4] proposes to focus on learning the differentiation between sibling nodes within the graph. For that, it proposed a masked evaluation of the cross-entropy loss. This mask filters out (turns to zero) the weights of the current prediction related to all non-adjacent nodes to the target path within the graph.

$$L_{Masked} = \sum_{n \in N} CE(y_n, \bar{y}_n) \cdot p(n), \tag{2}$$

where N, y_n, and $\bar{y}_n$ denote the set of graph nodes, the ground truth label of the node n, and its prediction. $p(n)$ is a binary function that returns 1 if of the parents of n is a ground truth label, 0 otherwise. For instance, if the target label is $A4C$, its ancestors are R, A, and/(outlined Fig. 1), then only the nodes in the red area of Fig. 1 will be considered for calculating the loss.

Proposed Model: Multi-Task Residual Neural Network (MTRNN). These two methods have demonstrated that they outperformed the regular cross-entropy loss upon their associated networks. However, how much each strategy is more efficient than the others is undisclosed. Even though Weighted loss and Masked loss have orthogonal approaches, they are not exclusive. In this study, we propose an ablation study that combines those two loss functions and analyses their impact on the learning of several network architectures. As an initial network, we used the BCNN, to which we proposed a few modifications and built three additional variations of this network (Fig. 2). The first additional network, R-BCNN: residual branch neural network, preserves all the connections of the BCNN but additionally concatenates the output of the branch of the upper level of the tree successor branch (black, green, and red connections). In the second additional architecture, we propose to translate the connections of branches 1 and 2 to the end of the features block of the VGG16 [18]. So we obtain a VGG16 with three classifier heads, named MTNN: multi-task neural network (black and grey connections). Finally, for the third additional network, we reuse the MTNN and add the red connections (black, grey, and red connections), defining the MTRNN: multi-task residual neural network. While the red connections aim to enforce the relationship between the adjacent nodes in the hierarchy, the grey connections propose a different depth for extracting features related to the higher classes. In our experimentation, we have tested combining and dissociating the two introduced methods for calculating the loss upon the four presented networks (BCNN, R-BCNN, MTNN, MTRNN).

2.2   Dataset and Pre-processing

In this work, we studied a hierarchical classification task on a Doppler echocardiography videos dataset of Massachusetts General Hospital composed of 249 aortic stenosis patients and 8292 videos acquired with Philips devices, with video labels of nine views (A2C, A3C, A4C, A5C, PLAX, PLAX_RV, PSAX_AV, PSAX_TV, and OTHERS) annotated by three sonographers. Parasternal long axis view focused on the left or right ventricle (PLAX_LV, PLAX_RV), Parasternal short axis view focused on the aortic valve or tricuspid valve (PSAX_AV, PSAX_TV). In the pre-processing phase, videos are decomposed into frame images. Images are masked, cropped, and resized to 224 squared with a black filling, so the embedded metadata surrounding the record is removed. Only the imaging sector of the ultrasound probe remains (Fig. 3). The field of view was not part of the metadata of the DICOM files. It has been estimated by extracting the largest convex hull over the pixels with high variability across the video frames. Table 1 shows the preparation of our dataset within the 9-class classification. According to the steps of sonographers in obtaining different views of the echocardiogram, including localizing, rotating, and tilting the probe, we established the tree structure of these nine views based on the similarity in their imaging procedure and visual appearance, as shown in Fig. 1.

Table 1. Composition of the echocardiography dataset used in our classification task. This table indicates the number of videos per view and splits. The split was made such that each video is exclusive to a unique split.

Split/View	A2C	A3C	A4C	A5C	PLAX	PLAX_RV	PSAX_AV	PSAX_TV	OTHERS
Training	209	446	702	374	775	201	475	133	2328
Validation	60	128	200	107	221	58	136	38	665
Testing	30	64	100	53	111	29	68	19	332

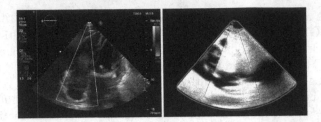

Fig. 3. ROI extraction from Doppler echocardiogram data. Left, original data. Right, the activity map was calculated across all the video frames with the largest convex hull extracted (red contour). (Color figure online)

3   Results

3.1   Model Implementation and Hyper-parameter Settings

The implementation of the neural networks was carried out over Pytorch and trained on an NVIDIA A100 GPU with 40 GB of VRAM. For the training parameters, we used a batch size of 124 and a learning rate of 0.001 with a scheduler that reduces it by 10^{-1} every 30 epochs. Each network was training over 100 epochs. The source code of all the models tested in this work and the echocardiogram video processing pipeline will be shared with the general public via GitHub (URL anonymized).

Table 2. Average accuracy among the tested combinations by different networks and the strategies for defining the training loss. Avg, W. Avg, and Masked stand for average loss, weighted average loss, and masked loss calculation, respectively. The accuracy is evaluated for each video by voting over all the frames.

Structure/Method	Avg	Avg + Masked	W. Avg + Masked
VGG16	0.90	NA	NA
BCNN	0.92	0.98	0.97
R-BCNN	0.91	0.98	0.97
MTNN	0.92	0.98	0.98
MTRNN	0.92	0.98	0.97

3.2   Running Example of the Classification Result

Figure 4 shows side by side the difference between the hierarchical multi-task architectures investigated in this work (BCNN, RBCNN, MTNN, and MTRNN) and the regular VGG-16, for the same input video. The additional labels predicted ("A" and "R") and the corresponding loss functions would be useful for improving model explainability and generalizability.

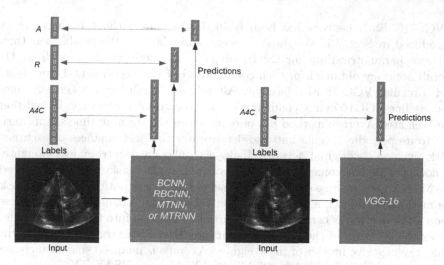

Fig. 4. The architectures observed in this study (left) take as an input an image and predict triple labels associated with a three-level hierarchical graph, where a regular VGG-16 (right) outputs only one prediction.

Table 3. Accuracy per class. The accuracy is evaluated for each video by voting over all the frames.

Average								
Structure	OTHERS	A2C	A3C	A4C	A5C	PLAX	PLAX_RV	PSAX_AV	PSAX_TV
VGG-16	0.86	0.87	0.92	0.93	0.91	0.96	0.90	0.94	0.95
BCNN	0.89	0.87	0.95	0.95	0.96	0.97	0.90	0.94	0.89
R-BCNN	0.88	0.90	0.94	0.95	0.92	0.98	0.83	0.91	0.79
MTNN	0.89	0.90	0.94	0.95	0.92	0.98	0.90	0.94	0.84
MTRNN	0.89	0.90	0.95	0.95	0.94	0.97	0.97	0.93	0.89

Average + Masked								
Structure	OTHERS	A2C	A3C	A4C	A5C	PLAX	PLAX_RV	PSAX_AV	PSAX_TV
BCNN	0.87	0.90	0.98	0.96	0.96	0.99	0.93	0.93	0.84
R-BCNN	0.88	0.97	0.89	0.92	0.94	0.95	0.86	0.90	0.68
MTNN	0.87	0.83	0.95	0.95	0.94	0.98	0.97	0.94	0.84
MTRNN	0.85	0.97	0.95	0.96	0.94	0.97	0.93	0.94	0.79

Weighted Average + Masked								
Structure	OTHERS	A2C	A3C	A4C	A5C	PLAX	PLAX_RV	PSAX_AV	PSAX_TV
BCNN	0.97	0.93	1.00	0.94	0.94	1.00	1.00	0.99	1.00
R-BCNN	0.97	0.93	1.00	0.95	0.96	1.00	1.00	0.99	1.00
MTNN	0.96	0.93	1.00	0.96	0.98	1.00	1.00	1.00	1.00
MTRNN	0.97	0.90	1.00	0.95	0.96	1.00	1.00	0.99	1.00

3.3 Performance Comparison

In the experimentation, the four architectures presented above (i.e., BCNN, R-BCNN, MTNN, and MTRNN) have been tested over the same backbone, a VGG-16. Each network has been trained with and without both strategies introduced in Sect. 2.1, Weighted Average and Masked. We established three different parametrisations for the training of each network. Table 2 shows the overall accuracy obtained for each combination of the experimental workbench and a regular VGG-16 as a baseline. All enhanced architectures outperformed the baseline VGG16 in any configuration based on overall accuracy. In addition, the Weighted Average method not only increases the training time significantly due to its periodic weights but also deteriorates the performances of each network, even on its original network. Using a regular cross-entropy loss (weighted or not), the BCNN comes on top. However, when the masking method is used, the MTNN gets an edge over the other networks. It was noticed that the masking method introduced a higher confusion between the A2c and OTHERS views upon all the networks compared in this article. Lowering into the details, Table 3 shows the accuracy of the tested configuration over each targeted class. At this scale, the negative impact of the Weighted Average is nuanced since it increases the accuracy on OTHER, A3c, PLAX, PLAX_AR, and PSAX_TV.

4   Conclusion and Discussion

This work proposed a framework for more effective learning on data with hierarchically organised labels: multi-task residual neural network (MTRNN) with masked loss. MTRNN integrated two schemes for multi-tasking learning and can perform better for an echocardiogram view classification task. While the proposed model is only validated for a specific task in this work, We envision that it can be easily adapted to other medical image analysis scenarios where the data labels are hierarchically organised, such as thoracic disease diagnosis by chest x-ray images. Furthermore, most object detection tasks in medical imaging can be formulated as a hierarchical multi-task learning problem, as a series of multi-scale regions inherently define the target. Examples of such tasks include but are not limited to skin lesion classification tasks from dermoscopic images [5] and gastrointestinal disease detection using colonoscopy imaging [6]. Furthermore, the proposed scheme can be integrated with the Knowledge Graph in the medical domain, providing knowledge-based guidance from integrated heterogeneous data resources [21]. Thus, we can achieve a more formalised modelling of interrelationships between imaging and its labels.

References

1. Balaji, G., Subashini, T., Chidambaram, N.: Automatic classification of cardiac views in echocardiogram using histogram and statistical features. Procedia Comput. Sci. **46**, 1569–1576 (2015)
2. Bannur, S., et al.: Hierarchical analysis of visual COVID-19 features from chest radiographs. ArXiv abs/2107.06618 (2021)
3. Charton, J., et al.: View classification of color doppler echocardiography via automatic alignment between doppler and b-mode imaging. In: Aylward, S., Noble, J.A., Hu, Y., Lee, S.L., Baum, Z., Min, Z. (eds.) ASMUS 2022. LNCS, pp. 64–71. Springer, Cham (2022). https://doi.org/10.1007/978-3-031-16902-1_7

4. Chen, H., Miao, S., Xu, D., Hager, G.D., Harrison, A.P.: Deep hiearchical multi-label classification applied to chest X-ray abnormality taxonomies. CoRR abs/2009.05609 (2020). https://arxiv.org/abs/2009.05609
5. Hsu, B.W.Y., Tseng, V.S.: Hierarchy-aware contrastive learning with late fusion for skin lesion classification. Comput. Methods Programs Biomed. **216**, 106666 (2022)
6. Khaleel, M., Tavanapong, W., Wong, J., Oh, J., De Groen, P.: Hierarchical visual concept interpretation for medical image classification. In: 2021 IEEE 34th International Symposium on Computer-Based Medical Systems (CBMS), pp. 25–30. IEEE (2021)
7. Khaleel, M., Tavanapong, W., Wong, J., Oh, J., de Groen, P.: Hierarchical visual concept interpretation for medical image classification. In: 2021 IEEE 34th International Symposium on Computer-Based Medical Systems (CBMS), pp. 25–30 (2021). https://doi.org/10.1109/CBMS52027.2021.00012
8. Kusunose, K.: Steps to use artificial intelligence in echocardiography. J. Echocardiogr. **19**(1), 21–27 (2021)
9. Liao, Z., et al.: Echocardiography view classification using quality transfer star generative adversarial networks. In: Shen, D., et al. (eds.) MICCAI 2019, Part II. LNCS, vol. 11765, pp. 687–695. Springer, Cham (2019). https://doi.org/10.1007/978-3-030-32245-8_76
10. Madani, A., Arnaout, R., Mofrad, M., Arnaout, R.: Fast and accurate view classification of echocardiograms using deep learning. NPJ Digit. Med. **1**(1), 6 (2018)
11. Mitchell, C., et al.: Guidelines for performing a comprehensive transthoracic echocardiographic examination in adults: recommendations from the American society of echocardiography. J. Am. Soc. Echocardiogr. **32**(1), 1–64 (2019)
12. Østvik, A., Smistad, E., Aase, S.A., Haugen, B.O., Lovstakken, L.: Real-time standard view classification in transthoracic echocardiography using convolutional neural networks. Ultras. Med. Biol. **45**(2), 374–384 (2019)
13. Otto, C.M.: Textbook of Clinical Echocardiography. Elsevier Health Sciences (2013)
14. Pham, H.H., Le, T.T., Tran, D.Q., Ngo, D.T., Nguyen, H.Q.: Interpreting chest X-rays via CNNs that exploit hierarchical disease dependencies and uncertainty labels. Neurocomputing **437**, 186–194 (2021)
15. Sanh, V., Wolf, T., Ruder, S.: A hierarchical multi-task approach for learning embeddings from semantic tasks. In: Proceedings of the AAAI Conference on Artificial Intelligence, vol. 33, no. 1, pp. 6949–6956 (2019)
16. Seetharam, K., Raina, S., Sengupta, P.P.: The role of artificial intelligence in echocardiography. Curr. Cardiol. Rep. **22**, 1–8 (2020)
17. Shen, D., Wu, G., Suk, H.I.: Deep learning in medical image analysis. Annu. Rev. Biomed. Eng. **19**, 221–248 (2017)
18. Simonyan, K., Zisserman, A.: Very deep convolutional networks for large-scale image recognition. arXiv preprint arXiv:1409.1556 (2014)
19. Vaseli, H., et al.: Designing lightweight deep learning models for echocardiography view classification. In: Medical Imaging 2019: Image-Guided Procedures, Robotic Interventions, and Modeling, vol. 10951, pp. 93–99. SPIE (2019)
20. Wu, H., Bowers, D.M., Huynh, T.T., Souvenir, R.: Echocardiogram view classification using low-level features. In: 2013 IEEE 10th International Symposium on Biomedical Imaging, pp. 752–755. IEEE (2013)

21. Zhang, Y., et al.: HKGB: an inclusive, extensible, intelligent, semi-auto-constructed knowledge graph framework for healthcare with clinicians' expertise incorporated. Inf. Process. Manag. **57**(6), 102324 (2020)
22. Zhao, J., Peng, Y., He, X.: Attribute hierarchy based multi-task learning for fine-grained image classification. Neurocomputing **395**, 150–159 (2020)
23. Zhu, X., Bain, M.: B-CNN: branch convolutional neural network for hierarchical classification. ArXiv (2017). https://doi.org/10.48550/ARXIV.1709.09890

Temporally Consistent Segmentations from Sparsely Labeled Echocardiograms Using Image Registration for Pseudo-labels Generation

Matteo Tafuro(✉) ⓘ, Gino Jansen ⓘ, and Ivana Išgum ⓘ

University of Amsterdam, Amsterdam, The Netherlands
tafuromatteo00@gmail.com, {g.e.jansen,i.isgum}@amsterdamumc.nl

Abstract. The segmentation of the left ventricle in echocardiograms is crucial for diagnosing cardiovascular diseases. However, current deep learning methods typically focus on 2D segmentations and overlook the temporal information in ultrasound sequences. This choice might be caused by the scarcity of manual annotations, which are typically limited to end-diastole and end-systole frames. Therefore, we propose a method that trains temporally consistent segmentation models from sparsely labeled echocardiograms. We leverage image registration to generate pseudo-labels for unlabeled frames enabling the training of 3D models. Using a state-of-the-art convolutional neural network, 3D nnU-Net, we delineate the left ventricle (LV) cavity, LV myocardium, and left atrium. Evaluation on the CAMUS dataset demonstrates the quality and robustness of the generated pseudo-labels, serving as effective training data for subsequent segmentation. Additionally, we evaluate the segmentation model both intrinsically, measuring accuracy and temporal consistency, and extrinsically, estimating cardiac function markers like ejection fraction and left ventricular volumes. The results show accurate delineation of the cardiac structures that evolves smoothly over time, effectively demonstrating the model's accuracy and temporal consistency.

Keywords: Left ventricle segmentation · Echocardiography · Image registration · Pseudo-labels

1 Introduction

The analysis of 2D transthoracic echocardiograms is crucial in clinical cardiology for disease diagnosis and treatment selection [2]. The analysis comprises the extraction of a number of quantitative markers of cardiac function, such as the ejection fraction (EF) and the chamber volumes [10]. Extraction of these quantitative markers requires accurate and precise delineation of the cardiac anatomy. However, manual expert annotation is a time-consuming task associated with high inter- and intra-rater variability [1]. Existing commercial solutions allow semi- or fully-automatic delineation of the cardiac structures, but they are

B. Kainz et al. (Eds.): ASMUS 2023, LNCS 14337, pp. 195–204, 2023.
https://doi.org/10.1007/978-3-031-44521-7_19

typically limited to the segmentation of the end-diastolic (ED) and end-systolic (ES) frames [14].

The focus on ED and ES frames is also reflected in most published research utilizing machine learning approaches [12]. As these methods require large and diverse datasets for training, collecting annotations of full sequences has not been the prime focus. The most commonly used public datasets for echocardiography segmentation, CAMUS [8] and EchoNet-Dynamic [11], provide manual labels[1] for the ED and ES frames only. Therefore, most current state-of-the-art (SoTA) segmentation methods rely solely on expert annotations for these two frames [12]. Despite achieving performance within the margins of intra-observer variability [15,18], these methods do not address the smooth evolution of the cardiac structures over time, leading to temporally inconsistent predictions [12].

Since preserving the temporal consistency of the segmentations is beneficial for precise EF estimation [18], several studies have addressed this issue. Some approaches combine temporal and multi-view information using 3D CNN and convolutional LSTM [9]. Others enforce temporal smoothness through postprocessing [12] or leverage optical flow for segmentation accuracy improvement [3,21]. Wei et al. introduced CLAS, an end-to-end approach that combines colearning of appearance and shape features with the generation of left ventricle (LV) pseudo-labels for the intermediate time points [18]. These LV pseudo-labels are obtained by warping the ground truth maps to other frames using optical flow. Chen et al. further added data augmentation (A-CLAS) [4], while Wei et al. introduced two auxiliary tasks, view classification and EF regression, and proposed the multi-task version of CLAS (MCLAS) [19].

Although these methods achieve temporally consistent segmentation, their reliance on co-learning and pseudo-labels makes them computationally complex. Moreover, their constrained end-to-end nature restricts their modularity. In contrast, we present a method that addresses pseudo-label generation and temporally smooth segmentation as separate components. It leverages an unsupervised image registration model to sequentially estimate the deformations between frames and generate pseudo-labels through the warping of the available segmentation maps. The generated pseudo-labels allow supervised training of arbitrary 3D (2D+time) segmentation networks. To this end, we train a 3D nnU-Net [7] to delineate the LV cavity, LV myocardium and left atrium. We evaluate the proposed approach on the public CAMUS dataset [8], demonstrating that it generates reliable pseudo-labels that bring significant benefits to the downstream segmentation task. The segmentation model exhibits remarkable accuracy in delineating cardiac structures while preserving spatiotemporal smoothness, ultimately yielding accurate EF estimations.

2   Method

To obtain accurate and temporally consistent 3D (2D+time) segmentations from a sparsely labeled dataset, the method first generates the pseudo-labels for those

---

[1] To aid readability, it may be worth specifying that "segmentations" and "labels" are used interchangeably throughout the paper.

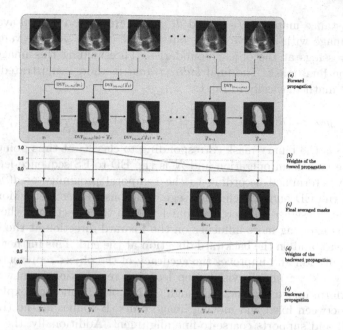

Fig. 1. The proposed image registration-based pseudo-labels generation method. The provided segmentations are propagated from ED to ES *(a)* and from ES to ED *(e)*. The masks from the two directions are aggregated as described in Sect. 2.1 and weighted according to a sinusoidal function *(b and d)*.

frames that lack reference segmentations. This is done through the sequential application of image registration. Thereafter, the method uses these pseudo-labels to augment sparse reference annotations and train a segmentation model.

2.1 Pseudo-labels Generation

Echocardiography acquisition consists of a sequence of image frames x_t, $\forall t \in \{1, 2, .., N\}$ showing the evolution of the heart over the cardiac cycle. Given the reference segmentation for the ED and ES frames, unsupervised deformable image registration (DIR) is exploited to segment the frames lacking segmentation masks. The registration's dense displacement vector field (DVF) is employed to warp the segmentation of frame x_t (y_t) to frame x_{t+1}, resulting in a pseudo-segmentation $\overrightarrow{y}_{t+1}$ of frame x_{t+1}. Specifically, the available ED segmentation is iteratively forward-propagated through the sequence to produce $\overrightarrow{y}_t$, $\forall t \in \{1, 2, .., N\}$. Akin, backward-propagating the ES segmentation mask returns a set of $\overleftarrow{y}_t$, $\forall t \in \{1, 2, .., N\}$.

To mitigate error accumulation caused by sequential registrations, the two sets of pseudo-labels $\overrightarrow{y}$ and $\overleftarrow{y}$ are combined using a weighted average of their class-wise signed distance maps. Specifically, for each class and time point, a binary mask is extracted and the signed distance to its edges is computed. The resulting distance maps, $d(\overrightarrow{y}_{t,C})$ and $d(\overleftarrow{y}_{t,C})$, are then weighted-averaged to return an image with negative values outside the object, positive values inside and zero crossings at the object boundaries. Thresholding this image at zero produces the final mask. The final *bidirectional* method is illustrated in Fig. 1 and defined mathematically in Eq. 1:

$$\tilde{y}_{t,C} = \left(d(\overrightarrow{y}_{t,C}) \cdot \cos^2 \frac{\pi}{2N}t + d(\overleftarrow{y}_{t,C}) \cdot \sin^2 \frac{\pi}{2N}t \right) > 0 \qquad (1)$$

where $\overleftrightarrow{y}_{t,C}$ is the binary mask corresponding to class C at time point t, $d(\cdot)$ is the distance transform operation and N is the ED-to-ES sequence length. The weights are determined according to the temporal proximity of $d(\overrightarrow{y}_{t,C})$ and $d(\overleftarrow{y}_{t,C})$ to the ED and ES reference segmentations, respectively. More specifically, they are designed to decrease from 1 to 0 in the direction of the propagation, thereby exerting more influence on the forward direction at the beginning of the sequence and on the backward direction at the end. This further mitigates error accumulation and improves the accuracy of the object representation.

In this work, an unsupervised deep learning registration framework is utilized to perform image alignment through CNNs [6]. The method exploits image similarity between fixed and moving image pairs, B-splines as the transformation model, and supports coarse-to-fine alignment. Additionally, the loss function combines the negative normalized cross correlation $\mathcal{L}_{NCC}$ with the bending energy penalty P: $\mathcal{L} = \mathcal{L}_{NCC} + \alpha P$ [13]. The regularization term P minimizes the second order derivative of local transformations, thereby enforcing global smoothness and preventing anatomically implausible image folding.

2.2 Segmentation

The reference segmentations of the echocardiograms are augmented with the pseudo-labels to provide densely labeled reference sequences. This enables the training of 3D (2D+time) segmentation models, which are designed to be trained on densely annotated data. By encoding the time dimension as the third dimension in convolutional space, a 3D model can learn spatiotemporal features that encourage temporally smooth predictions. To this end, a 3D nnU-Net is trained on the augmented dataset (*3D Dense* nnU-Net) [7].

2.3 Evaluation

Both the generated pseudo-labels and the predicted segmentations are intrinsically evaluated by overlap and boundary metrics: the DICE coefficient (DC), the mean absolute surface distance (MAD) and the 2D Hausdorff Distance (HD). The metrics are calculated per frame and subsequently averaged over an entire video. Additionally, the segmentation models are evaluated extrinsically through quantification of EF and LV volumes at end-diastole and end-systole, EDV and ESV. To aggregate dataset-level statistics for these indices, the correlation coefficient, bias and mean absolute error (MAE) are calculated between the reference and automatically obtained values. Finally, the temporal consistency of the automatic segmentation is assessed by tracking the area of a given class over time. The smoothness of a sequence is computed as the integral of the second derivative of the resulting curve (*area curve*). To account for changes in the slope of the area curve and to prevent the loss of information due to opposite bending, the second derivative is squared prior to integration. The final smoothness metric is defined in Eq. 2, with N being the ED-to-ES sequence length and $a_C(t)$ the area of class C at time point t.

$$ \text{Smoothness} = \int_1^N \left(a_C''(t) \right)^2 dt, \tag{2} $$

3 Experiments

Two main experiments were conducted[2]. First, the pseudo-labels were generated and evaluated against reference segmentations. Second, the pseudo-labels were utilized to complement the original dataset and train the segmentation network.

All the models were implemented in PyTorch 1.12.1 and trained using 2 Intel Xeon Gold 6128 CPUs (6 cores, 3.40GHz) and a GeForce RTX 2080 Ti.

3.1 Data and Preprocessing

This study uses two public datasets: CAMUS [8] and TED [12]. CAMUS contains 2D echocardiograms with 2-chambers (2CH) and 4-chambers (4CH) views of half-cycle sequences (from ED to ES) of 500 patients (450 training, 50 test). Manual annotations of the LV cavity, LV myocardium and LA are provided for the ED and ES frames only. TED is a subset of CAMUS that comprises 98 full cycle 4CH sequences, with manual segmentations of the LV cavity and the LV myocardium for the *whole* cardiac cycle. 94 sequences are part of the CAMUS training set and 4 of the test set.

Prior to analysis, all images are resized to 512×512 px, and the pixel spacing is scaled proportionally to preserve the anisotropic nature of the data.

3.2 Pseudo-label Generation

The DIR model was trained on the CAMUS training set after leaving out the overlapping 94 TED echocardiograms, resulting in a set of 806 echo sequences. Successively, the frame-wise alignment quality was evaluated against these 94 left-out TED sequences. The DIR network was trained on every intra-patient combination of two frames from the registration training set. The training was performed in 10,000 iterations and used a batch size of 32, the AMSGrad variant of the ADAM optimizer and a learning rate of 10^{-3}. Hyperparameters such as

---

[2] The code is publicly available at https://github.com/matteo-tafuro/temporally-consistent-echosegmentation.

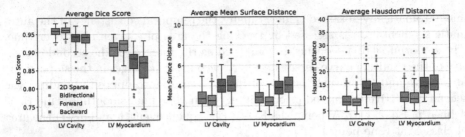

Fig. 2. Comparison of the pseudo-labels quality in terms of geometric metrics evaluated on the densely annotated TED dataset.

the size, the number of kernels and the B-spline grid spacing were determined in preliminary experiments by testing values between 2 and 128. Optimal results were obtained with 32 kernels of size 32 × 32, a grid spacing of 32 and a regularization hyperparameter of 1.0 to prevent folding. Coarse-to-fine registration did not improve performance, hence simple one-stage alignment was employed.

Figure 2 demonstrates the performance of pseudo-label generation using different approaches. Pseudo-labels were compared with predictions from a SoTA 2D nnU-Net trained on the original sparsely labeled CAMUS dataset (*2D Sparse nnU-Net*). Figure 3 highlights the effectiveness of our label propagation method in generating temporally consistent pseudo-labeled segmentation maps, promoting coherent feature learning during the segmentation step.

3.3   Segmentation

The *3D Dense* nnU-Net was trained and tested on the sparsely labeled CAMUS datasets augmented with pseudo-labels, allowing direct comparison with related works. In addition, the *3D Dense* model was evaluated against two baselines: a 2D nnU-Net trained on the sparsely labeled CAMUS dataset (*2D sparse* nnU-Net) and a 2D nnU-Net trained on the *augmented* CAMUS dataset (*2D Dense* nnU-Net). Each nnU-Net was trained for 1,000 epochs, using 5-fold cross-validation with an interleaved test setup. After training, the framework automatically selected the best U-Net configuration. Finally, three SoTA CLAS-based methods [4,18,19] were included for comparison. The models were compared in terms of (i) accuracy of the LV cavity, LV myocardium and LA segmentation at ED and ES; (ii) estimation of EF, EDV, and ESV; (iii) temporal smoothness.

The average segmentation performance on the ED and ES frames of the test set is listed in Table 1; the results of the EDV, ESV and EF estimation are displayed in Table 2; the observed temporal consistency of frame-by-frame predictions is shown in Fig. 4; finally, the area curve of a test patient is depicted in Fig. 5 along with the corresponding ED and ES predictions.

Table 1. Average segmentation results at ED and ES on the (sparsely annotated) CAMUS test set. The intra-observer variability results (in blue) are taken from the official CAMUS website and are not provided for the left atrium. The best value per column is indicated in bold.

	ED									ES								
	LV Cavity			LV Myocardium			LA			LV Cavity			LV Myocardium			LA		
	DC	HD	MAD	DC	HD	MAD	DC	HD	MAD	DC	HD	MAD	DC	HD	MAD	DC	HD	MAD
Intra-observer	0.945	4.6	1.4	0.957	5.0	1.7	–	–	–	0.930	4.5	1.3	0.951	5.0	1.7	–	–	–
CLAS [18]	0.947	4.6	1.4	0.961	4.8	1.5	0.902	5.2	1.9	0.929	4.6	1.4	0.955	4.9	1.6	0.927	4.8	1.8
A-CLAS [4]	0.942	–	–	0.955	–	–	0.887	–	–	0.923	–	–	0.950	–	–	0.916	–	–
2D Sparse	**0.955**	**4.1**	**1.2**	**0.965**	4.4	1.4	**0.906**	**4.9**	**1.9**	0.938	**4.0**	**1.2**	**0.959**	**4.3**	**1.5**	**0.937**	**4.3**	**1.5**
2D Dense	0.950	4.2	1.3	0.963	**4.3**	**1.4**	0.902	5.0	2.0	0.934	4.2	1.3	0.957	4.5	**1.5**	0.933	4.5	1.7
3D Dense	0.952	4.2	1.3	0.961	4.6	1.5	0.899	5.2	2.0	**0.939**	**4.0**	**1.2**	0.958	4.8	**1.5**	0.932	4.7	1.6

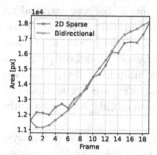

Fig. 3. Left atrium area over time from the pseudolabels of `patient0010` (4CH).

Table 2. LV volume and EF estimation on the CAMUS test set. The intra-observer variability is indicated in blue, and the best column-wise value is displayed in bold.

Methods	EDV			ESV			EF		
	Corr	Bias	MAE	Corr	Bias	MAE	Corr	Bias	MAE
Intra-observer	0.978	−2.8	6.5	0.981	−0.1	4.5	0.896	−2.3	4.7
CLAS [18]	0.958	−0.7	7.7	0.979	0.0	4.4	0.926	−0.1	**4.0**
A-CLAS [4]	0.969	–	–	0.983	–	–	0.883	–	–
MCLAS [19]	0.975	−1.0	–	0.983	−1.2	–	**0.946**	1.0	–
2D Sparse	0.972	0.0	6.0	0.980	0.6	4.8	0.827	1.3	5.0
2D Dense	0.972	0.4	5.7	**0.986**	−0.3	4.2	0.841	1.3	4.6
3D Dense	**0.978**	−1.4	**4.8**	**0.986**	−0.1	**4.0**	0.859	−0.1	4.6

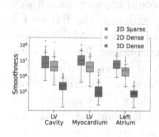

Fig. 4. Temporal smoothness of the CAMUS test set predictions in terms of the metric from Eq. 2 (lower values, higher smoothness). Note the logarithmic y-axis.

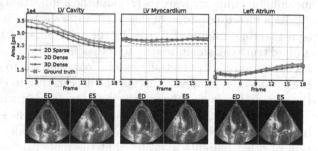

Fig. 5. Evaluation of the temporal consistency on `patient0002` from the test set. *Top row:* area curves. *Bottom row:* predictions at ED and ES. The green contours refers to the ground truth and the magenta outline is the prediction of the *3D Dense* model.

4 Discussion and Conclusion

This paper presented a method for temporally consistent segmentation of echocardiography using sparsely labeled data. The method exploits pseudo-labels generated by the use of DIR to complement the original set of sparsely annotated frames and allow the training of a 3D nnU-Net.

The analysis of the generated pseudo-label revealed the benefits of bidirectional over unidirectional label propagation. Results on the subsequent ED and ES segmentation task demonstrate that exploiting the pseudo-labels retains or improves the performance of the model trained on the sparsely labeled dataset, thereby endorsing their quality for downstream applications. The geometric metrics show that all three evaluated models perform *at least* as well as the SoTA methods, achieving a level of accuracy on par with intra-observer variability. However, evaluation of the temporal smoothness showed that the *2D Dense* model outperforms the *2D Sparse* model and that the *3D Dense*, in turn, outperforms both. For quantification of LV volumes, the *3D Dense* model outperforms all SoTA methods with EDV and ESV values closely matching intra-observer variability. EF estimation, however, is less remarkable. Yet, we argue that our method's very low bias and MAE akin to intra-rater variability advocate sufficiently good estimations of the measure.

A more notable limitation of our approach is its exclusive focus on the systolic function. Longer sequences can be analyzed by identifying and extracting the systolic phase from the entire heart cycle [4], but this would still preclude the characterization of the diastolic function, which is relevant to various heart diseases [16]. To this end, related studies have investigated the extraction of more meaningful temporal features [21] and the application of cyclical self-supervision [5]. As a direct extension of this work, future research could explore the efficacy of registering unlabeled frames to the same image (specifically, the ED or ES ground truth) as an alternative to the sequential approach. This could limit error accumulation and potentially extend our method to encompass full- or multi-cycle sequences. However, this may be detrimental to the temporal consistency of the pseudo-labels and thus to the downstream segmentation and quantification.

Figure 5 shows that *3D Dense* model results in slightly offset quantitative indices from ground truth and 2D models, especially at ED and ES. Examination of other patients indicates that the model does not favor over- or under-segmentation. Rather, Fig. 5 suggests the presence of uncertain boundaries in the data. Disagreements between manual and automatic segmentations arise when the endocardium is occluded, or when the LV myocardium and/or the LA extend beyond the field of view. In these cases, the ambiguous position of the structures likely influences the creation of manual annotations. Accordingly, the ambiguity is reflected in the predictions of the models, resulting in the observed discrepancy. Future work could model this randomness in order to convey the reliability of a given estimation. Extensions of this study may also attempt to limit the aforementioned uncertainty, for instance by selectively choosing high-quality pseudo-labels for training, or by leveraging distinct loss functions (or weighting schemes) for ground truth and pseudo-labeled frames [17, 20].

In conclusion, our approach achieves accurate segmentation comparable to SoTA methods while offering remarkable temporal consistency. Unlike ond-to-end frameworks such as CLAS [4,18,19], our approach separates pseudo-label generation and segmentation, offering flexibility and modularity.

References

1. Armstrong, A.C., et al.: Quality control and reproducibility in M-mode, two-dimensional, and speckle tracking echocardiography acquisition and analysis: the CARDIA study, year 25 examination experience. Echocardiography **32**(8), 1233–1240 (2014). https://doi.org/10.1111/echo.12832
2. Chen, C., et al.: Deep learning for cardiac image segmentation: a review. Front. Cardiovasc. Med. **7** (2020). https://doi.org/10.3389/fcvm.2020.00025
3. Chen, S., Ma, K., Zheng, Y.: Tan: Temporal affine network for real-time left ventricle anatomical structure analysis based on 2D ultrasound videos. ArXiv (2019). https://doi.org/10.48550/ARXIV.1904.00631
4. Chen, Y., Zhang, X., Haggerty, C.M., Stough, J.V.: Assessing the generalizability of temporally coherent echocardiography video segmentation. In: Išgum, I., Landman, B.A. (eds.) Medical Imaging 2021: Image Processing. vol. 11596, p. 115961O. International Society for Optics and Photonics, SPIE (2021). https://doi.org/10.1117/12.2580874
5. Dai, W., Li, X., Ding, X., Cheng, K.T.: Cyclical self-supervision for semi-supervised ejection fraction prediction from echocardiogram videos. IEEE Trans. Med. Imaging **42**(5), 1446–1461 (2023). https://doi.org/10.1109/TMI.2022.3229136
6. de Vos, B.D., Berendsen, F.F., Viergever, M.A., Sokooti, H., Staring, M., Išgum, I.: A deep learning framework for unsupervised affine and deformable image registration. Med. Image Anal. **52**, 128–143 (2019). https://doi.org/10.1016/j.media.2018.11.010
7. Isensee, F., Jaeger, P.F., Kohl, S.A.A., Petersen, J., Maier-Hein, K.H.: nnU-net: a self-configuring method for deep learning-based biomedical image segmentation. Nat. Methods **18**(2), 203–211 (2020). https://doi.org/10.1038/s41592-020-01008-z
8. Leclerc, S., et al.: Deep learning for segmentation using an open large-scale dataset in 2D echocardiography. IEEE Trans. Med. Imaging **38**(9), 2198–2210 (2019). https://doi.org/10.1109/tmi.2019.2900516
9. Li, M., Wang, C., Zhang, H., Yang, G.: MV-RAN: multiview recurrent aggregation network for echocardiographic sequences segmentation and full cardiac cycle analysis. Comput. Biol. Med. **120**, 103728 (2020). https://doi.org/10.1016/j.compbiomed.2020.103728
10. Moal, O., et al.: Explicit and automatic ejection fraction assessment on 2D cardiac ultrasound with a deep learning-based approach. Comput. Biol. Med. **146**, 105637 (2022). https://doi.org/10.1016/j.compbiomed.2022.105637
11. Ouyang, D., et al.: Video-based AI for beat-to-beat assessment of cardiac function. Nature **580**(7802), 252–256 (2020). https://doi.org/10.1038/s41586-020-2145-8
12. Painchaud, N., Duchateau, N., Bernard, O., Jodoin, P.M.: Echocardiography segmentation with enforced temporal consistency. IEEE Trans. Med. Imaging **41**(10), 2867–2878 (2022). https://doi.org/10.1109/TMI.2022.3173669
13. Rueckert, D.: Nonrigid registration using free-form deformations: application to breast MRI images. IEEE Trans. Med. Imaging **18**(8), 712–721 (1999). https://doi.org/10.1109/42.796284

14. Schuuring, M.J., Išgum, I., Cosyns, B., Chamuleau, S.A.J., Bouma, B.J.: Routine echocardiography and artificial intelligence solutions. Front. Cardiovasc. Med. **8**, 648877 (2021)

15. Sfakianakis, C., Simantiris, G., Tziritas, G.: GUDU: geometrically-constrained ultrasound data augmentation in U-net for echocardiography semantic segmentation. Biomed. Signal Process. Control **82**, 104557 (2023). https://doi.org/10.1016/j.bspc.2022.104557

16. Thomas, L., Marwick, T.H., Popescu, B.A., Donal, E., Badano, L.P.: Left atrial structure and function, and left ventricular diastolic dysfunction: JACC state-of-the-art review. J. Am. Coll. Cardiol. **73**(15), 1961–1977 (2019). https://doi.org/10.1016/j.jacc.2019.01.059

17. Wang, C., et al.: Pseudo-labeled auto-curriculum learning for semi-supervised keypoint localization (2022)

18. Wei, H., et al.: Temporal-consistent segmentation of echocardiography with co-learning from appearance and shape. In: Martel, A.L., et al. (eds.) MICCAI 2020. LNCS, vol. 12262, pp. 623–632. Springer, Cham (2020). https://doi.org/10.1007/978-3-030-59713-9_60

19. Wei, H., Ma, J., Zhou, Y., Xue, W., Ni, D.: Co-learning of appearance and shape for precise ejection fraction estimation from echocardiographic sequences. Med. Image Anal. **84**, 102686 (2023). https://doi.org/10.1016/j.media.2022.102686

20. Xia, Y., et al.: 3D semi-supervised learning with uncertainty-aware multi-view co-training (2020)

21. Xue, W., Cao, H., Ma, J., Bai, T., Wang, T., Ni, D.: Improved segmentation of echocardiography with orientation-congruency of optical flow and motion-enhanced segmentation. IEEE J. Biomed. Health Inform. **26**(12), 6105–6115 (2022). https://doi.org/10.1109/JBHI.2022.3221429

Author Index

B. Kainz et al. (Eds.): ASMUS 2023, LNCS 14337, pp. 205–206, 2023.
https://doi.org/10.1007/978-3-031-44521-7

Printed in the United States
by Baker & Taylor Publisher Services

Printed in the United States
by Baker & Taylor Publisher Services